INVITATION TO PORTUGAL

Mary Jean Kempner

INVITATION TO PORTUGAL

Photographs by Russell Lynes

Introduction by Alan Pryce-Jones

Atheneum New York
1969

Map drawn by Ava Morgan
(Facing the first page of text)

Library of Congress catalog card number 75-80956
Published simultaneously in Canada by McClelland and Stewart Ltd.
Manufactured in the United States of America by
Kingsport Press, Inc., Kingsport, Tennessee
Designed by Harry Ford
First Edition

To Gladys

MY MUCH LOVED AUNT WHO WAS MORE LIKE A SISTER

INTRODUCTION

Alan Pryce-Jones

LUCKILY FOR those who love Portugal, it remains one of the least discovered countries in Europe. Partly this is due to a number of popular misconceptions among foreigners. Portugal, they repeat, is a police state. The Portuguese are dull, by comparison with the Spaniards. The country is poor and backward. There are no Portuguese painters, and what of Portuguese art there is is derivative. Besides, the language is hermetic.

A handful of writers, beginning with William Beckford in the late eighteenth century, have labored to dispel these legends, but there has remained a need for some book which is personal, informed, and affectionate. The late Rose Macaulay used to note with surprise the number of what she called "Turkey books" which suddenly burst on the world. There is no comparable number of Portugal books, but I shall not be surprised if Mary Jean Kempner's companionable excursion into an unfamiliar landscape sets a fashion.

For the truth about Portugal is far more endearing than those who know it only by hearsay are likely to admit. For one thing, the Portuguese are among the kindest of people. There is no trouble they will not take to make the stranger feel at ease. The Atlantic breezes have softened their natural Iberian toughness, so that even to children and animals—normally the victims of a Southern European temperament—they behave with perfect good humor.

Simply to pass the Pillars of Hercules westward is to leave—along with a troublesome and, in winter, almost perpetual wind—the disadvantages of the Mediterranean civilizations behind. The shameless charm of Italy, the fire of southern France (which burns as much as it illuminates), the tattered majesty of Spain, have no counterparts in Portugal. There you will find a charming softness, the kind of soft grace that Victorian lithographers depict in their scenes of domestic life. But you will also find, beneath that softness, a resilience, a determination to make the best of things, and a degree of unostentatious national pride, which are peculiar to these green Atlantic provinces.

It is important to remember that Portugal has spent the last thirty-five years awakening from a sleep of centuries. Should you wish to know what the nineteenth century in Lisbon was like—and Lisbon is the quintessence of Portugal—you can find it all in the novels of Eça de Queiroz. By 1932, when Dr. Salazar came to power, the little republic, its vitality sapped by the legacy of an incompetent monarchy, was in a piteous condition. It was then that I first visited it, crossing the Guadiana out of Spain into what was still an unspoiled Algarve. If it was unspoiled, it was also extremely uncomfortable. The hotel pillows were filled with sand, banks and stores generally (except for such commodities as cartwheels and rope) were universally to seek, the roads were deplorable, and poverty oppressive.

Not for nearly twenty-five years after that did I have the chance of a talk with Dr. Salazar himself, and by that time Portugal was already dismissed by the Western democracies as a Fascist tyranny. The honest observer, however, could not but observe that the tyranny, if it existed at all, was of a very mild order. Nor did Dr. Salazar defend it on ideological grounds. He wished, he said, that he were governing a people with a long democratic tradition behind it, rather than one which had known nothing but misgovernment, apathy, and decay since the seventeenth century. He wished he had cadres of eager young administrators, cut to the pattern of Harvard, Oxford, or Heidelberg. Instead, he must make do with the human material before him. And was he likely to sacrifice a generation of progress to a theory of democracy, however alluring?

Since that talk, twenty more years have passed: and now that the reign of Dr. Salazar has drawn to a close, it is possible to see it for the astonishing achievement it has proved to be. Facile judgments as to whether or no the Portuguese renaissance can be equated with Fascist experience elsewhere is totally irrelevant. A handful of leaders—and the builders of modern Portugal remain extremely few—have managed to create out of misery and disorder a stable, solvent, evolving society. Certainly the division between rich and poor is unpleasantly sharp. On the other hand, to be poor in Portugal is much less disagreeable than to be poor in the outworn industrial communities of northern Europe or the slums of, say, Boston. Like their Andalusian neighbors, the peasants of Portugal live in glittering cleanliness. And when it is remembered that a prosperous middle-class existence, with servants in the kitchen and a car in the garage, can be financed on an income of $500 a month, it will be seen that the value of money in Portugal cannot easily be assessed by those who normally think of income solely in terms of the dollar, the mark, or the franc.

Not that the Portuguese are a self-satisfied people. They see quite clearly that they have a long way to go before they can count on the consolidation of the gains made since 1932. They have to step up a sense of national purpose; they have to flex mental muscles which have been encouraged to relax under the discipline of a paternal government.

It is a merit of Mary Jean Kempner's book that she writes as a discerning American by no means automatically impressed by what she finds. It is her special skill to take one aspect of Portugal after another—historical, picturesque, visual, architectural, social—and build them into a kind of polyptych—a form of art at which the Portuguese themselves excel. Under her eye, and helped by the camera of Mr. Russell Lynes, the country assumes a shape and a context. It comes alive as it could not in a guidebook, however wide-ranging. For what she gives us is her own view of the country, set together by a selective talent and given life because her own voice can be heard throughout. There will be more Portugal books to come, I have no doubt, but none more useful nor more evocative.

Foreword

WHAT IS it you like about our country?" is a question I have been asked repeatedly in the course of my four-year love affair with Portugal. The attentiveness that inevitably follows tends to assume awesome proportions, particularly as the Portuguese are brilliant talkers and poor listeners. Individually and chauvinistically proud and profoundly insecure, they appear uneasy in the presence of unqualified foreign enthusiasm, fearful that it might conceal a note of scorn and derision. To admire their beaches is easy—the sandy stretches that rim the country are renowned objects of praise. But when it comes to national monuments—matters involving architecture, painting, sculpture, or the decorative arts—one often senses wary withdrawal. A note of cautious cultural self-deprecation may be sounded. The scion of a great Portuguese banking family once sought refuge under just such an umbrella of understatement when I raved over the infinite charms of the ravishing pink Rococo palace at Queluz. "It's a nice little palace," he admitted reluctantly, "not bad at all."

There is much I like about Portugal, and a few things I like less well—the way one feels about a dear friend. So I have decided to put some of them down on these pages in the hope of answering my Portuguese friends and sharing with others the fascinations of this lovely country.

This, then, is my invitation to the reader to accompany me on a voyage of exploration. In its course we will take a brief canter through the somewhat turbulent and frequently remarkable history of Portugal. We will visit the great Portuguese abbeys and monasteries, explore palaces, prowl through great private houses, tarry in fascinating provincial towns. There are foods and wines to be sampled; the mournful, pervasive rhythms of the *fado* to listen to; the peculiarly Portuguese and infinitely elegant bullfights to watch. We will go to country fairs to be amazed by the gamut of merchandise, including cattle, bibelots, ceramics, fur pelts, and potted plants. We will look at gardens, at museums, watch fireworks, take part in native *festas*.

The armchair reader can go with me on a trip that starts in Lisbon, goes far south past the harbors from which Henry the Navigator sent out his caravels to sail the unknown oceans. In small towns we find architectural treasures. We drive past fertile slopes covered with vineyards, eucalyptus, or wild flowers. We probe the most northern frontiers before again turning south and following the rich coastline back to Lisbon. The last section of this book is a journal of just such a trip, taken at a headlong pace that I do not commend to anyone else. It will, however, serve the reader as a table d'hôte of visual delights to be savored, and will suggest the means of discovering them. Neither the author nor the photographer presumes to "tell all" in either words or pictures. We prefer instead that our readers use us as a springboard from which to make their own Portuguese discoveries.

Acknowledgments

THIS BOOK could never have been written were it not for the encouragement and help provided by a number of people. Heading this list are Russell Lynes, who not only took the splendid photographs illuminating its pages but who conscientiously read each chapter as it was written, with a critical eye, making his keen editorial judgments in a kindly tone of voice designed not to frighten the tentative author; Vere Pilkington, whose expertise and enthusiasm were both instructive and stimulating; and the author's teen-age son, Daniel Thorne, who suffered good-humoredly through long sightseeing junkets.

And there are others, many of them, persons in important positions, hospitable persons, informed persons, frivolous persons, along with countless anonymous, friendly Portuguese men and women to whom a visitor might turn for routine assistance. To these latter, I can only extend my general thanks and enduring affection. More specifically, some names must be recalled. To each, I bow my appreciation and offer the hope that on perusing *Invitation to Portugal* they will feel that their time and effort were not wholly wasted.

H.E. the United States Ambassador to Portugal and Mrs. Bennett

H.E. the Portuguese Ambassador to the United States and Mrs. Garin

H.E. the French Ambassador to Portugal and the Comtesse de Rose
The Hon. Roswell Gilpatric
Dr. Gonçalo C. Caldeiro Coelho, Minister Plenipotentiary for Foreign Affairs
Dr. Luis Forjaz Trigueiros
Monsignor Dom João de Castro
The Duque de Palmella
The Marquesa de Cadaval
The Conde de Mangualde
The Conde de Anadia
Dom Luis de Albuquerque a Cáceres
Jose Vilella
Marcellino de Salles Gomez
Dr. Ayres da Carvalho
Dr. Hellmut Wohl
Dr. Brian Head
Dr. Robert Smith
Dr. Carlos de Azevedo
Dr. I. E. Jago
Brendan Gill
Karl Kup
Joseph Rankin
Lady Elles
Mrs. Keith Newall
Felix Vigne
Fernando Von Zeller
Alvaro Burmester Martin
The Banco Português do Atlantico
The New York Public Library
The New York Society Library
St. Paul's School Library
Heyward Associates
Alberto Rapetti
Carlos, of the Palácio Seteais

Contents

Illustrations

INVITATION TO PORTUGAL

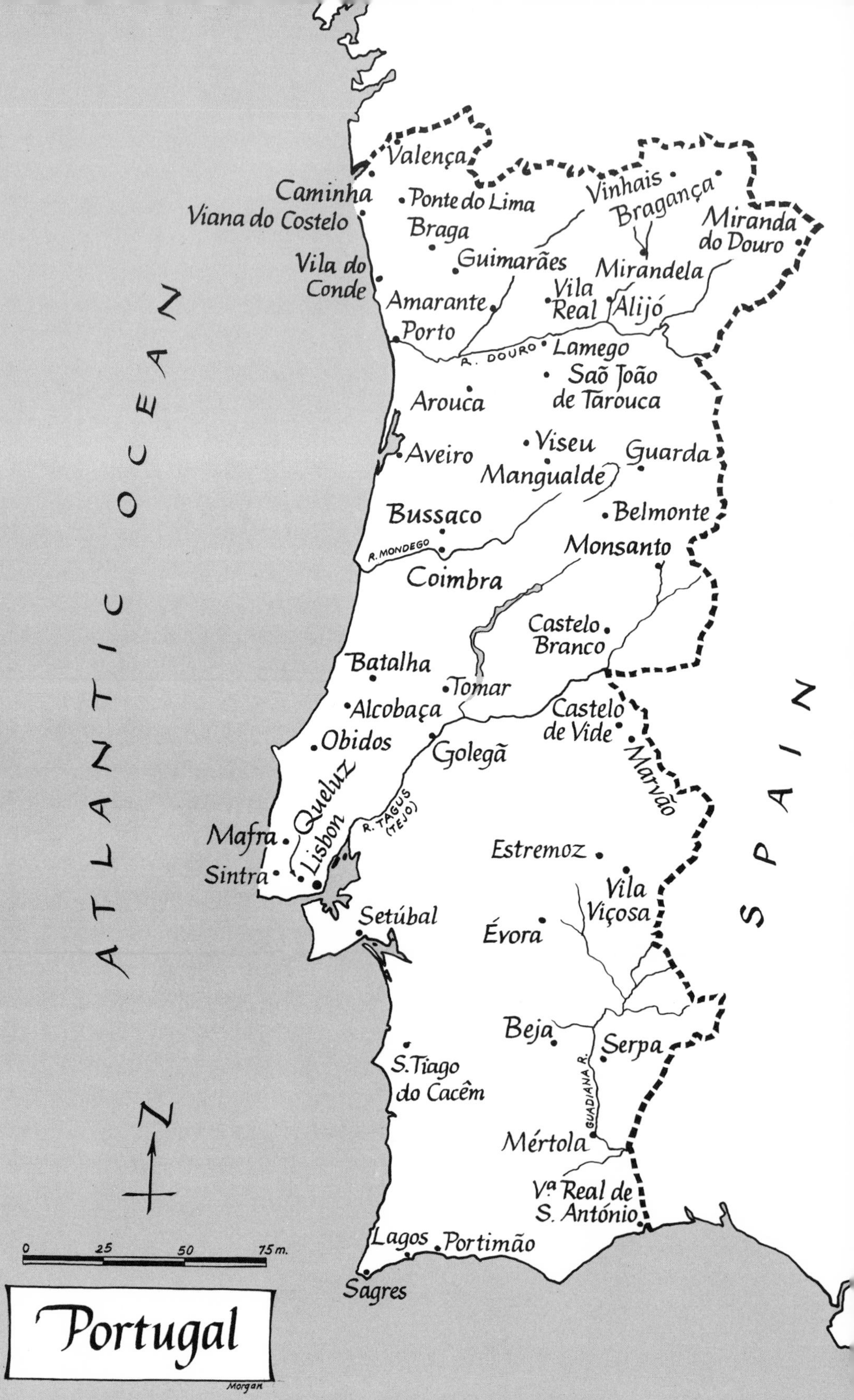
Valença
Caminha
Ponte do Lima
Viana do Costelo
Braga
Vinhais
Bragança
Miranda do Douro
Vila do Conde
Guimarães
Mirandela
Amarante
Vila Real
Alijó
Porto
R. Douro
Lamego
São João de Tarouca
Arouca
Aveiro
Viseu
Guarda
Mangualde
Bussaco
Belmonte
R. Mondego
Monsanto
Coimbra
Castelo Branco
Batalha
Tomar
Alcobaça
Castelo de Vide
Obidos
Golegã
Queluz
Marvão
R. Tagus (Tejo)
Mafra
Lisbon
Estremoz
Sintra
Vila Viçosa
Setúbal
Évora
Beja
Serpa
S. Tiago do Cacêm
Guadiana R.
Mértola
Vª Real de S. António
Lagos
Portimão
Sagres
0 25 50 75 m.
ATLANTIC OCEAN
SPAIN
N
Morgan

Portugal

CHAPTER I

Landscape with Figures

PORTUGAL BEHAVES like an island. In a world where most places are only a few hours' flying time one from another, it manages to appear remote. Stitched onto the flank of an often predatory Spain, it appears withdrawn, its back firmly turned against Europe, determined to look outward—to Africa, Brazil, England, the Indies, Japan—anywhere that happens to be across the sea. An 18th-century Chinese statesman described the Portuguese he encountered as being "like fish; remove them from the water and they die"; while in the more contemporary opinion of John Gunther, "they are basically coastline people."

This state of mind, or geographical accident, or historical expedient—most likely a combination of all three—paid off. Portugal has been independent for more than 800 years. Its boundaries have not changed since the 13th century. Its kings have been Portuguese except for a sixty-year mishap (1580–1640) when the crown carelessly slipped onto Spanish heads. Bonaparte, who was never able to conquer this indigestible morsel, believed the seed for his ultimate defeat was sown by Portuguese obstinacy. A hundred years before England had a single warship, Portugal had a navy busily making war on the Moors and exploring the seas. Prowess, determination, and daring won her control over three empires. Although she has lost two of them, she resolutely clings to what remains of her colonial territory—an impressive area that is twenty-three times bigger than the Portuguese mainland. For a country less than half the size of Great Britain, this takes tenacity, a stubborn sense of destiny, and impressive cheek.

Mesmerized by past glories and determined to ignore the reality of foreign policy in the world today, the Portuguese tend to delude themselves with the idea that they are practical progressives, as they were in the 15th century, when "they entered upon modern life three generations ahead of the rest of Christendom." Looking between rose-tinted blinkers, they seek the new Camelot which they believe exists just beyond the horizon. "Realists would never have attempted the early Voyages of Discovery," a friend in Lisbon argued, "not in the face of the superstition of that time. Those projects were for dreamers—call them constructive escapists, if you like." A more detached view probably was taken as far back as the turn of the century by a historian who wrote, "The country glows in the sunset of the day before yesterday, or the dawn of the day after tomorrow." Although it is afternoon in Portuguese history, it never seems too late. Time is unimportant. I have been told that there are four public clocks in Lisbon, but I have never found one of them.

The majority of the people still live by farming and fishing as they have since the Roman invaders called the country Lusitania

Fishermen checking their nets

and officially gave it dual importance, as a resort for tired soldiers and functionaries, and as a breadbasket of empire. Today some 153,000,000 pounds of canned fish—roughly $39,000,000 worth—is exported annually. Along much of the coast, fishing boats come in with their catch from dawn till dusk. They unload on the beaches and the fish are promptly auctioned off to buyers who come with refrigerated trucks from all over Europe. Like many other things in Portugal, these auctions follow an eccentric pattern: the auctioneer starts at a peak price and works down till he gets a buyer, a method that accelerates the procedure—an important factor in dealing with un-iced fish.

Sixty percent of the national economy is based on the land. More than half the world's cork is grown in Portugal. The country is a leading producer of wine and olive oil. It raises enough cereal grain for domestic consumption, and no by-product is allowed to be wasted. Corn, for instance, not only provides human food as well as animal fodder, but the shucks are used as bedding for cattle, and the cobs as fuel for farmhouses. Motoring recently from Lisbon to the northern frontier, I counted only five tractors. Although this is partially due to a shortage of modern farm equipment, it also testifies to the wisdom of government agronomists. Mechanized devices may be rural status symbols, but they are not necessarily synonymous with efficiency and high yield per acreage. This is particularly true in a country like Portugal where land is often broken into small plots owned by proud and touchy peasants unwilling to tolerate any intrusion on their domain. For them the ox-drawn plow is a better implement than the tractor, making it possible to cultivate every inch of arable land. Skillfully they dig transverse furrows or lay intricate dry-stone walls to prevent erosion—giving an Oriental cast to the landscape. Wherever fields run up hillsides, the plow is likely to be supplanted by a man (or woman or child) with a hoe. At harvest time magnificent oxen with long, lyre-shaped horns are seen along rural roads hauling the crops—hay, wheat, olives, grapes, and casks of wine. Usually worked in pairs yoked together with wooden headboards that often are elaborately carved, these enormous, docile creatures are dwarfed by their loads; so are the delicate-looking tough little burros, ridden by women sitting sidesaddle between pairs of deep baskets filled with farm produce. The briskly moving horse or donkey carts are the sports cars of this remote, placid, rural world.

A third of Portugal is wooded, either in eucalyptus, pine, oak, or chestnut, much of it recently planted as a result of the government's reforestation program. Portuguese kings were generally concerned with protecting their trees, although in the Age of Discoveries shipbuilding swallowed up whole forests. A 17th-century Pope went so far as to issue a Papal Bull threatening excommunication to anyone who damaged the great cypresses of Bussaco, in the forest near Coimbra, which by now have grown almost as tall as redwoods. Before cutting down a cork oak, one is required to obtain government permission. The rules for cork harvest are stringently enforced: trees are stripped once every nine years—a process of removing the bark, reminiscent of martyrdom by flaying, which leaves the trunk raw and angry-looking, the color of red-lead paint. However, it does no damage, and the top-quality cork is known to come from middle-aged trees which already have been stripped several times.

Compared to the rest of Europe, the inroads of the machine age in Portugal are negligible. Small industries and assembly plants persist in cropping up, but the industrial revolution barely grazed the country. According to a 1967 United Nations census, the population is 9,440,000 people; of these about 800,000 live in Lisbon and 300,000 in Oporto, and there are no other towns of over 50,000. There has always been considerable rivalry between the two major cities. Until recently Oporto proudly pointed to its steel suspension bridge, which was built toward the end of the last century. Now Lisbon has the largest steel suspension bridge in Europe, spanning the Tagus River, and Oporto people call attention to the sparsity of the toll-paying traffic which goes across it. Traffic outside urban centers, however, is generally light. Gasoline, like all other imports, is expensive—about one dollar a gallon—and motoring is a luxury primarily indulged in on Sundays, when the entire population rushes to the beach or a roadside picnic. Roads throughout the country are generally good even though the pace of life is more attuned to the pony cart than to jet planes. This gentle ambiance probably contributes as much as the present puritanical government to the fact that Lisbon today is a capital city where one is safe on the streets at any hour of the night.

PATIENCE AND RED TAPE

There are no more intuitively polite and gracious people than the Portuguese. It does not necessarily mean they like you, it definitely does not invite familiarity, but it is a spontaneous expression of warmth and good manners without any overtone of either servility or scorn. "Your Excellency" is not a term reserved for ambassadors, but remains in colloquial use. Strangers will go out of their way to escort you to your destination. To ask a favor or a service is regarded as a tribute to an individual's ingenuity and importance, and as such it is regarded as an act of faith rather than an imposition or a chore. The Portuguese tend to be sensitive, however, and imagine hurts easily, rather like the Chinese; to them it is unseemly to show petty anger or raise one's voice in irritation. (To summon a waiter one hisses.)

They understand deep-rooted rage or a passionate scene, but demonstrations of lesser emotions seem to them like bad manners or the behavior of a spoiled child. They are unimpressed by threats of all sorts. On the other hand, they dote on red tape as a challenge and are wonderfully adept at getting around it. They are fundamentally efficient as well as resourceful; it is no wonder that Lisbon is one of the rare Pan American World Airways stations entirely staffed by locals.

Unlike the French, the Portuguese are immensely patient with persons who struggle to speak their complex, sibilant language. They are quick with smiling praise for those who say anything properly, and never presume to correct faulty pronunciation. Philologists consider Portuguese to be the contemporary language closest to ancient Latin, although they recognize heavy borrowings from the Moors. There are close to 600 Arabic words assimilated into the language. Pidgin English, the old *lingua franca* of the Far East, "is as much Portuguese as it is English," according to many old China hands.

The basic kindness of the Portuguese is well illustrated by the way they treat criminals, animals, and foreigners. While the Frenchman feels *he* is in France, and acts accordingly, the Portuguese feels *you* are in Portugal and entitled to the treatment accorded honored guests. Generally speaking, animals are better treated than in most Latin countries. Livestock is sleek and well-fed, burros are bright-eyed, sheep seem more like the shepherd's pets than a flock of scatterbrains, bullocks are rarely mud-caked. Dogs sleep flagrantly on sidewalks and village streets while pedestrians step around them rather than interrupt these canine siestas, although the word *cão,* or dog, is often printed as c-- like a minor obscenity—a custom inherited from the Moors.

Naturally permissive, the Portuguese have never been looked on as good persecutors. Robert Southey, the English poet, in a book of letters published in 1797, commented on current "auto-da-fé." "You will be surprised by the mildness of the sentences," he wrote and went on to list those he had noted as being "one to three years confinement in a monastery." Portugal became the first European nation to abolish capital punishment. Up to that time executions had been subject to strict rules of protocol: *fidalgos* (gentry) traditionally were entitled to be decapitated, while more plebeian offenders were simply hanged. According to Southey, the last man to be executed under the old law had been found guilty of killing his father and his brother in order to inherit the estate. When the death penalty was pronounced he claimed the honor of being beheaded as a *fidalgo*, but as only one of his parents enjoyed the title the council of *fidalgos* rejected his demands and insisted he be hanged like common folk. For a while the man indulged in the national game of etiquette and legal quibbling, but in the end, Southey reported, "The matter was compromised, for the poor fellow had not interest enough to make a law suit out of it, and his head was only half cut off to satisfy both parties."

TEMPERAMENT AND EUROPE'S WILD GARDEN

Because of geographical juxtaposition, the uninitiated are tempted to compare Spain and Portugal. This is a booby trap which serves only to antagonize the people of both countries. They probably are as different as the Irish and the Scots, and along something of the same lines. It shows in their attitudes about almost everything—from love to religion. Like the Irish, the Portuguese enjoy their melancholy; they cherish what they call their *saudades* or longings. They admit to being happiest when they are mildly sad. They are neither as gay nor as implacable as their Spanish neighbors: the theme of the Spanish *flamenco* is desire and the tempo of the dancer's heels clearly says, "I want you"; the theme of the Portuguese *fadista* is one of longing and despair, a lament crying out how much "I miss you." Both are clear expressions of a national temperament. When it comes to religion one notices primarily a variation in the tone of voice. Both peoples are deeply religious, deeply Catholic. But their tribute to God is expressed differently. Spain built magnificent monasteries and churches to the glory of God, beseeching His blessing on the land and its people. Portugal waited for the *fait accompli*, promising equally grandiose monuments, provided the favors were granted, as thanksgiving for God's blessings already received.

Visually the Spanish landscape is more dramatic. But Portugal makes up in variety for what its landscape lacks in grandeur. Here there are no vast plains, canyons, deserts, jungles, or mountains over 7,000 feet. Instead it is like going from one garden to another—all of them seemingly laid out by Capability Brown, the greatest English landscape designer of the 18th century. Even the wildest, boldest stretches of country appear to be in the highest state of cultivation. This is the wild garden of Europe, its flora acknowledged to be the richest on the continent. Wild flowers abound—dwarf iris, narcissus, pink bluebells—varieties famous for their rarity grow in profuse splendor. The moors are thick with heather, golden broom, and aromatic cistus. It is as if all the best landscape paintings by classical or romantic artists were lined up in an open-air studio for a lordly patron of the arts. And as wherever one goes one is never far from the Atlantic Ocean, an awareness of the sea is all-pervasive.

Like engravings out of Don Quixote, conically shaped stone windmills—for grinding grain rather than pumping water—top the softly rounded hills. The miller sets the triangular sails—fixed to their slender spars—to suit the day's wind. Clay whistles and/or wooden clackers in the rigging summon him from his other chores should the wind shift and his mill sails need to be reefed or let out. (Sometimes when a miller's family is in mourning these clay whistles are taken off the rigging.) Highways slope past Roman ruins, walled towns, palace-monasteries, elegant aqueducts, somber fortresses, Moorish ruins. Like exclamation points, they provoke the traveler's attention; it takes longer than one expects to motor fifty miles in Portugal because of such temptations to tarry.

Although grapes grow in practically every backyard, the principal wine-producing regions are the Minho, the Douro and the Dão in the north, and parts of Estremadura near Lisbon. The vineyards look greener than those of France and Italy. There is more insouciance in the way grapes are grown and trellised, sometimes over granite posts, or encouraged into trees to romp and run from branch to branch, forming verdant screens on either side of the roads. In the Algarve, in February, the blossoming almond trees, like sweet-scented snowdrifts, inevitably call to mind the legend of the Nordic princess captured by a rich Moor who imprisoned her in his Algarve palace. In spite of his rich gifts and great tenderness, the princess sighed, cried, and wasted away. Doctors and sorcerers were summoned to no avail. One night as her distraught captor watched her tossing in sleep, he heard her cry out a single word: "Snow!" Immediately he ordered all his lands planted with almond trees, so that as January ended, the lovely princess looked out on a blanket of snowy petals. It was said that she smiled with joy, pressed his hand, and ate the orange he had peeled for her. But, more important, she was never heard to sigh again.

Portugal is famous for her fruit, and rightly so. All of it is tree-ripened, and it is rarely marketed outside the country.

Bacalhoa . . . topiary garden

There are the sweet figs of Sintra, plums from Elvas, melons from Amarante, oranges from Setúbal, and huge succulent peaches from Alcobaça, which the 18th-century traveler William Beckford called "delight of fruit." Everyone throughout the country seems to have a green thumb. Geraniums and bougainvillea cascade off country walls and town balconies, sometimes growing together in a blast of color that is loud as a brass band. Hydrangeas bloom big as a man's head and are often used to bank sharp curves. Magnolias and tree ferns grow taller than oaks. Oleanders and camellias are big as apple trees. Women with flat willow baskets balanced on their heads carry piles of blossoms to sell in the town streets—blue agapanthus in July, mimosa in February, camellias in March—for roughly pennies a flower.

Highways, especially in the north, are lined with clipped hedges—made of privet or bush cedar—suggesting the approach to a private estate rather than a public thoroughfare. River beds take the place of laundromats, waterwheels irrigate rice fields, the village pump remains a meeting place for young women who carry their filled jugs on their heads with an air of infinite ease and grace. One becomes accustomed to the face of streets swept with brooms made of leafy branches clumped together; in private gardens, these are often made of rosemary. Everything looks clean, neat, inviting. There is no litter anywhere, not even at the close of a village fair or market.

Market day is the peasant's equivalent of the businessman's cocktail party. Everyone comes dressed in well-worn regional clothes to gossip, sell, and have a good time. Along with the ubiquitous plastic shoes and dishes, the cheap nylon lingerie, market stalls are filled with quality produce: willow baskets, chairs woven of palm leaves, baked earthenware pots, urns, and cooking utensils similar to those brought by Phoenician sailors to the Portuguese shores. There are piles of vegetables and fruit,

Lisbon . . . a house in the Alfama

1

yards of homespun, rabbitskin throws, and *garrafões* of local wine—wicker-covered jugs with a seven-liter capacity. Gypsies mingle in the crowd begging money for milk for their dirty, doe-eyed, exquisite babies. Farmers haggle over livestock. Women sell embroidery, potted plants, live fowl. There are usually a couple of stands selling curios. Fresh sardines are cooked over open braziers. Roast suckling pig, local cheese, olives, and sweetmeats are on sale. Inevitably there is the blare of some ancient carousel. At dusk there are fireworks—the Portuguese, who still find them as irresistible as when they first encountered them on the China shores, shoot them off in broad daylight or thick fog on saints' days or other holidays. Hardworking people, they have a talent for getting fun out of their chores. Harvest time is particularly joyous, much of the labor accompanied by the sound of music. Olive-picking is like an overgrown family picnic enlivened by the strumming of guitars. Grape-cutters and grape-treaders arrive at the vineyards with tambourines as well as guitars and bagpipes. Corn-shucking and courting go together with musical accompaniment; traditionally the lad who finds a red cob is allowed to kiss *all* the girls, while a girl who finds it can kiss only one youth. Tradition or law governs almost everything.

Villages have a pristine look stemming from a law which requires houses to be painted at proscribed intervals. Stucco façades washed in white or pale color—pink, green, ocher predominate—accented by door and window frames painted a contrasting color or sharpened by plain granite surrounds, have the two-dimensional look of stage scenery. Rust-colored tile roofs that turn up at the corners, to keep evil spirits away, suggest pagodas or Arab tents. Dried lavender is burned in country houses to sweeten the air. Hans Christian Andersen, on a brief visit from his native Denmark, admired the broad, clean Portu-

Peniche . . . fishermen's houses

guese streets, the friendly houses, the blossoming jacaranda trees, the fragrant air. He wrote in his journal, "It is as if one stood in a spice shop or a confectioner, just when the vanilla ices were prepared and presented."

CHAPTER II

Instant History

"Seldom any splendid story is wholly true," Dr. Johnson once wrote. Here are twelve splendid Portuguese stories concerning seven kings, three queens, one king's brother, and one prime minister. They purport to be factual; they are here necessarily brief, and they add immeasurably to the traveler's delight and understanding of Portugal. These personages are landmarks of a nation's 800-year existence. In spite of time passing, their names remain miraculously topical in the 20th century. They are the builders of palaces, libraries, churches, and monasteries; patrons of the arts in general; scientists, poets, farmers, and liberals.

When the tomb of the first king of Portugal, Dom Afonso Henriques, was opened sometime in the 16th century—roughly 400 years after his death—witnesses claimed to have found the perfectly preserved body of a giant clad in royal armor. Obviously he was marked for greatness from the date of his birth, which was in 1111.* Afonso's father, the French Count Henry of Burgundy, married—considerably above his station—a Spanish princess, Doña Teresa, who brought as her dowry the land lying south of the Minho River and stretching as far down the peninsula as Coimbra. A Portuguese saying, "No good comes from a Spanish match or a Spanish wind," may stem from this wedding. Teresa was proud, scornful of a husband of inferior status, particularly one who seemed more concerned with the Burgundy grapes he had planted than with the title of "Lord of All Portugal" which went with her fiefdom. An unfaithful wife, an unloving mother, when Count Henry died prematurely, she flaunted her lovers and refused to surrender the fiefdom to her son, the rightful heir. Afonso was twenty-seven before he finally wrenched the title from this grasping mother with the acclaim of his barons ringing in his ears. The new ruler placed his country under the protection of Our Lady of Clairvaux and dispatched messengers to that French town beseeching the Cistercian monks to pray for him.

Although something of a parvenu in the king business, Afonso Henriques understood its subtle intricacies. Fearful of antagonizing his powerful neighbors, the touchy cousins of Spain, and anxious to gain favor and recognition with the Pope in Rome—at that time the most influential international power in Christendom—Afonso found an expedient way to achieve both goals. He proposed to engage himself and his nation in the Crusades by opening a second front against the Infidels who were entrenched south of Coimbra. This won acclaim from Rome and thereby provided a vital safeguard against Spanish encroachment.

Strategically his most important move was to dislodge the Moorish garrison holding Santarém, the key town for the entire Tagus River area. Heavily fortified, the town was considered

* Some historians place it a year earlier, others a year later.

impregnable by both sides—defenders and attackers. Only with God's help could he hope for victory. Afonso swore a solemn oath to build a great Cistercian monastery on nearby land between the Alcoa and the Baça rivers if he successfully ousted the Moors. He planned his attack with greatest secrecy. From spies he learned where to place twelve strategic scaling ladders and chose the hour of midnight for his attack. The King himself was in the first wave of fighting men to engulf the over-confident enemy. Victory came quickly. Because Afonso felt the enemy must be taught to look on him as a merciless opponent, he ordered a massacre, specifying that it end with the first light of day. It was reported that the King shed tears at the violence he witnessed and prayed for the coming of an early dawn. Four months later, his forces bolstered with English, French, and Flemish Crusaders who had sought refuge from a storm in a Portuguese harbor, Afonso took Lisbon after a long, arduous siege.

Afonso Henriques hated war, but never knew peace. Whenever possible, however, he encouraged his countrymen in peaceful endeavors. He fixed the prices for commodities such as shoes, rabbits, and wheat. He sponsored farming and forestry and invited Bernard de Clairvaux (later to be known as St. Bernard) to send a colony of his white-robed monks—all of whom were expert agrarians—to São João da Tarouca and to the abbey of Alcobaça, which he had built (at vast cost in time and money) for their order in acknowledgment of his pre-battle vow. Afonso died in 1185 at the age of seventy-four, in the knowledge that the succession of his young kingdom was secure and in good hands; his marriage to Mafalda, daughter of the Count of Savoy, had produced four daughters and seven sons, the oldest of whom had been trained by his father for kingship over the past eighteen years.

POET AND LIBERAL

Ninety-four years and four kings later—in 1279—Portugal was ruled by a man of versatile talent. He was a farmer, a poet, an intellectual, a pragmatist, and a liberal in terms of the 13th century. In deference to his ancestors' Burgundian line, the young Infante Diniz was educated by tutors brought over from France. Latin and French were spoken exclusively at the court, but when the eighteen-year-old prince succeeded to the throne, he ordered all official acts inscribed in Portuguese. Further to nationalize the language, he composed amorous poems and madrigals in the "people's tongue," and it was not long before the prettiest ladies at his court—and their mothers and jealous husbands—made sure they could read the King's lyric *billets-doux.*

Like any handsome, lusty young male, Diniz enjoyed his bachelor freedom; he had a roving eye and a lordly manner, and few resisted his advances. Two years passed happily in hunting, dancing, and writing verse, but responsibility to the throne prevailed and it was apparent that he must marry soon and well. The royal catch of Europe was the Princess Isabella, daughter of the King of Aragon, an alliance which seemed ambitious; but, to the surprise and delight of all Portugal, the betrothal of Isabella and Diniz was announced.

In order to shorten the fifteen-year-old bride-to-be's journey from Aragon (in the northeastern section of present-day Spain) the wedding was held in the fortified castle of Trancoso, less than 100 miles from the northern Portuguese frontier. With his usual gusto, the King attended to all details; the entertainment included jongleurs, troubadours, hawking, and bull-baiting. He saw that tapestries and banners not only decorated the great halls but also hung outside between the double ramparts. When Isabella and her entourage were sighted riding along the craggy Serra da Lapa, Diniz abandoned protocol and rushed to meet his young Princess. With a practiced and appreciative eye, he noted the slim figure dressed in brocaded silks, bejeweled and becomingly crowned. She approached him smiling, and although court gossips remarked that she kept her eyes downcast and her hands clasped as if in prayer, others defended her attitude as a suitable demonstration of girlish modesty. During the long days and nights of festivity—plays, balls, and hunts—the new Queen, with her pretty manners, remained attentive although somewhat withdrawn. Then one day she announced that she had invited all the poor of the neighborhood to be her guests, and that, furthermore, she proposed to wash their feet and feed them bread and soup with her own hands. The court was startled and impressed. The King was deeply touched by such sweet gentleness and humility.

It was good public relations but a private disaster. An army of beggars followed Their Majesties on their honeymoon, growing to ominous size, clamoring for the Queen's attention, and receiving it, at the King's expense, at every halt in the royal progress. The ardent, fun-loving young monarch was understandably shaken. He had bargained for a wife, not a saintly social worker. Aware, however, of her dynastic responsibilities, Isabella in due time produced two children—one of them a healthy heir—before withdrawing entirely into good works. Only then did someone recall the young Princess' attachment to her pious aunt, the sainted Queen Elizabeth of Hungary: Isabella was henceforth labeled a religious fanatic, and it became apparent how Portugal happened to have won such a "prize" in the royal marriage derby.

No one was surprised when the King sought gayer company, and Isabella made no attempt to draw him to her. Apparently she understood the depth of the gulf that separated them. Perhaps she was relieved by his detachment. She even welcomed his bastards to her presence—there were nine of them—and undertook their education along with that of her own children. She never complained, not even when her oldest, the legitimate heir, was taken from her to be educated in Évora. Her whole being was absorbed by church and charity, and she spent ruinous sums on their support. Alarmed by her raids on the exchequer, the King reluctantly denied her further means for largess. According to legend, one morning he stopped her as she was leaving the palace through a side gate carrying loaves of bread for the local poor concealed beneath her mantle. When he demanded to know what she was carrying so surreptitiously, she opened her cloak and red roses instead of bread fell at her feet. (The same story was told about her pious aunt of Hungary.) Another equally charming version concerns the convent of Santa Clara Velha in Coimbra, which was built at her command. When it came time to pay the masons, the Queen had only roses to offer them. When the astonished workmen begrudgingly accepted the flowers, each rose turned into a bag of gold.

A wise and far-sighted monarch, King Diniz in his public life struggled to improve his country's welfare. He concerned himself with its natural resources, its farms, vineyards, and forests. The great pine wood near Leiria, planted at his command to hold shifting sand dunes, still exists, possibly the only state forest with a nearly 700-year-old history. He encouraged farming and viticulture by offering bonuses and came to be known affectionately as "The Farmer." (In much the same way Salazar was sometimes called "The Schoolmaster.") He organized model farms, agricultural schools, institutes to educate and establish orphans on the land, a 13th-century industrial movement. According to the historian Sir George Young, he was "inspired by strong pacifist and socialist principles." When at last the country produced more than it consumed, he diverted the surpluses to export, in exchange for textiles and metals. He built a merchant marine and invited a Genoese admiral to advise him on such matters. He gave literature a boost by his verse-making, and in 1290 founded a university in Lisbon—one of Europe's earliest seats of learning—which later moved to the more austere and scholarly ambiance of Coimbra.

A man who appreciated expertise, Diniz turned the nation's fiscal policy over to the Portuguese Jews, inviting the renowned Rabbi Novarros to leave Lisbon's ghetto and become financial adviser to the Crown. This radical departure from custom displeased Pope Clement V, but Diniz was a man of conviction and remained unmoved. He nationalized the Order of Santiago, changing its name to Aviz, and defended the estates of the Knights Templar when Philip IV of France had convinced the Pope at Avignon that the powerful Templars were guilty of "heresy, immorality and abuses" and should be stripped of their properties. Diniz preferred to investigate Templar activity in Portugal and, finding it satisfactory, proceeded to devise a letter to the Pope which complied with his demands but preserved Templar wealth.

Some years before his death, Diniz ordered a Cistercian monastery constructed at Odivelas and a great Gothic tomb in which he wanted to be buried. A lonely man and a great King, he died at the age of sixty-three. The Queen immediately retired to her beloved convent of Santa Clara Velha, which she left only to make two pilgrimages to Santiago de Compostela in Spain. Her time was spent in prayer and supervising her sarcophagus, which was cut from a single block of limestone and placed in the convent's crypt awaiting her demise. Even in death there was no reconciling this royal pair. In the 17th century when Santa Clara had been hopelessly flooded by the rising waters of the Mondego River, the Queen's body was removed, placed in an elaborate crystal-and-silver casket and transported to the newly built Santa Clara Nova. Isabella was by now officially a saint, canonized in Rome some 300 years after she had first been known to her people of Portugal as The Sainted Queen.

THE CORONATION OF A DEAD QUEEN

Isabella was a true citizen of the Middle Ages in which she lived, but King Diniz, her husband, already reflected the trend toward change that would pervade Europe within the coming century. Prematurely, he had instinctively stepped into the transition that would lead to the Renaissance. In implacably opposing the Church, Diniz struck a blow for a new freedom of the human spirit from the orthodoxy that had shackled men for centuries. Thirty-two years later, when his grandson Pedro finally came to the throne, this burgeoning respect for the natural right of reason and the senses was quickening throughout Europe. Dante had written *The Divine Comedy;* Boccaccio, *The Decameron;* Petrarch, *Le Rime.* Andrea Pisano had cast in bronze the south doors of the Baptistery in Florence, Giotto's frescoes were much admired in Santa Croce. But the Renaissance came about eighty years late to Portugal, and subsequently its flowering lasted longer, lingering right through the 17th century.

Diniz' grandson was only four years old when the old King died and the succession passed to the boy's father, Afonso IV. The small boy would be a man of thirty-seven before he became Pedro I, and by then a scarred man. He was affianced to the Infanta Constança of Spain when they were both in their teens, and almost immediately their life was singed by tragedy. Among

Coimbra . . . in Machado de Castro museum, "The Sainted Queen"

the Infanta's favorite ladies-in-waiting was a beautiful and aristocratic Galician, Inés de Castro. Fair-haired, slim, with the neck of a swan, Inés was said to be descended from the Cid, that fabled figure in Spanish history and literature. Although Pedro became infatuated with her at sight, the young girl remained aloof to his advances, loyal to her friend the Infanta. But not for long. Pedro and Inés were young and they were passionately attracted one to the other.

Even court gossips were touched and silenced by these youthful lovers. Pedro's father, Afonso IV, however, was an intolerant man, lacking in compassion, who reacted violently against all illicit romance, much less adultery. He had never recovered from bitter childhood slights—mostly imaginary—on the part of his father, King Diniz, brooding over the nine bastards that had been "forced on my sainted mother, the Queen." A possible repetition of such matters seemed intolerable to him. Inés was ordered to leave the realm, but, in order to remain as close as possible to her lover, the young woman chose to live with an aunt just across the Portuguese frontier. Ironically this aunt was the widow of the eldest of those same bastards.

Hardly more than a year after her lady-in-waiting's exile, the frail Infanta died in giving birth to a healthy son and heir. Pedro barely took time to mourn her demise; then, taking refuge in a widower's prerogative, and possibly even with the King's tacit acquiescence, he brought Inés back to Portugal. With her beside him, he settled into the palace adjoining Santa Clara (later to become known as the Quinta das Lágrimas) which had been left by his grandmother, Queen Isabella, specifically for the "use of the royal family." With Inés he lived there openly and royally. It seemed as if he wanted all to regard her as his wife, which, in the light of subsequent events, she may indeed have been. The irregularity of the situation left Inés untroubled; she appeared content with her love, detached from worldly ambition, happy in their children—for whom she seemed to make no royal claims. The legitimate heir, the deceased Infanta's small son, Fernando, was placed in the hands of tutors and servants in a household of his own, while Pedro's bastards seemingly enjoyed a warm, happy home life with their doting parents. To old King Afonso, history appeared to be repeating itself.

Inés and Pedro seemed unaware of the tensions building up around them. Perhaps a whispering campaign was planted—it hardly mattered how the talk started once public disapproval was avowed. The heir apparent and his fancy woman were criticized—in court circles and in taverns—for flagrantly living together in the residence of the "Sainted Queen." A series of national disasters struck the country; in 1346 an earthquake rocked all Lisbon's church bells and set them tolling; in 1348 the plague ravaged the country and "six bodies were buried in every grave"; in the summer of 1354 a fierce heat wave combined with drought killed the crops and "the cattle knelt in the fields to die." A scapegoat was needed. Suddenly ugly voices whispered, "Death to her, life to Portugal!"

King Afonso listened and took note. His legitimate grandson had been pushed aside—just as Afonso believed he had been rejected—and was threatened by the favorite's sons. Rumor falsely accused her of planning a power grab in their name with the help of her important relatives in Castile. The King's advisers urged that she be eliminated before it was too late. But Afonso was loath to endorse assassination even for reasons of state. He preferred to confront the lovers in their palace. Inés' enemies apparently left little to chance, and the moment for this visit was well chosen; when the King called at the palace of Santa Clara, Pedro was out hunting and was not expected back till after dark.

If Inés de Castro was alarmed by her royal visitor on that afternoon—which, according to the great Portuguese epic poet

Camões, was in January 1355—she gave no sign of it. Contemporary accounts say she received him surrounded by her four children, who were instructed to kiss the stranger's hand, as he was their grandfather, the King. Their obeisance, sweetly and prettily performed for their tender years, disturbed Afonso. So did the sight of Inés, beautiful, respectful, and serene. Cutting short the visit, he returned to where his advisers waited. The King refused to make a decision, ostensibly wiping his hands of the matter; he told them, "Do as you like."

Even before Pedro rode through the gates later that same night, he sensed that something was wrong. The palace was dark and threatening; there was no one at the entry to welcome him. As he rushed to the garden, where torches were burning, he heard a strange muted sound rising over the splash of the fountain. There he found the children hysterical, the servants distraught and incapable of ministering to them, and Inés dead, lying in a pool of blood, her body pierced by dagger wounds, her beautiful swan's neck severed. Momentarily stunned and revived only by the passion of his grief and rage, Pedro rushed out to find the assassins, all three of whom had been recognized by the servants as the King's men. Naturally, it was too late. Wisely they had fled the country. Pedro was left with his dream of revenge, and many who knew him feared "he might go mad."

Afonso IV lived less than two years after Inés' murder, and on his death in 1357 his anguished son became Pedro I. Manic from grief and the frustrated desire for revenge, Pedro spent his nights riding on horseback through the sleeping Portuguese countryside, or dancing in the streets of Lisbon to tunes played by his hunt servants on silver horns. Sometimes a pretty woman caught his fancy for an hour or a night. He encouraged public feasting at his expense, gave generously to the poor, reputedly ruled with "justice and sagacity." And all the while he secretly negotiated and planned his revenge.

Two years after he assumed the throne, Pedro announced to his State Council that he had no intention of remarrying. He considered himself the husband of Inés de Castro before God and man, and he claimed that he had married her immediately after the Infanta's death. Their union, he said, had been blessed by the Archbishop of Guarda. (Neither confirmation nor denial was ever produced.) Having announced this explosive "fact," Pedro planned two tombs, to be sculpted in the finest white Portuguese marble. He specified the subject matter for the exquisite carving and insisted on having the work done on the palace grounds in order to supervise its progress. (Only later did it become evident that precise timing was an essential of his scheme.) At last he persuaded the King of Castile to extradite the assassins, although one of them, Diogo Pacheco, managed to escape to France. (Apparently a beggar to whom Diogo had been kind warned him just in time, hence the familiar Portuguese saying, "Lucky as Diogo Pacheco.") The other two unfortunates were brought in chains to the palace in Santarém, where the King passed judgment. They were to be tortured and their "worthless hearts cut from their body while they still retained consciousness." It is recounted that Pedro watched the procedure from a palace window while eating what is described as "a hearty lunch."

Now, with the assassins disposed of, the King had one further step to take in order to avenge Inés. Members of the court were, in his mind, responsible for events leading up to the tragedy. It was impossible to ferret out the guilty, so the entire court must pay. Although by now Inés de Castro had been dead and buried for close to four years, Pedro had her body disinterred in great secrecy. He saw her dressed in regal robes and adorned with state jewels. Then he summoned the court to attend a mysterious ceremony in the church of Santa Clara Velha in Coimbra, close to where they had lived with such happiness. Inside the church, the courtiers were astonished to see two thrones placed just in front of the altar, both of which at first glance seemed to be occupied. Perhaps the eccentric King secretly had chosen a wife after all? They crowded in, pushing to see, and those in the rear wondered why those ahead seemed to be pressing back rather than moving forward. They were all too soon to discover why. There sat the King, as might be expected, and beside him a richly dressed royal cadaver. Mesmerized by the macabre scene, the court watched Pedro crown his beloved and in a stentorian voice pronounce her Queen of Portugal. No one moved, or spoke, and when the King with a sweeping gesture ordered them to make obeisance to his Queen, a shudder was said to have run through the elaborately dressed assemblage. Only then did they realize that the church doors were shut and bolted. Slowly they came forward, hardly believing what was required of them. But the implacable King stood watching to see that all bowed and pressed their lips to the hand of his dead Queen.

That night when it was dark, the royally attired corpse was placed on a litter and lifted to the shoulders of Pedro's loyal friends. The cortege, with Pedro in the lead, set off on foot for Alcobaça, forty miles away, along roads lit on both sides by men holding tapers, while dirges were sung by many of the same peasants who had called for her destruction. The body was placed in the marvelous sarcophagus, which now lay in that great Cistercian abbey, and the whole community of 700 White Monks joined in the service for Inés.

Pedro lived for only six more years and died in 1367 after a ten-year reign during which the country was at peace and justice was stringently observed. Sometimes called Pedro the Cruel, sometimes Pedro the Just, he too was buried at Alcobaça.

Alcobaça . . . tomb of Inés

A PAIR OF BASTARDS

"Sins write histories, goodness is silent," Goethe remarked. When Pedro I died, his son, the legitimate heir, came to the throne. (It was in order to ensure the rightful succession of this young prince that twelve years earlier his grandfather had become accessory to the murder of Inés de Castro.) Fernando was twenty-two when he became King and he pictured himself as the prototype of his father; unfortunately for his country, his facsimile was weakly drawn and the brush strokes were undistinguished. True, he was keen on hunting and skilled at falconry, but the new King was willful, sickly, and generally lacking in discipline and character. Haughtily ignoring the fact that his beautiful, conniving mistress was married to another man, with no further ado he went through a marriage service with her in an obscure church outside Oporto. The cuckolded husband discreetly left the country as a convenience to his monarch, and the King's half-brother—Pedro's natural son by Inés—stayed around long enough to refuse to kiss the new Queen's hand before he too sought exile.

A daughter was the only child of this unsavory union, and she was said to have been "affianced five times before she was twelve," probably an all-time record in nubility *manqué*. Finally, and foolishly, she was married in 1383 to the King of Castile in a short-sighted piece of matchmaking almost certain to endanger Portuguese sovereignty. Apprehension on this matter among the more astute members of the court was justified before the year was up, with the death of King Fernando. Wasting no time, the opportunist King of Castile—ignoring his rightful title of Consort—proclaimed himself King of Portugal. The nation faced the unpalatable choice of submitting to Castile or fighting for survival. Although reluctant to accept the claimant, the court and the Church were too lethargic to fight a war of succession. The people, however, forcefully opposed the idea of Spanish domination, and the popular will, along with the leadership of two young bastards, saved the nation.

The *Côrtes*, a body drawn from the Portuguese gentry, met in emergency session at Coimbra and declared the throne to be elective. They then proceeded to nominate their candidate, one of Pedro's other bastards, this one by "a certain Teresa Lourienço" with whom he had spent a few nights after the murder of his beloved Inés. Pedro had recognized the child's birthright before the assembled court, naming the seven-year-old boy João, Master of Aviz. Now, by unanimous vote, the *Côrtes* elected this Master of Aviz as King of Portugal, an unusual move in the history of royal successions. It was so daring that it met Papal opposition. A Bull proclaiming João's illegitimacy was read at his coronation in the Sé * Velha at Coimbra, and he was crowned João the Bastard, a sobriquet soon to be changed to João the Good.

João I faced a brief reign indeed, unless the Spanish pretenders were kept out. He was only twenty-six and it seemed natural for him to choose a contemporary and a fellow bastard, Nuno Alvares Pereira, as Constable of Portugal, general of the armies. Nun'Alvares was the son of a prior, a susceptible ecclesiastical gentleman who was said to have sired thirty-two children. Nourished on tales of chivalry, the handsome young Nun'Alvares had been soldiering since he was fifteen. As bright as he was good-looking, he had learned much about the strategy of defense which was to stand him in good stead. He chose to make his stand against the Castilian enemy on the plateau of Aljubarrota, eighty miles north of Lisbon, and based his battle

* "Sé" means "cathedral."

plan on one he had seen effectively used by English mercenaries. The Constable counted himself lucky to have some 500 English bowmen to bolster his people's army, peasants who flocked to his side carrying scythe blades as if they were sabers, and the knightly sons of the *fidalgos* who had voted the King into office. They were faced by the best armies of Castile, strengthened by 2,000 French mercenaries. Scouts reported on the awesome size of this approaching army, but Nun'Alvares remained calm and drew his men into a tight square formation.* In the front ranks he placed men with lances braced on the ground at an angle calculated to impale the attacking cavalry; on their flank were the archers, and inside the square, peasants who vowed to die rather than surrender.

There was no shade from the August sun on the elevated ground upon which the Portuguese prepared to make their stand. They were thirsty and hungry, for it was the eve of the Assumption of the Virgin and a fast day, but they wryly consoled themselves that, if only in that respect, they were no worse off than their enemy. There was consternation when it was noted that the King of Castile had brought along sixteen cannon—he had planned to use these to flatten Lisbon, but decided to test them here at Aljubarrota. One round was fired, wounding two Portuguese brothers (who had been accused of killing a monk the previous night), but otherwise the damage was largely among the Spaniards, for the cannon exploded in their midst, killing all those in the vicinity. A subsequent Spanish cavalry charge aborted when the horses ran into a thicket of lances and bolted under a deadly rain of arrows. King João fought along with his men with such disregard for his own safety that he narrowly missed being killed by a Spanish sword. But the invasion fire of the Castilians was extinguished—they had been prepared to annex Portugal provided it fell like an overripe plum, but not if it meant an all-out war.

* The British were still using this formation at Waterloo.

Watching their retreat, King João recalled his oath to build a monastery-church to Our Lady of Victory, and within three years the construction of Santa Maria da Vitório was well under way. The village that grew up around the great abbey and the church itself were soon known as Batalha—The Battle. No less conscious of the need for thanksgiving, Nun'Alvares endowed a chapel to St. George, patron of chivalry, on the field of Aljubarrota, where it stands today exactly as the Constable specified—even to the jug of fresh water and the loaf of bread commemorating "that day of great thirst and hunger."

João I was a man of medium height with flashing black eyes, a strong chin, and a prominent nose. He was intelligent, fearless, a shrewd judge of character, and, generally speaking, a man's man. He had sown some wild oats, in spite of the religious vows he had assumed at the age of seven. At twenty-nine he applied for permission to be relieved of these pledges to the Order of Aviz in order to meet responsibilities to the dynasty of Aviz, of which he was the first king. Shortly after this dispensation was granted on February 2, 1387, João married Philippa, daughter of John of Gaunt, Duke of Lancaster, in the Sé at Oporto. England and Portugal have been allies ever since.

It was apparent to João from the start that he had picked a winner as his wife, personally as well as politically. As for Philippa, she recognized that "God had given her a husband to her liking and she was careful never to displease him." She did much more than that. It was the Queen who won over the aloof members of the Church and the aristocracy, who were alienated more by his popularity than by his illegitimacy. From the beginning of their reign, the King and Queen traveled almost continuously through the realm, looking, listening, learning about their people and the problems of their land—so much so that only two of their six children were born in the same town. The bourgoisie burgeoned, the country prospered, trade flourished. Wine, hides, dried fish, wax, honey, cork, figs, almonds, olive oil were shipped to France, England, Flanders, and Venice, where they were exchanged for fine woolens, silks, and linens. Luxuries such as spices were coming into greater demand—sugar, pepper, bay, cloves, ginger, nutmeg. Lisbon became the official capital of Portugal, and its port before long was to be known as "the wharf of Europe."

More fortunate or more determined than the rest of Europe, Portugal had been a united kingdom for more than 200 years. There were no robber barons to contend with, no feudal lords or provincial dialects to impede communication between people in different parts of the nation. The gentry lived in their *quintas*, as country manors were called. Fiefs were held only from the King. Town councils had more autonomy than was customary elsewhere in medieval Europe. King João seemed convinced that "all the good customs here in Portugal had been introduced by the Constable," but it was not entirely true. The Crown had done much in the way of reform. But João enjoyed giving credit to others when it was their due, and Nun'Alvares was not only a trusted friend but also the champion of all those who lived in this age of chivalry.

The legend of the Twelve Gentlemen of Portugal dates from this time, although to hear it told locally one might think it happened yesterday instead of 500 years ago. It seems that there were twelve beautiful English ladies in distress; some say they had been slandered, others that they were determined to teach the English knights a lesson in manners. (Even then the Portuguese were renowned for their courtesy.) These ladies quite sensibly sought the support of their compatriot, the Queen of Portugal, who responded with alacrity out of pride in her new subjects and affection for her native land. She commanded that their request be published in her Court Circular and interested herself in the selection of twelve Portuguese knights to defend their honor. Now, it appears that one of the chosen knights

Lisbon . . . azulejos *surrounding the water tank of the Fronteira Palace garden depict the Twelve Gentlemen of Portugal*

suffered acutely from seasickness and decided to make the journey as far as a Channel port by land while his eleven companions set sail from Lisbon. The winds were fair, and their journey speedy; the land-bound knight, however, who delayed in pleasurable dalliance on the Continent, arrived late to find the tourney nearing completion. His companions had roundly trounced their English opponents—in jousts and various feats of "hand, head, and heart," to the delight of eleven elaborately garbed damsels. But as the tardy knight entered the lists, he noted to his dismay a lovely, disconsolate lady in mourning sitting apart, probably in contemplation of spending the rest of her days in a nunnery. With supernatural ease and celerity, he bested every adversary in the games, "thereby restoring to the lady her pride, her honor and her zest for life." *

The reign of João I and Philippa was most deeply incised on the memory of the world with the birth of their third surviving son, Henriques, an especially blessed event which occurred on March 4, 1394, in Oporto,† the town where they had been wed. This son, when he reached manhood, did more than anyone before or since to revolutionize the maps of the world. In doing so, he brought immense wealth and power to his native land and earned for himself the title of Henry the Navigator. Although his father, King João, was a level-headed man, perceptive and even progressive in the light of his time, he was always a medieval man. His sons, however, were part of the *avant-garde* of thought that refused to accept hearsay—whether historic, scientific, or religious—as fact. They demanded tangible proof by asking why, where, and how, most especially the Infante Henry. Although in the Middle Ages family affection and togetherness

* Supposedly the Twelve Gentlemen of Portugal are the horsemen who are flamboyantly portrayed in tile in the great 18th-century gardens of the Fronteira Palace at Benfica, a Lisbon suburb.

† Lieutenant General Wauwermans, a Belgian historian writing in 1890, claimed it was at Vila Viçosa.

were not typical of royal life, the First Family of Aviz seemed unusually close. The Infante Duarte, Henry's eldest brother and the heir to the throne, wrote in his *O Leal Conselheiro:* " . . . never was there any jealousy among us. . . . Above all, we felt that we were very fortunate in having such a father and mother." The five princes and their sister also shared an unusual enthusiasm for things of the intellect, and they inherited their mother's piety and respect for chivalry.

It is no wonder, then, that when the three eldest Infantes were aged seventeen, nineteen, and twenty, they dreamed of the time when they would be knighted. They agreed among themselves, however, that they must win the accolade and not accept it as the privilege of princes. The King sympathized with their wish, but the country was at peace, which ruled out the battlefield as a testing ground. Instead, he suggested that an international tournament be held in Portugal to which every nation would be invited to send a champion. There would be competitive jousts and rich pageantry, and his sons could win their knighthood in the presence of the elite of Europe. The young men found his idea tame, contrived, and unacceptable. Instead, they suggested a crusading expedition to conquer Moorish Ceuta on the coast of Africa just across from Gibraltar. Many consultations followed the young men's proposal before the King was prepared to look favorably on their scheme. Even when he had come around to their way of thinking, he withheld final consent until Nun'Alvares and the Queen had been consulted. As any mother's would, Philippa's heart shrank from encouraging her sons to risk their lives, but in addition to being a mother and a queen, she was the daughter of John of Gaunt and the niece of England's Black Prince. She knew only too well that she could not be the one to hold them back.

The months that followed the decision to take Ceuta were busy ones for Portugal. All able-bodied men were drafted. Trees were laid low. All carpenters, shipbuilders, sailmakers, and coopers were requisitioned. Cattle and fish were butchered and salted. Armorers were flooded with orders for coats of mail, and the Queen ordered swords for her sons. Public conjecture as to the reason for this feverish activity was wild and rampant. Abroad the preparations were viewed with alarm. Envoys came from all over Europe to inquire, and although the King refused to divulge his objective, he managed to reassure them one by one, except the Moors of Granada, who started strengthening their coastal fortifications. It was essential that such Moorish alarm not spread panic among neighboring tribesmen, particularly the garrison at Ceuta. In order to guarantee this, João played a trump card.

It is a tribute to his ingenuity that he thought of a ruse that not only would effectively camouflage his invasion plans but also would serve a second, ulterior purpose. He leaked the news that he was preparing to go to war against Holland and sent envoys to inform Count William of his intended hostility. Privately, these emissaries informed Count William that King João would be very much obliged if he would play along with a stratagem. Publically, before the Dutch court and the foreign ambassadors gathered there, João's representatives accused the Dutch of piracy on the high seas and declared Portugal at war with Holland. The Count played his part magnificently, accepting Portugal's challenge with a proper show of bluster and angry denial, insisting that although Holland was guiltless, she was prepared to defend her honor. The whole performance provided the required cover for a surprise attack on the Moorish defenses of Ceuta and a subsequent victory. It also put an end to Dutch acts of piracy which had indeed occurred and which, according to Zurara's *Cronica*, "from that date were discontinued."

While these negotiations were taking place, summer lay heavy on Portugal. There was a terrifying eclipse of the sun in June, and in July a plague swept the country. The Queen fell ill, and there was as little doubt as to the diagnosis of her malady as there was hope for her recovery. Historic deathbed scenes are usually subject to considerable contradiction, but Philippa's last illness has been explicitly recorded by several court chroniclers (including Zurara) in similar fashion. Lying in her room in the monastery-palace of Odivelas, the fifty-seven-year-old Queen asked to have the three swords she had commissioned from the royal armorers brought to her bedside. Carefully she examined the slim blades and ran a fevered hand over the three hilts fashioned of gold and seed pearls. She called for her husband, the King, and for her three eldest sons. To each of the Infantes she gave her blessing. Then she took her most precious relic, a fragment of the True Cross, and broke it into four parts, one for each of the grief-numbed men standing helplessly beside her bed. She called the fragments "bucklers of defense" and asked each man to wear his always. The next day she gave her sons their swords. Not for a moment did she lose her calm; her voice never broke and she remained lucid and aware of everything about her. Furthermore, she insisted that her approaching death must not interfere with the imminent departure of the expedition against Ceuta. When the wind rose and whistled through the palace rooms—riffling rugs and tugging at the arras—she asked, "What wind is that?" And when they said it came from the north, she replied knowingly, "That is a good wind for your voyage. . . . You will sail by the feast of St. James." It was less than two weeks off, but Queen Philippa knew of what she spoke, and the very next day she died.

The order went out that the great and good Queen had prophesied that the fleet would sail on St. James' Day. The Infantes and the other knights were instructed to forgo mourning as a gesture to raise the morale of the 80,000 men involved—50,000 of them soldiers, the rest oarsmen and sailors. The invasion fleet lying off Lisbon was uncertain of what would happen next. According to an Italian eyewitness, Mateus Pisano, "The fleet stood bleakly like a forest when it has lost its leaves and fruit. . . . Suddenly it was brilliant with many colored flags and standards, changed into a flowing orchard. . . . One might imagine that strange birds had suddenly begun to sing there, for from every ship there sounded musical instruments. . . . " There were those who blamed Prince Henry for driving his father to derring-do at a time when mourning and meditation were more appropriate; it was not the first nor the last time that his implacable nature was to run counter to conventional, petty minds.

THE NAVIGATOR

Just as Albert Einstein pushed 20th-century horizons into space, Henry the Navigator, Prince of Portugal, pushed the horizons of the 15th century out to the ends of the world. Without Einstein there might have been no astronauts; without Henry, neither Columbus, da Gama, Cabral, nor Magellan could have sailed. According to descriptions of Prince Henry by his contemporaries, he was ". . . big and strong of limb, the hair of his head was erect, his color naturally fair. . . . His bearing was dignified, his speech and address gentle." Intellectually, the man was a giant who would have left a mark on whatever age he had lived in. His stature was so impressive that several European rulers bid, although unsuccessfully, to enlist his services, among them the Kings of France and Castile, the Emperor of Germany, and Pope Martin V. But Henry the Navigator was his own man, and Portugal's.

On the Sunday following the Portuguese capture of Ceuta,

Serra da Arrábida . . . Troia in the distance

the King and his followers heard Mass in the great mosque, which had been thoroughly purified with salt and water and consecrated to Christ. After the service was over, King João walked to the makeshift altar and there he knighted his three sons with the swords their dying mother had blessed: ". . . and this was a noble sight indeed, for all three princes were tall with well-built bodies, and their new armor was gleaming and richly adorned. . . . Before them went trumpets and drums. . . . I do not believe that there was a single man there who did not take pleasure in beholding them." The King distributed many honors among his sons, endowing Henry with the titles of Duke of Viseu and Lord of Covilhã. This was a triumphant moment in the annals of the Crusades, but no one realized until centuries later that it was also a turning point in world knowledge, or that the pivot was to be a young Portuguese prince.

During the three years it had taken to build the invasion fleet which triumphed at Ceuta, Henry had been exposed to nautical talk at many levels. The scuttlebutt of the 15th century was particularly bizarre and rich in unsubstantiated "fact." Sea monsters had been observed devouring whole ships. Sailors spotted serpent rocks and water unicorns. The sun poured down "sheets of liquid flame," causing seas and rivers to boil. Mariners admitted it was possible to sail along the African coast as far south as Cape Non, but they insisted it was fatal to go farther. Cape Bojador ("the paunch," in Portuguese), which lay a couple of hundred miles farther south, was the cut-off place where, it was believed, the ocean started to run downhill.

A few educated men, of course, knew that Herodotus had in 600 B.C. described the African continent as "washed on all sides by the sea except where it was attached to Asia." Herodotus also claimed that Phoenicians had told of sailing from the Red Sea into the Mediterranean and back. In 1291 the Vivaldi brothers, sailing from Genoa, tried to make their way around Africa, but no word was ever heard from them. The famous Florentine map of 1351, the *Laurentian portolano,* which the distinguished turn-of-the-century historian Sir C. R. Beazley calls "a wonderful triumph of guess-work," showed Africa as an island. Except for detailed sketches of the shoreline of Europe and the Mediterranean coast, there was no such thing as a navigational chart.

Exploration of the seas had been sporadic, quixotic, and rarely purposeful. It was left to Henry of Portugal to make it systematic, consistent, scientific, and continuous. As a prince-scientist of royal blood and high rank, he had resources of wealth and power at his disposal: as Grand Master of the Knights of Christ, he was a prelate of the Church and unlikely to be bothered by charges of witchcraft or heresy. In a later age this might have been only a minor asset, but in the 15th century it was essential. It gave superstitious men confidence to obey his commands and allowed him to gather information from the most learned sources regardless of whether they were Muslim, Christian, or Jew. On the western tip of Europe, at Sagres, a bleak promontory jutting out into the Atlantic, Henry built his equivalent to Cape Kennedy. It included a palace, a chapel, a library-study, a hospital, a village for the staff, and an observatory. " . . . . At great expense [he] procured the aid of one Master Jacomo of Majorca, a man skilled in the art of navigation and in the making of maps and instruments." He invited wise men and crackpots of the day to join him at Sagres, for he had need of many intellectual disciplines—astrology, astronomy, mathematics, cosmography, medicine. They were joined in their deliberations by experienced mariners, sailmakers, shipbuilders.

By nature a man of action, Henry practiced the most arduous forms of self-denial. He was said to fast more than half the year, to allot himself only a few hours' sleep, never to touch wine. Only with himself was he severe. Recognizing that the scientist's place was in the laboratory pressing research, he denied himself participation in the great voyages. There was no time for him to spare in such indulgences. Working in what Beazley calls "the mist that so long hung over Christendom, chilling every enterprise," Henry ignored the climate of his age. He turned "his cold temper of will" on all who impeded progress. He wanted to know what the world was like, not what people thought it should be like. His captains and crews were urged always to "go farther."

In spite of the heavy cost of failure, he rarely showed disappointment or anger when his mariners turned back either because of honest misadventure or overwhelming, superstitious fear. Much was to be learned even from failure, provided the men returned to report facts concerning the voyage. He urged them to observe the flights of birds, the color of the sea, the timbers cast on beaches. He cautioned them against evaluating the trivia; he would do the processing. He listened with eager curiosity to achievements and alibis. But he was not taken in by sailors' yarns and was apt to suggest curtly that the observer go back and get the facts straight. One day a captain reported on a cloud that tenaciously hovered over a spot in the vast Atlantic. To Henry this suggested the existence of an island. He congratulated his informant, ordered the ship careened and reprovisioned, and told its captain to "go farther" until he sailed under the cloud. There, it so happened, was found a heavily wooded island which was named Madeira—the Portuguese word for timber.

Everything the mariners observed and reported was grist to the Sagres mill. Sailors were still dependent on the Polar Star at night, but as exploration proceeded south, that star dipped low on the horizon until it disappeared completely. Henry and his research team worked to develop better navigational aids—compasses, astrolabes, quadrants—and taught men the skill to use such tools effectively. The square-sailed *barca* which was in general use at the time was difficult to sail close into the wind and was soon replaced by the caravel. This faster, finer-lined, shallow-draft craft, developed at Sagres, had triangular sails which responded to the lightest breeze and could go hard to windward, a feat that had been considered impossible. Ranging in size from 40 to 100 tons, the caravels with the red cross of the Order of Christ painted on their sails won such a reputation for seaworthy performance that it was soon believed that only Portuguese-built ships could successfully navigate African waters, a legend that lasted many hundred years. Henry's captains and navigators were instructed to be secretive about the courses they steered, the wind and weather conditions they encountered, the nature of the coasts they visited, the maps they used. Throughout the ages, nations have guarded the secret of their explorations—whether on earth or to the planets.

When Gil Eanes, one of the first to round Cape Non, was instructed to go beyond Cape Bojador, he accepted the mission but faltered short of his goal. Henry listened sympathetically to the description of the black funk that paralyzed the trustworthy sailor, then urged Eanes to try again. "If you do no more than pass the Cape, you will have honor and reward," he told him. Henry of Portugal was a compelling man with a will to smother the smoke of superstition, and it is not surprising that Eanes was persuaded to set out once more in the summer of 1434. When his ship passed Cape Non, one can imagine the chill that enveloped the crew and their captain. As they neared the redoubtable Cape, they saw and heard huge breakers bursting along the reefs, strong currents seemed to suck the ship landward and the water turned a strange bottle green. To avoid all risk of running aground, Eanes gave orders to stand off, sailing well beyond the Cape before turning landward. Fear was peeled away like onion's skin as all hands observed that the ocean was not running downhill. When finally land was sighted south of Bojador, the seas were placid—calm, indeed—and a small boat put out to explore the shore for signs of life. The men found only desert, but growing in the sand were flowers they recognized—the Rosa da Santa Maria, as commonplace in Portugal as geraniums. It was remarkably comforting, and Eanes ordered several of the plants tenderly packed to take back to the Lord Infante Henriques at Sagres.

Henry was a man of all seasons, whose crusading spirit was linked with a critical, inquiring mind. His aims were primarily scientific, but he was also concerned with religious, educational, agricultural, and commercial matters. He was interested in souls as well as geography. He founded a chair of theology at the University, personally revised the curriculum and teaching of mathematics, astronomy, and medicine. No Master of the Knights of Christ ruled the Order's extensive land holdings as well as or more profitably than Henry. He owned dye-works and soap factories, coral and tuna fisheries. He levied tribute on the Guinea trade and the lucrative sugar industry of Madeira. (Portuguese sugar was regularly entered in the British custom accounts in London before 1456.) The money that poured in was swallowed up by shipbuilding, by pensions for mariner's widows, by distribution among successful captains and their crews.

Primarily Henry wanted to find a sea route around Africa to India for the sake of knowledge and for the power that knowledge would bring Portugal—an overseas empire and immense riches. The wealth of the East—spices, silks, gold—had traveled until now by caravan through the greedy hands of middlemen in the Levant, to Venice and Genoa. If such goods were shipped by caravel over a direct sea route to Lisbon, Portugal would profit and the European consumer would benefit by a price cut. "For the service of God and the Infante our Lord, and honor and profit to ourselves" became his sailors' creed. When Henry's

Batalha . . . center aisle of nave of Santa Maria da Vitória

The caption for the photograph facing page 50 should read:
Alcobaça . . . center aisle of nave of Santa Maria de Alcobaça.

sea route was finally established, Venice reeled and never recovered its financial stride. Riches and religion—the mighty R's—had done them in.

Although Henry was not legend-led, he was preoccupied with the idea of finding the fabulous kingdom of Prester John. Scholars today view the persistence of the Prester John myth as evidence that it must have been based on a nucleus of fact concerning a Christian personage who was thought to rule "the countries of Asia and Ethiopia." The great king was said to be so well born that he was descended from the Magi, so rich that he ate only off tables of emeralds. Furthermore, "within his domain was to be found the Fountain of Youth and the pebbles that restore sight and make their possessor invisible." Although the land of Prester John and his emeralds were never found, Henry's seamen brought exotic objects back to him and he sent these as princely gifts to European courts, tangible evidence of his exploits and of a very human royal tease. Ostrich eggs went to Italy and England, where goldsmiths deftly cut them in two and mounted them in silver and gold as goblets. A pair of live monkeys and an elephant's foot went to his only sister in Burgundy. But the strangest of all—a live African lion—was sent to an ailing captain in Galway, Ireland.

Henry died on November 13, 1460, at his beloved Vila do Infante. He was sixty-six years old, and still wore the fragment of the True Cross which his mother had given him. His will was specific and like the man. As Elaine Sanceau, in a definitive biography, observed, "No public figure ever sought the limelight less. As King's son, brother and uncle, successively . . . he always stepped aside." He forbade court mourning: "I will have none for me, only let me be simply and decorously commended to God." His body was laid out in the nearby church, where it was guarded by his faithful companion, Diogo Gomes. Some four weeks later, when his tomb had been made ready in the

Royal Chapel, the King (Henry's nephew Afonso V) ordered it transferred to Batalha. According to Gomes, "I was bidden to look at the Lord Infante Henriques to see if the body of the Prince were at all corrupted. . . . I found it dry and sound, clad in a rough shirt of horsehair. Well doth the Church repeat 'Thou shall not suffer thine Holy One to see corruption.' "

The breakthrough in the 15th century's obtuse climate of superstition regarding the universe was entirely due to Henry, who made navigators out of squires, deep-sea sailors of local fishermen, and lived to see his caravels sail as far south as Cape Palmas, off the Ivory Coast, as far north as the Newfoundland banks. In doing so they discovered islands, deserts, rivers, trading posts, and even identified a constellation—with its four stars set in a diamond pattern—which they called the Southern Cross. Henry the Navigator, Infante of Portugal, had many lofty titles. He was Grand Master of the Order of Christ, Governor of Ceuta and the Algarves, Duke of Viseu, Lord of Covilhã, King of Cyprus, Knight of the Garter. But it is as the self-made man of science that the world remembers him. He lived and died by the motto he chose in his youth—*Talant de Bien Fere*—which is engraved on his tomb at Batalha.

THE NAVIGATOR'S HEIRS

Two of Henry's great-nephews—João II and his cousin Manuel I—reaped the harvest of Prince Henry's vision and tenacity. For the next three quarters of a century, Portuguese exploration lost little of its momentum, although it was apparent that the dedication and the scientific exactitude that The Navigator brought to it was missing. Even before 1490 Portuguese sailors had traveled around the Cape of Good Hope, had visited Greenland, the mouth of the St. Lawrence River, and Labrador—which they mistook for a part of Greenland and named for one of the captains who was nicknamed *lavrador*, or farmer. After Henry's death, however, the decision to encourage and subsidize discoveries was turned over to a committee which was to study their possible merits and advise the Crown. Such a committee warned João II against Christopher Columbus. This Genoese, married to a daughter of a Lisbon map-maker who had been much influenced by Henry, was far from a popular fellow. He was boastful and demanding. Columbus' demands included three caravels, the rank of Admiral, ten percent of the profits from the venture should it be successful, the permanent title of Viceroy of whatever land he discovered. The committee of four, annoyed by his presumptions, kept Columbus hanging on their decision. Surreptitously, they sent out a caravel to test his projected route, but after a few days the inexperienced, craven-hearted crew turned back with the very tales of monsters and impenetrable mists that Henry the Navigator despised and ignored. As the committee was aware, João II was prepared to spend money on exploration, but admittedly he was no innovator and this so-called route to the Indies did not jibe with the Navigator's studies. In any case, Columbus was turned down, but not without his finding out how they had tried to dupe him. In a rightful rage he left for Spain, where after much delay and indecisive action he managed to persuade Isabella and Ferdinand to back his scheme, and in the end sailed under their aegis.

Often referred to as the Perfect Prince, perhaps because he seemed so like the prototype for Machiavelli's hero, João II bolstered the national treasury by opening the Portuguese frontier to the Jews banished by Spain. Twenty thousand Jewish families sought exile in Portugal, where they were heavily taxed but not persecuted, and the income from this head tax provided moneys to mount an expedition to India under the youthful Vasco da Gama. João II died before the success of this voyage was known; according to a loyal courtier, Garcia de Resende, the King did penance as he lay dying and chose for his deathbed the bare tiled floor of his chamber. In spite of this act of humility, however, he insisted on the observance of all the rules of protocol, saying loftily, "Even dying, a king is always King."

Some time before this, João II's son and heir had been killed in a hunting accident and the King had named his young cousin Manuel as his rightful successor. It therefore was Manuel I who welcomed da Gama on his return from the momentous voyage to Calicut on the Malabar coast of southwestern India. The journey had taken a crippling toll of the four ships; of 170 men who had set out—the officers wearing full armor with swords, the men in leather jerkins and breastplates—only 55 returned. Scurvy was second to shipwreck in deadliness, but the small band of survivors were now rich beyond their fondest dreams. The spices in the ship's cargo paid for the expedition sixty times over. Vasco da Gama was rewarded with the prestigious prefix Dom before his name, a generous share of spices, and tax-free benefits for himself and his descendants. The King now assumed the awesome title of "Lord of the Conquest, Navigation, and Commerce, of India, Ethiopia, Arabia, and Persia," a resounding mouthful intended to serve notice on other European rulers to keep hands off. In all this excitement, Portugal barely noticed that another of her sons, Pedro Álvares Cabral, by a fluke of winds, tides, and drifts, had discovered Brazil in the name of Manuel the Fortunate.

As a result of his first (of three) marriages with Spain, Manuel I was forced to threaten to expel the Jews—welcomed by his cousin and predecessor, João II, only four years earlier—except for those who were willing to change their faith. Sir George

Young suggests that "had the Jews been let alone, Lisbon might have become the commercial capital of Europe, a position she was firmly headed toward a good hundred years before London was." Even so, for the next thirty-six years the Crown did not inquire very profoundly into the belief of these former Jews who claimed to be *conversos.* Dogmatism, religious intolerance and its vile instrument, the Inquisition, were still alien to Portugal. There were too many other things to think about.

Lisbon had earned her title of "the entrepôt of Europe." She also ruled as queen of the Tagus, a city straight out of the Arabian nights, ostentatious and exotic. Manuel was the richest monarch in Christendom. He ordered streets to be widened for aesthetic reasons and to allow the four elephants who now proceeded his royal progress to move through the capital city. With the revenue of pepper alone—which sold in Lisbon at sixty times its cost in India—the King paid for building Santa Maria de Belém, the great monastery-church of the Jerónimos. Manuel is probably best remembered for the uniquely Portuguese, flamboyant architecture called Manueline, * which marked his twenty-six-year reign, an enduring statement in stone and mortar that bespeaks the nation's obsession with the ocean and the East. These Manueline monuments are marvels of Portugal today.

Although his country was the most important world power of its age, Manuel felt the rest of Europe was insufficiently aware of its position. François I, King of France, referred to him disparagingly as *le roi épicier.* To remedy the situation, King Manuel sent his ambassador Tristão da Cunha on a special mission to the Pope in Rome. It was designed to knock all Europe's eyes out, and did. Da Cunha announced that the presentation to His Holiness the Pope must take place outdoors; all the cardinals and foreign ambassadors, as well as the members of the Sacred Col-

* See page 158.

Lisbon . . . Tagus River from the Torre de Belém

lege, were invited to attend. It was an unnecessary precaution, as all Rome flocked to see what Portugal had up its sleeve. The parade that made its way majestically through the streets to the dais on which the Papal throne had been installed was a show indeed. First came elaborately garbed, mounted musicians playing gay tunes; then 300 bedecked white mules laden with silks and rare Oriental rugs for His Holiness; next came fifty knights of Portugal riding Arab horses with jeweled bridles and solid gold stirrups. But the *pièce de résistance* was a bedizened elephant loaded with presentation caskets of unset precious stones for Pope Leo X, who appeared somewhat startled when the great beast genuflected three times before him and moved off to shower members of the Sacred College with sweet-scented water sprayed through his trunk.

Obviously there was money for circuses, but when another explorer, Magellan, who had already served his country well, asked for a larger allowance of oats for his mule, the request was denied. As a result of this ignominious rebuff, Magellan offered his services to Spain, under whose flag he circumnavigated the world and named the great peaceful stretches of ocean, north and west of Cape Horn, the Pacific Ocean.

THE OTHER SIDE OF THE BLANKET

Manuel's great-grandson, Sebastian, was the next-to-last king of the Aviz dynasty. Following his needless death on a Moroccan battlefield in 1578, the throne passed to his cardinal uncle, who within two years allowed the Spanish take-over known as the "Sixty Years' Captivity." This ugly interim ended abruptly on December 1, 1640, with an uprising which W. C. Atkinson describes as "a triumph of spontaneity."

To grasp the measure of what actually took place, we must go back. Soon after he was crowned king in 1385, João I sired a bastard son: two years later, when he married the strait-laced Philippa of Lancaster, his former mistress quite properly retired to a nunnery. Her son, however, was brought up at court as Count of Barcelos and eventually married Nun'Alvares' only child; later he acquired the additional title of Duke of Bragança. With this firmly in mind we can better appreciate the events of 1640. It took Lisboans just three hours on that December morning to overthrow the hated Spanish authority, and within twenty-four hours Portugal acclaimed a Bragança as their new king. The Portuguese nobility delighted in noting the parallel of these historic events. Two hundred and fifty-five years before, the founder of the Aviz dynasty, a bastard called João, had been elected king; his bastard had been the first Bragança, from whose line—again by will of the people—a new king, João IV, had now been chosen.

The Sixty Years' Captivity was costly in many ways, ranging from damaged pride to lost sovereignty. The Dutch, the French, the Danes, the Swedes, even the English had wasted no time. Taking advantages of Portugal's reduced circumstances, they had cut their slices of East India cake and New World pie. The Portuguese overseas monopoly was broken. Referring to her lost colonial empire, the authoritative historian W. C. Atkinson notes, "the wonder would be not that Portugal recovered so little of her overseas territory but that she had recovered so much." These reclaimed areas included sovereignty in Africa and in Brazil—soon to be labeled the Crown's "milch cow."

In 1706, some sixty-six years after that first Bragança came to the throne, his grandson, João V, was crowned king. This young prince was intelligent, handsome, and just seventeen. Possessed of a firmer jaw than many Bragança men, he took as his pattern of an enlightened despot Louis XIV of France, whom he held in high esteem. João became a patron of the arts, a builder of impressive public works. Some said he found relaxation in "mathematics and languages"; others claimed it was in a more basic masculine diversion—women. This elaborately pious man who attended Mass no less than three times a day loved only nuns. He had at least one natural son by a lady cloistered in the convent of Odivelas, which he was said to have turned into a kind of royal seraglio. "João tried to outdo Louis XIV as a devotee and Louis XV as a debauchee," according to Sir George Young.

Brazilian gold and diamonds abounded to pay for His Majesty's indulgences. His prodigal munificence is visible in beautiful, lavish buildings, palaces and churches strung like jewels throughout all of Portugal, treasures to delight today's sightseers. There is the vast Baroque monastery-palace at Mafra. There are Lisbon's splendid aqueduct of Águas Livres, and the extravagant Capela de São João Baptista in the church of São Roque. In Coimbra there is the great university library, and dotting the countryside are Baroque and Rococo churches with magnificent organs, marbles, polychrome figures, and gilded interiors that take on a ballroom air. Life was too easy; everyone took bribes; there was too much gold to be good. "Courtiers swarmed about the King while officers of the Royal army were reduced to waiting on table in noble houses and soldiers and sailors begged on the streets." Nothing seemed as important as grandeur and keeping up (or slightly ahead) of one's royal cousins.

In 1716, João V persuaded the Pope to give him a foot up in this game of royal one-upmanship. A Cardinal-Patriarch was created for Portugal, entitled to say Mass like the Pope, facing the congregation; the dress worn by this prelate was similar to that of the Pope, and when he appeared in public he rode on a

Coimbra . . . organ in the university chapel

white mule as the Holy Father did. When it came time for the new Patriarch to officiate at his first great service, it was discovered that an important particular had been forgotten, and, according to the poet Robert Southey, "the service was therefore suspended, whilst a courier was sent to Rome to know whether the Pope fastened his breeches with a buckle or a string. . . . His Holiness returned for answer 'sometimes with the one, sometimes with the other' and that the Patriarch might use either at his discretion."

Even this honor did not quite satisfy the insatiable Portuguese appetite for prestige. For years her kings had envied the title of Most Catholic and Most Christian which traditionally belonged to their Spanish and French cousins. Late in João V's reign this nagging discrepancy was finally corrected when the Pope named João "Most Faithful." Such an honor could be accepted only with Portuguese splendor. The King ordered three great coaches constructed—extravanganzas in gilded wood elaborately carved with mermen, tritons, conches, nets. (They are exhibited today in Lisbon's Coach Museum. *) These provided appropriate, if slow, transportation for the ambassador arriving from Rome with the Papal accolade for the sovereign. It seems miraculous that these golden Rococo behemoths survived the journey over Europe's rutted 18th-century roads—although it took them eighteen months to make the trip.

Toward the close of his reign, illness loosened João's hold on the throne. The church by now ruled the state with a cardinal as Prime Minister, and another as Inquisitor-General; one tenth of the total population consisted of monks, priests, or nuns, and there were said to be 8,000 monasteries in Portugal. According to Voltaire, "João's gaieties were religious processions. When he took to building, he built monasteries; when he took a mistress, he always chose a nun."

* See page 222.

THE GREAT DICTATOR

The reign of João V's son and heir, José I, was notable for three things: an exquisite pink Rococo palace at Queluz,* a world-shaking earthquake, and a great dictator. Sebastião José de Carvalho e Melo, later Conde of Oeiras and Marquês de Pombal, was the son of a country gentleman. He studied law at the University in Coimbra, served a short tour as a private in the army, enjoyed the pleasures of a gay but penniless man-about-town, and eloped with a young widow, Teresa de Noronha, daughter of a distinguished Portuguese family. Her parents, reacting as parents do under such circumstances, raged, slammed their door on the couple, and then set out to do what they could to promote their new son-in-law. Influential in court circles (João V was still alive), they prevailed on the King to assign Carvalho to London as Portuguese ambassador. "His fine presence and proficiency in gentlemanly accomplishments" made him a much-admired member of the diplomatic set for five years, after which time he was transferred to a highly sensitive ambassadorial post in Vienna. Teresa had died and he soon married again—this time the daughter of a prominent and aristocratic Austrian marshal. When José I came to the throne, he appointed Carvalho Minister of State for Foreign Affairs and War, a curiously ambivalent, double-headed assignment.

Carvalho was fifty-one years old at the time, with little practical experience in government. Nonetheless, within six years he managed to make the nation discharge its personal debts; he reorganized the army and navy; promoted new industry and commerce; ended English interference with the domestic econ-

* See page 209.

omy of Portugal; prohibited the export of silver and gold, whether in bullion or coin. As King José had neither talent for, nor interest in, these matters, he was only too glad to give Carvalho authority in public affairs, and the Minister was as little intimidated by the magnitude of the job as he was by his royal master. An often-told anecdote concerns the day the King inquired of his Council whether it would be advisable to have all persons of Jewish extraction wear some sort of distinguishing garment—such as a white hat. No decision was reached on the rather delicate matter until the next Council meeting, when Carvalho arrived carrying two white hats, "One for His Majesty and one for me," he explained.

It would not have taken a national disaster to make him powerful, but when one occurred he became a world-famous figure. On All Saints' Day, which in 1755 fell on Saturday the first of November, a calamity struck Lisbon that shook the world. It led to Voltaire's writing *Candide*, to the fall from power of the Society of Jesus, to a revolution in philosophical thought in Europe. Conservative death tolls ran from 10,000 to 15,000 people. All Lisbon was in church at nine-thirty that Saturday morning when three separate shocks at about one-minute intervals caused the city to sway like a wind-blown wheat field. According to T. D. Kendrick, who has written the authoritative book on the Lisbon earthquake, the congregation in the vast basilica of São Vicente de Fora "felt the great grey marble church suddenly rock and sway like an unsteady ship at sea." (One can still see the columns that support the dome sitting askew on their pediments.)

In ten minutes two thirds of the city collapsed. The Tagus River, under the stress of subterranean shocks, poured over the lower city in several great tidal waves. Fires, started largely by the thousands of lighted tapers in every church and private chapel, turned the town into an inferno. Churches, palaces, monasteries, convents, prisons, slums, public buildings, rich private dwellings, along with their contents—art treasures, books, manuscripts, archives—all vanished. Everyone lost his head except for Carvalho and the Marquês de Alorna, who made the celebrated remark to the King, often attributed to Carvalho. "Sire," Alorna is supposed to have said, "bury the dead, care for the living, close the ports."

Carvalho set about coping with the dead by informing the Patriarch that the only efficient way of dealing with the problem was to stack the bodies on barges and sink them at sea. He fed the living by commandeering the supplies of the entire countryside; by seizing ships' cargoes in Lisbon harbor; by placing harsh controls on food prices. Anyone caught looting was given a summary trial and immediately executed on the nearest gibbet, and Carvalho ordered that these be erected on every square. He was tireless, efficient, ruthless, powerful, and irreplaceable in the crisis.

Once the rubble of Lisbon had been cleared away, he calmly set about the reconstruction. Much of the old town had simply vanished. (There is still considerable snobbery about being able to claim that any part of a house dates from "before the earthquake.") Carvalho had the spirit of a city-planner. He ordered broad, straight avenues where there had been winding, narrow streets. On the site of the Royal Palace, fronting the Tagus estuary, he built the beautiful almond-green buildings to surround three sides of the Praça do Comércio—making it look more like a drawing room than an open city square. He set about reforming the whole country, encouraging architecture, building roads, improving communications, encouraging the Portuguese to become self-sufficient rather than dependent on overseas revenues. And he kept a suspicious eye cocked on the aristocracy, who continued to treat him as an upstart, and on the Jesuits, who insisted that the earthquake was retribution for the people's sins. Both played into his hands.

A realist, Carvalho weighed his chances of assassination and took care to be well guarded. The King, without whose support Carvalho would fall from power, was prone to embark on amorous assignations and proved an easier mark. One moonlit September night in 1758, when His Majesty was returning from such a delicate adventure, there were sudden shots. Unfortunately for his assassins, José was wounded so slightly that nothing was said except for an announcement that the King was indisposed. Three months passed before any arrests took place; when they did, they included two of the great names of Portugal. The Duke of Aveiro and seven other men were broken on the wheel and strangled; the Marchioness of Tavora was guillotined. Under torture they implicated ten Jesuits, including the fiery preacher Malagrida, all of whom were rounded up, jailed, and apparently forgotten. Then a decree expelled from Portugal all members of the Society of Jesus, which was accused of being "corrupt and perfidious." Over a thousand Jesuits were shipped out of the country. Malagrida was dragged from prison, accused of heresy, and handed over to the Inquisitor-General—conveniently enough, Carvalho's brother—who sentenced the priest to burn in an auto-da-fé.

Two years later Carvalho became Count of Oeiras, and eleven years after, Marquês of Pombal. Aware that his power could not survive the King, Pombal was indefatigable in the eighteen years that remained. Realizing that a lack of education impeded all reform, he created grammar schools, the College of Nobles, and a royal board of censorship to clear much material the Inquisition had barred. He reformed and liberalized the University, abolished slavery in Portugal, ended the old distinction between "old" and "new" Christians. His most celebrated failure was an attempt to teach punctuality to Portuguese officialdom; several hundred grandfather clocks which he imported from England for use in government offices were almost immediately relegated to church sacristies, where they remain to this day. Although

Lisbon . . . Praça do Comércio

Pombal filled the jails with those who opposed him, he stood out in a period of great administrators, probably as the most famous of them all.

As he expected, immediately following the death of José I he was banished to live on his estates and forbidden to come within twenty leagues of Lisbon. Always realistic, the old man considered himself fortunate.

THE VACUUM AND THE APATHY

Portugal's days of glory were passing, if not already past. No strong monarch followed José I. Napoleon's "Peninsular Wars" engulfed the country, and the French invasion caused the royal family to flee to Brazil, which in 1815 was declared of equal rank with Portugal. João VI, when he came to the throne, chose to rule from there, pretending that Portugal proper was a colony of the New World. It sounded better than being a king-in-exile. General Junot, heading Napoleon's occupation forces, was billeted at Queluz, which was hard for the Portuguese to swallow, but, aside from looting, Napoleon's army left little mark on the nation except for stimulating an acquisitive appreciation for French *objets d'art*, silver, and furniture. By 1811, Portuguese and English forces under Wellington had pushed the French out of the country, and by 1822 João VI was back in Lisbon. But the monarchy was losing power. In 1889 Brazil became an autonomous republic. In 1908 Carlos I, King of Portugal, and his Heir Apparent were struck by an assassin's bullets as they rode in an open carriage through Lisbon. The eighteen-year-old younger son, Manuel II, ruled for a bare two years before it became expedient for him and the Queen Mother to escape in the royal yacht to England, where they spent the rest of their lives.

So the Republic was born. But the change from king to president was no guarantee of representative parliamentary government, or of stability, or of financial soundness. From 1910 to 1926 Portugal—for lack of one or the other or all three—averaged one revolution and three governments a year. The turnover in cabinet officers ran into the hundreds. The country was bankrupt—financially and spiritually. In 1928 Portugal applied for a large loan from the League of Nations, but could not stomach the terms. In 1932 the professor of finance and economics at Coimbra, Dr. Oliveira Salazar, demanded similar guarantees before taking the job of Prime Minister—primarily that the nation live within a budget based on its means, not its dreams; and that as the new head of government he be given complete control of the purse strings. He was reassured and urgently welcomed. Salazar remained in power for thirty-six years, philosophically convinced that "The people have more need of being governed than they have need of being sovereign." Whether his successors will follow this principle remains to be seen.

CHAPTER III

Bullfights and Fado

TWO INTANGIBLE characteristics are basic to the Portuguese: a mild but chronic tendency toward melancholia, which they label *saudade* and indulge by listening to *fado;* and a passion for artifice and ornament, which they gratify by attending bullfights.

Fado is a musical tale of unrequited love, of passion spent, of sensuous despair related in song by either a man or a woman: to the uninitiated, it may sound at first like an incongruous mixture of old-fashioned blues and the muezzin's call to prayer, but before long one succumbs to its strident, haunting plaint. The male *fadista* wears a black suit; if the *fadista* is female, which is most likely, she will draw a coarse black shawl over her head before beginning to sing a note. Two guitarists provide a contrapuntal accompaniment as they sit facing each other across a small table, their instruments engaged in a musical gossip or quarrel which seems independent of the singer. The audience sits in rapt attention until at the end of the number the *fadista* throws his, or her, head back in defiance of Fate. Then listeners are expected to respond enthusiastically pro or con. It is the tune (or lack of it), the tone of voice, that characterize *fado;* the words deal with love, or lost glories, or far-off lands, and are insignificant to the uninitiated.

Fado has a shady past and a murky history. It probably originated in African Angola, traveled to Brazil, and from there to the docks of Lisbon. (Other towns and cities, Coimbra in particular, have local versions of this hypnotic music, often more sentimental and melodic than the purer Lisbon brand; there is even pop-*fado*, popular among the young.) From the taverns along Lisbon's water front where it was first heard sung by sailors and tarts, *fado* gradually made its way into society, starting in the city's fancier *demi-monde*. It retained its umbrageous reputation until one of the most talented and flamboyant 19th-century cocottes introduced it in the drawing room of her lover, the Conde do Vimioso, an *avant-garde* man-about-town and bullfighter. Maria Severa, as she was called, might have vanished into obscurity in spite of her charms and *fado* fame, had it not been for the circumstances of her early death. She died at twenty-six "from eating too many squabs."

Not long ago there was said to have been an official move to prohibit *fado* as "demoralizing and decadent," but this attack of puritanical fervor was short-lived. Today's *prima fadista*, Amalia Rodrigues, is immensely respected, rich, and aloof. She rarely sings in public and then usually abroad, where she demands and receives huge fees; a great pity it is, too, for her recordings create a desire for her presence. Her sister, however, has a dedicated *fado* following. In any case, there is little chance that this old lament of gloom will lose its hold on Lisbon, as is evident when one wanders at night through the streets of the old town, where it is heard spilling out into the night. One can feel safe in entering the most modest *fado* inn, usually to find oneself in a darkened room with small tables covered with checked cloths, a bar, and paper lanterns—often shaped like barnyard animals. Sipping the coarse purple-red wine, one slips easily into the general ambiance of vicarious melancholy.

JANUS' OTHER CHEEK

The Portuguese relish such superficial tear-letting, they enjoy these *saudades*, sung in a darkened room. But their ambivalent nature drives them in the opposite direction as well—to the brilliant elegance of the *praça de touros*, where the bull is neither injured nor killed. The "moment of truth" may be lacking in the Portuguese bullfight, but tensions feed and build on the juxtaposition of fighting bull, educated stallion, and brilliant equestrian skill and daring. Thanks to Ernest Hemingway's enthusiasm (not shared by this writer), almost every literate English-speaking person is aware of the form of the Spanish bullfight. What takes place in Portugal * is totally different. The crowds that gather in the bullrings, whether in Spain, Mexico, or Portugal, are not perceptibly unlike those who attend an American baseball game. The undercurrent of excitement may be keyed a little higher. There is a different smell on the air—pervasively sweet and made up of cheap scent, hair oil, and a dash of stale garlic. Butcher boys sell red seat-pads, mineral water, and fruit ices. The music—the *pasodoble*—is specific. These events usually

* The season for bullfighting generally runs from May through All Saints' Day, which comes at the end of October.

Ribatejo . . . crowds waiting for the running of the bulls

take place under a blazing late-afternoon sun, although some arenas are floodlit for night fights, which start around ten o'clock. Seating plans show three locations, *sol*, *sol e sombra*, and *sombra*, or shade, and these last are the most expensive. (Front-row center-aisle *sombra* seats in Lisbon cost as much as ten dollars each, and all are likely to be snatched up by the *aficionados* in advance.)

Although punctuality is commonly a trifling matter in Portugal, bullfights start on time. People tend to be at the arena a half-hour early, milling around and clogging the aisles as they gossip. But they keep an eye on the box of the president or referee, who is in charge of the proceedings and has a bugler at his side to signal the order of events. Inevitably there are a few bars of the national anthem, then a bugle call to summon the performers into the ring for a preliminary parade, known as "the courtesies." As the gates swing open, the participants come swaggering in: the *campinos*, or herdsmen, in scarlet waistcoats and white stockings, carrying the forked pole or goad which is the tool of their trade; the *forcados*, or bull-catchers, in buff-colored breeches, flowered coats, and red or green stocking caps; the *espadas*, or foot fighters, with heavily embroidered capes of silver and gold; lastly, the *cavalheiros* in 17th-century court attire—tricorn hats, gold-lace ruffles, brocaded jackets—mounted on splendid stallions. Trained in *haute école* dressage, these proud and showy creatures—plumes attached to their headpieces, tails flying, bright ribbons in their manes, fox-fur blankets under their saddles—fairly take one's breath away.

THE CULT OF THE BULL

The Minoans of ancient Crete, in the frieze of Knossus, left a memorable record of bull-jumping in the royal bull court. Minos, their greatest king, is often classified as a Phoenician. Historians agree not only that Phoenicians visited the Lusitanian shores, but also that many of them lingered there. The Phoenician cast of feature seen among the fishing people of Nazaré seems to confirm the theory. It is not farfetched to surmise that a uniquely Portuguese part of the bullring drama—the *pega* or catch, in which a man hurls himself between the horns of a charging bull—is a holdover from Minoan bull-jumping tradition. (Precisely how the *pega* is executed will be described later.)

For centuries past, man has risked his life against a wild bull to prove his masculinity. The *cavalheiro*, or mounted bullfighter, is said to have existed long before the *matador*. Rameses III speared bulls from a chariot drawn by two horses; Julius Caesar was said to have fought a bull on horseback in Seville; so did the Cid, Spain's legendary hero. Thirteenth-century Portuguese aristocrats fought bulls from horses as a form of battle training; the exercise helped horse and rider perfect their technique for attack and retreat in combat.

No *corrida* is any better than the combined speed and courage of the brave bulls entering the arena. A Spanish or Portuguese rancher breeding for the ring looks to develop those two characteristics, just as the American cattleman breeds for heavier beef. As a result, the best of these Iberian bulls are fighting animals full of cunning and murderous intent. Naturalists have always considered the African buffalo when aroused as one of the most vicious and dangerous of animals. But when these were tried in bullrings in Angola, they proved cowardly. Removed from their natural habitat, they compared poorly with domestic bulls produced by selective breeding when it came to mustering the guts for purposeful attack.

According to Huldine Beamish, the author of an explicit and highly readable book called *Cavaliers of Portugal,* calves are branded with the owner's earmark nicked into an ear, and subsequently left to run together for about a year. Then these young bulls face the *tenta,* or testing, where for the first time they feel the sting of the spike administered by a man on horseback. Breeders prefer to limit the number of these *pics* to three or four at the most; sometimes one suffices to show the animal's mettle. Experienced observers note speed, reaction, behavior, and a culling process takes place. Some rejected yearlings are butchered as young beef. Some are castrated, to be used to lure a fighting bull from the ring. Those which show the potentials which in maturity make for "brave bulls" are allowed to grow up to fight. Testing for stud bulls (and breeding cows, a more intricate procedure) comes when the animals are between the ages of three and four, and bulls are rarely bred under four years of age.

A six-year-old bull entering the ring is in his prime, an animal bred to be a killer. For the uninitiated it is easy to misread his intent, particularly because when he seems most uninterested and stupid he may be at his most vicious. In all probability he is thinking and looking for his favorable moment; according to bullfighters, the longer a bull is allowed to think, the more dangerous he becomes. Legally a bull is fought only once, primarily because experienced *touros* learn to fight dirty. In small towns this law is not always observed, and the results often lead to serious human casualty. To the Portuguese breeder the Lisbon bullring is what the Chicago Livestock Exposition is to the Hereford cattleman, and he is often invited to share the final applause after a *corrida* for which he has provided especially brave bulls.

Strictly speaking, after a solo fight the bull is butchered, although in some cases he shows so much courage and endurance that it is decided to retire him to stud. If, as is most often the case, his hours are numbered, he is allowed a twenty-four-hour rest before dying. The butcher comes to him, and Portuguese rules for slaughtering animals are rigid. According to Huldine Beamish, "the bull goes out of the ring almost as fresh as when he came in, and after a quiet spell is sure of a swift and certain death."

DOCILE STALLIONS

As a rule, stallions are not known to be docile, except for two celebrated exceptions, the Peninsular stallion and the Lippizaners (of Vienna), who came from the Iberian peninsula in mid-16th century. Thus both descend from similar stock, a mix of Arab and Barb, much favored by the Moors. An American horseman on a recent visit to some Portuguese stud farms spotted this similarity; in a well-deserved compliment to both blood lines, he told me, "I saw marvelous animals, some good Arabs and lots of great Lippizaners." Although the Lippizaner almost always turns white at maturity, the Peninsular may be gray, bay, or occasionally piebald. But it is not their dissimilarities which are important; the qualities they share in common are what count. They both tend to aristocratic Roman noses, arched necks, long manes and tails, and extravagant action. Both breeds are intelligent, sensitive, interested in improving their communication with man. At heart they are equine perfectionists. They respond to what horsemen call "gentling," a characteristic they might easily have inherited from their Arab forebears, who were doted on by the Moors; mares were so highly prized that they were often fed precious camel's milk as a rich dietary supplement.

Xenophon, the ancient Greek general, was probably one of the earliest advocates of training a young horse with praise for achievement and gentle, firm correction for mistakes. Patience works better than anger in dealing with these well-bred Peninsular horses; the rule of thumb is to end the day's instruction when a particular exercise has been well executed. The young stallion must learn a multitude of things—both simple and sophisticated—before he can perform in the bullring. He must develop his innate courage and ingenuity, while at the same time he learns to place complete faith in his rider. He is expected to acquire a whole vocabulary of movement, learning the techniques of dressage and *haute école*, a kind of Ph.D. in equine performance that takes five to six years to acquire. The Peninsular strain is slow in developing, but it is conscientious and has a strong will to learn; other blood lines mature faster, but when faced with the exigencies of the bullring often prove timid, too high strung, or hard to handle. Portuguese breeders * and *cavalheiros* believe in handling foals and colts much earlier than is customary in America and England. In a kind of behavioral kindergarten, they teach them that man is their friend and worthy of their respect and confidence.

Watching the magnificent Peninsular stallion in action in the bullring is a thrilling experience. The change of tempo is incredibly fast. The stallion will be marking time, prancing, and in an instant he is wheeling in highly controlled fashion so that he seems to be turning "a complete circle on one hind foot." He

* Among the outstanding Portuguese studs with names going back a hundred years are Veiga, Infante da Câmara, Ervideira, Assunção Coimbra.

will rear, or stand like a statue—the reins lying loose on his neck—seeming almost relaxed and carefree except for the excitement of his distended nostrils. His repertoire is not as extensive nor is he as much of a classicist as his Lippizaner cousins, who perform in a great white hall—one of the most beautiful Baroque rooms in Baroque Vienna—beneath three massive chandeliers. There is no sound to break the Lippizaner stallion's concentration on the intricate maneuvers he is invited to perform at his rider's command, nothing but rippling applause. He is alone or among his own kind, in a room that resembles a ballroom. How different this is from the noise of the bullring, where a spirited horse is asked to carry out complex commands while taking chances that must often seem to him unnecessarily risky. His signals come from leg pressure and neck reining. He must behave as if he were being ridden with "reins made of ribbons." He must master his own feelings as the bull charges at terrific speed within inches of his flank. "Dodging and turning like a leaping flame, facing the wild animal for whom he feels not only great distaste but also an inborn fear . . . His temperament, long training (often six years) and confidence in his rider's judgment, all contribute to this finished performance . . . the cavalier and his Peninsular horse act as a centaur."

Cavalheiros—amateur or professional—are immensely proud of their horses, their equestrian skill, and their history. In the past, only the elder sons of aristocrats—bearing the proudest names of Portugal, Cadaval, Castelo-Melhor, Marialva—were *cavalheiros*. It was, in fact, the death of the Marquês de Marialva's heir, the dashing Conde dos Arcos, that irrevocably altered the form of the Portuguese fight. The accident happened before the entire court, and although the youth's father, the Marquês, sprang into the ring to attempt to rescue his son, it was already too late. Pombal, the all-powerful Prime Minister, immediately announced: "Portugal is not rich enough to lose such a man to a bull." It was, of course true, but Pombal had an ulterior motive as well in making the announcement. Determined to diminish the power of the nobles, he understood that by denying them the prestige of such public heroics he weakened their hold on the people. When Pombal spoke, the King commanded. José I immediately ordered reforms, and although they were not all stringently observed until 1834, they changed the nature of bullfighting. Henceforth, the bull's horns had to be *embolados*, sheathed in leather, to protect the *cavalheiros*. And in a memorable gesture of fair play, it was ordained that henceforth "the kill" would be symbolized by placing a foreshortened dart in the bull's withers.

There are more farmers' sons than gentry fighting bulls from horseback today, but economics prevent it from being a poor man's avocation. Harnesses cost around $300; the 17th-century ensemble the *cavalheiro* wears another $600. The cost of a trained stallion is in the thousands, and no man fights without at least two of them—one acting as back-up "man," saddled and ready should the *cavalheiro* wish to change mounts. Such a change is made for any number of reasons; the first horse may tire, or the *cavalheiro* may think that a more experienced mount could get more out of a particularly brave bull, or that a bull might react with more ferocity to a different-colored opponent—like a trout taking one lure and not another. The *cavalheiro* must, however, first obtain permission from the president of the *corrida* in order to do so. This must be done by prescribed hand signals.

SCENE I: "MAJOR COMPETITORS"

"The courtesies," or parade into the ring, end on a signal from the president's bugler. Then the ring empties, and the arena concentrates on the *cavalheiro* and his stallion, motionless at the far side just opposite the gates through which the bull must enter. Horse and man know what to expect, a fast fighting machine, "a killer who could destroy a tiger in a couple of minutes." They wait until suddenly he is there, charging violently round the barrier searching for some object on which to vent his spleen. A cape man on the right engages the animal's attention, then one on the left. In the brief period that they play the bull, the *cavalheiro* observes the enemy's strategy. Vaulting over the barrier, the cape men are out of the ring, leaving the two protagonists alone, brute strength matched against disciplined daring. (The average Portuguese *corrida* includes three *espadas,* or foot fighters, alternating with three *cavalheiros* on a six-bull fight program, but in this writer's opinion the *espada* without the kill is pedestrian in spirit as well as fact.)

Part of the *cavalheiro's* * skill is reflected by his ability to encourage and, more important, sustain the bull's natural animosity. When he first prepares to challenge the bull, he does so with his voice. He holds the long *farpa* (dart) between two fingers: stylistically it must hang down perpendicularly at a precise right angle to the outstretched arm, which must remain at shoulder level. Either horse or bull may initiate a charge, but a true *touro bravo* is likely to charge every time he is challenged.

* The most famous among those fighting today are the two Nuncios, Conde, Teles, Ataide da Veiga, Mestre Baptista.

The *cavalheiro* tries to set the course of this attack so that it brings the angry bull at right angles to the horse's body, close enough so that he can lean over and place the *farpa* in the beast's withers. With each subsequent charge, the dart becomes shorter than the one before, drawing the antagonists closer until a split-second swerve of the stallion at his rider's command separates the two animals by the operative fraction of an inch. Incidentally, the darts are tipped with small barbs only long enough to penetrate the skin like a pinprick, yet sometimes they hit a capillary, causing a trickle of blood. Their primary purpose is to annoy the bull but not to damage him as in the Spanish fight, when the objective of the *banderillas* is to weary the neck muscles, forcing the beast to lower his head to a position suited to the kill.

Just as the Spanish *matador* occasionally indulges in *adornos*—like turning his back on a bull or patting his horns—the Portuguese *cavalheiro* has his form of histrionics, the most exciting of which is when he places two darts simultaneously. In order to do this, he must drop the reins onto the horse's neck and control the excited stallion solely by body and knee signals. Handling a spirited steed in this manner—making him charge the bull to the exact point of contact and curve away at the correct angle for the rider to place the two darts, one in either hand—requires the highest mastery of the equestrian art. (Purists in both Spain and Portugal denounce such *adornos* as tricks, but the audience cheers them lustily.)

SCENE II: "THE PEGA"

After the *cavalheiro* has placed all his darts, he sweeps his *tricorne* hat off his head, makes a deep bow to the president's box, another to the audience, and gallops from the ring. Again the bugle sounds and the *forcados*, a team of eight unarmed men, swarms over the barrier. The bull's attention has been captured by the cape men in a brief interlude serving the double purpose of letting him catch his breath while the *forcados* get into position. They string out in single file behind their leader, all dressed alike in red or green stocking caps, patterned jackets, buff breeches, scarlet cummerbunds, and white stockings.

The *pega* (catch) team is always listed as amateur. They may be farm hands or gentry, paid or unpaid. (In the 18th century, if the elder son became a *cavalheiro*, a second son might become a *forcado* to show his manhood and courage.) The leader, with hands on hips or clasped behind his head, struts slowly toward the bull, shouting a challenge in order to distract him from the cape man, who now retreats from the ring. At the sound of this insolent abusive voice and the moving human object which must seem as menacing as a bantam rooster, the bull charges. Clasping his hands behind his back, the *forcado* stands his ground. At the last second he takes a step back—to cushion the moment of impact—and hurls himself between the bull's horns, simultaneously trying to lock his hands under the animal's neck. His seven teammates move in, three to a side, with one at the tail, and if all goes according to plan, the bull is immobilized. At a signal they all let go simultaneously, except for the tail man, who hangs on while the frustrated bull spins in circles trying to reach him. When he finally relinquishes his hold, the bull is too puzzled to move and his late captor turns his back on the animal. With mock dignity, he strides from the ring. This is when everything works. Often the *forcado* is unable to make the catch and protects himself by jumping over the horns. This means another try. A quick hook by a crafty bull can upset all eight *forcados* like a bowler's strike; worse still, bulls have been known to ram them against the barrier. There is no doubt that the *pega* is an exciting spectacle of guts and determination.

SCENE III: "THE FALSE FRIENDS"

A final signal from the official bugler announces the entrance of a herd of clowns—tame oxen wearing clanking bells—who are expected to lure the bull from the ring by encircling him and sweeping him along in their midst like courtiers in the king's train. It often takes more than one entrance and exit, and each time they reappear it is with the same enthusiastic look of stupid self-importance. Sometimes the bull, still simmering with rage, takes umbrage at their treachery and butts them about like rag dolls. But the whole of this finale tends to loosen tensions and provoke laughter. Even so, one leaves the bullring in a mood in which fatigue often mixes with exhilaration but never with overtones of sadness.

CHAPTER IV

Four Provincial Towns for Tarrying . . .

Évora, Coimbra, Viseu, Braga

ÉVORA

A TOWN OF some 39,000 people, Évora is located in the rich plains of the Alentejo, less than 100 miles southeast of Lisbon. Famous for mules, cork plantations, cereal grains, olives, pigs, antiquities, it is said to contain seven public swimming pools, one of them "large enough for Olympic competition." Originally a Roman colony called Ebora, it changed its name to Liberalitas Julia as a result of municipal benefits bestowed by Julius Caesar. Even the most unobservant visitor walking through Évora streets recognizes signs of a long and rich past. Street names have remained unchanged for centuries: for example, Carta Velha (Old Map), Cosinha de Sua Altesa (His Highness' Kitchen), Amas do Cardeal (The Cardinal's Wet Nurses), Alfaiata da Condessa (The Countess' Seamstress), or Odreseiros (The Leather Bottle-Makers). Spotlessly clean, these often tortuous passages wind between high whitewashed garden walls overhung with flowers. In Évora it is almost always hot and dry, as in Tucson, Arizona, and under the blazing sun the town assumes a checkered cloak—white on the sunny side of buildings, and near-black in the shade. Winters are short but often chill and damp.

Évora has a fascinating story to relate to anyone except possibly those visual perfectionists who refuse to fix their eyes on anything but an ultimate example. Here are the remains of a Roman temple, a portion of a Visigothic wall, a hint of Moorish domination, samplings of Romanesque, Gothic, Renaissance, and Baroque. The town is small, but not necessarily a "toy city" as it is sometimes described. Fortunately it remains unscathed (or almost so) by "restoration"; it has not been embalmed by antiquarians. This is a vigorous agricultural community. Farmers in characteristic Alentejo carts—shaped like inverted half-casks on wheels—bring produce into town to sell to the stalwart middle-class small businessmen, many of whom eat their midday meal at Gião's restaurant. "Meals are made of many dishes" is an old Portuguese saying; a glance at the plates piled in front of the customers shows the number of dishes to be served, and the management at Gião's expects one to eat one's way through to the bottom plate.

Gone are the days when Évora was headquarters for the sophisticated Order of Aviz, or when it was a center of *avant-garde* intellectuals, of rich art patrons, powerful kings, prelates, and dread Inquisitors. Monarchs in the 14th century sent their heirs to study here when it seemed appropriate to remove the tender princelings from overprotective maternal influences. To Évora, too, came high-born ladies to enter convents in the environs. Probably one of the most romantic of all nunnery tales concerns the aristocratic Coutinho family, whose fourteen-year-old daughter was compelled to marry Pombal's son against

Évora . . . Temple of Diana and (at right) Convento dos Lóios

her will. (Pombal was not the kind of man to whom one said no.) This child bride already loved another—a Sousa Holstein, the son of noble neighbors, with whom she shared a tutor—and the enforced marriage was never consummated. The girl vowed she would never speak to her husband. After three years of this mute protest, he faltered, and she was allowed to retire to a convent in Évora. Fortunately, the story does not end behind cloistered walls. After Pombal's fall from power, the marriage was annulled and the still youthful woman allowed to marry her beloved. Their son became the first Duke of Palmela. The chest that this stubborn girl packed for her cloistered retreat is shown guests at the great Palmela summer palace, Calhariz, on the Serra da Arrábida, where the present Duchess thinks of a weekend in terms of "a hundred beds to be slept in."

Most visitors in Évora stay at the Pousada dos Lóios, a former monastery, and its chapel has remarkable early tombs, dramatic in their simplicity; blue-and-white *azulejos* that line the walls, depicting events in the life of St. Lawrence, are signed and date from the 18th century. It is only natural to gravitate straight from there to the Roman temple opposite, an entrancing ghost of a building generally spoken of as the Temple of Diana, although there is no evidence for or against its having been dedicated to that goddess. Columns remain only on three sides, but even so the French, who are loath to compare anything outside of France favorably with what is in it, admit that the proportions resemble those of the Maison Carrée at Nîmes. During the Middle Ages the temple was walled up, crenelated, and transformed into a fortress; much later it was used as a slaughterhouse, and not till late in the last century were these external walls stripped off, allowing it to assume its full aesthetic grandeur. Today, children playing between the slender old pillars give an air of liveliness to the silver-gray stones.

Standing there, one is at the hub of Évora. Down the street

rise the severely handsome façade of the early Sé, and the Archbishop's Palace, now converted into a regional museum. As in most of these provincial storehouses scattered throughout Portugal, the treasures are varied, both in kind and quality. But this does not mean they are not worth looking at. Here, for instance, one finds fine 16th-century church plate and ornaments, including a triptych in Limoges enamel. There is an early Roman female torso that seems to move across the room, and an exquisitely carved 16th-century ivory cenotaph. But it is the Renaissance sculpture by Nicolau Chanterene that one remembers best. A true Renaissance man, Chanterene was a friend of prelates, humanists, and the aristocracy; he had a strong sense of the architecture of sculpture, the rhythm of clothing, and the dignity of human grief.

Although the museum's sculpture is richer and better than the painting—it always tends to be in Portugal—in Évora one can see the work of two notable painters, Frei Carlos and Josefa d'Obidos. A Flemish monk who is known to have spent at least twenty-three years in Évora (1517–1540), Frei Carlos treated religious subjects with special charm. His saintly personages were richly robed (one can almost feel the embroidery), he persisted in scattering flowers throughout his compositions, and his angels were blessed with fluttery wings that make them hover as tenderly as dragonflies. He painted with sophistication, an ethereal quality of light, and a perspective that stays in one's mind's eye. Reynaldo dos Santos, president of the Lisbon Fine Arts Academy, describes him as "a sort of Fra Angelico."

Josefa d'Obidos also leaned toward religious themes, but the best paintings by this 17th-century artist are her still-life studies —usually fruit and vegetables—several of which hang in Évora's museum. Here, too, the collection of decorative arts should not be overlooked—antique Portuguese faïences, Arraiolos rugs (the town of Arraiolos is nearby), and furniture; Portuguese

Chippendale is easily distinguished from its English and American relations by the unusually heavy Brazilian wood of which it was made.

Cathedrals inevitably tend toward solemnity and the no-nonsense look of buildings consciously carrying the weight of authority. This is particularly true in Portugal, where many of the lesser churches indulge in all kinds of enchanting exuberance. The Sé in Évora is massive, forbidding, provocative, and almost as Gothic as it is Romanesque. The thing one notices first, and remembers longest, is the high lantern tower with its six pepperpot domes rising over the transept. The façade of the church consists of two dissimilar towers flanking a porch, and a portal decorated with 14th-century carved marble figures of the Apostles. The sculptor apparently used Alentejo peasants as his models, particularly for a big-nosed impatient St. Peter. Inside, the church consists of three aisles, with seven bays and a fine triforium; the white cement pointing recently inserted between the stone building blocks seems disconcerting, but the appreciative eye has no trouble spotting the fine gold woodwork of the side altars and the handsome *côro alto*. A rare 16th-century organ has recently been repaired (thanks to the Gulbenkian Foundation), and experts claim it has a most unusual and magnificent tone. The High Altar and chancel are immensely grand, a mix of pink, gray, and green marble, the result of renovations commissioned by João V in the 18th century and executed by Ludovice, the great Baroque architect of Mafra Palace.* A pair of life-size polychrome angels stand on either side dressed in elegant stoles that appear to waver in a non-existent breeze. There are a 14th-century cloister, a lovely 17th-century sacristy, and a room filled with church treasures—vestments, chalices, patens, monstrances. Most unusual of these is a small 13th-century ivory vir-

* See page 203.

gin of French origin, carved with great feeling, which opens up into a triptych with all the important events of Our Lady's life carved in high relief within her . . . a rather disconcerting concept in spite of the beauty of the workmanship.

Near the Sé, the public library, housed in the former school for choirboys, contains rare incunabula along with a half-million other manuscripts, among them the original Braga missal of 1494; but as few libraries on the Iberian peninsula have been thoroughly catalogued in the past 200 years (indeed, if ever), there is no telling what treasure may be in these stacks. In any case, only a highly accredited bibliophile would be (or should be) allowed to handle such material.

Travel has become so routine and easy today—almost anyone can see practically everything—that the Portuguese detachment from tourist whim and curiosity adds a fillip to sightseeing. The difficulty of getting access to monuments presents a not unsurmountable challenge. Whether one gets inside the 15th-century convent of Santa Clara in Évora, for instance, depends on the humors of its aged caretaker, a peasant woman who may well be out marketing or may simply refuse to absent herself from home to take one round until after the milkman has called at her door. (Such dilemmas can be resolved most often by patience, firmness, and ingenuity; anger is of no avail in Portugal, and frustration bad for the digestion.) The exterior of the convent of Santa Clara has little to recommend it except some unusual brickwork, particularly on the bell-tower, where there are brick latticed arches, like *moucharabis,* a kind of Moorish window screen. The Poor Clares, as the nuns were called, liked to live it up, decoratively speaking, and the interior of the chapel of this Évora convent is infinitely rich, although in a state of alarming disrepair. *Azulejos* around the walls reach up to meet a barrel ceiling covered with 17th-century paintings; the carved and gilded altar, the *côro alto*, and the elegant grilles all show signs of a lavishness that was characteristic of the order.

One cannot remain long in Portugal without taking a stand on *azulejos*, as the reader has been warned. To reject them means taking against a segment of almost everything one sees; the alternative is to accept them as decoration at the risk of going overboard along with thousands of *azulejos* cultists. It is indeed hard to resist the dazzling assortment of these decorative tiles to be found in Évora. In the old Jesuit College, for instance, they appear as facings on stairways and in the refectory, they line monastic cells, they decorate the walls of cloisters and chapels, and most date from the 17th–18th centuries. An early center of learning, the College of the Holy Spirit, was said to have been visited in the 16th century by Francisco Borgia, Duke of Gambia, a disciple and a contemporary of St. Ignatius. When Pombal determined to expel the Jesuits from Portugal, this was one of the first institutions he shut down.

The Ermida de São Bras, a little fortress-like hermitage on the far side of the public gardens, has fine early diamond-shaped green-and-white *azulejos* decorating the otherwise uninteresting interior, but its façade is curious. São Bras is one of the early churches often attributed to Boytac, one of four great Manueline architects * responsible for the most significant late 15th- and early 16th-century buildings in Portugal. Because Boytac was thought to be French-born, there is a tendency to see his Gallic roots in this toy-like, battlemented church building. But it seems likely that its pepper-pots and turrets reflect a sophisticated approach to what was indigenous to the Alentejo—in Mértola, Serpa, and Beja †—translated into the more elegant idiom of a chess castle.

* See page 158.

† See page 85. These three towns, along with Vila Viçosa, are easy excursions out of Évora.

Évora . . . street near the center of town

No church in Portugal has more indigenous facets than the church of São Francisco. (The visitor should not be put off, as this writer was, by the gruesome Casa dos Ossos, always mentioned along with São Francisco: it need never be seen, although my son, when he was thirteen, ventured inside and reported with a sickly look that it indeed was lined with human bones and skulls.) There is a Gothic-Moorish flavor to the carved horseshoe arches of the porch, but the church proper is Gothic with Portuguese accents—twisted columns at either side of the porch, and the pelican (emblem of the Royal Founder, João II) along with the armillary sphere (of his heir, Manuel I) over the church portal. The interior consists of a wide single stone nave of a severity that serves to point up the beauty and richness of the side chapels. One especially—all paneled in white and gold—looks like a drawing room constructed for frivolous prayer. There is marvelous balustrading all around, a pleasant demonstration of the fact that the Portuguese handle stairs, balustrades, and balconies with immense imagination. There are the usual number of cheerful polychrome guardian angels, a couple of Gothic tombs, two royal galleries in the Renaissance manner. But nothing is as impressive as the chapel on the left, richly carved and gilded, with its great ivory Christ crucified. Its conflict of moods—from opulence to agony—produces a tremendous impact.

As a town, Évora has a special evening charm. As the air turns cool, people walk around its lovely squares, less in the patterned way of the Spanish *paseo*, more like Anglo-Saxons "taking a breath of fresh air." There is the sound of water splashing in marble fountains, most of them plain (used in the complimentary sense), either round or vase-shaped, and often topped off with some symbolic ornament like the armillary sphere. The streets are often narrow, and houses on either side appear to be

Évora . . . Nossa Senhora da Graça

leaning out as though trying to meet for a gossip at the top. There are strange and elegant graffiti on some of the white-washed walls; pot-bellied balconies made of intricate ironwork; arcades, arches, palace ruins, flat roofs and Alentejo chimneys with their Moorish air. Twilight, or better still, moonlight, is the moment to see the astonishing silhouette of the façade of the church of the Graça. (The interior has been "closed for repairs" for years.) Its Doric and Ionic columns support a pediment where four stone giants sit, dangling their legs over the side like small boys perched on the edge of a bridge. The effect is tongue-in-cheek, classic Baroque, particularly fanciful and grand seen in half-light which obscures telephone wires carelessly strung across the square.

Évora's town houses and palaces become repossessed by their ghostly past after dark. There are the remains of Vasco da Gama's house, the ancient crested door at the Conde de Soure's, the palace of the Inquisition where 22,000 souls were convicted, although mercifully few persons were actually burned to death. Portugal's zealous religious excesses did not compare with those which took place in France and Spain. One sees the delicate traceries of the Conde de Basto's palace, its gray ribs visible against the blue-black Alentejo sky. Catherine of Bragança lived here immediately after her return from England following the death of her royal, profligate husband, Charles II. (It was she who introduced the English court to tea with bread and butter served in the late afternoon.) Finally, there is the Cadaval palace with pyramids on top of its towers (rather like those which William Kent was to design for Worcester Lodge at Badminton) which Sacheverell Sitwell wittily describes as "a crypto-arabic throw forward."

COIMBRA

No town in Portugal has a richer or more distinguished past than Coimbra. It was the nation's second capital (after Guimarães * and before Lisbon), a Romanesque and Renaissance art center, an early university town, and a thriving community before the end of the 16th century. Today, with a population close to 50,000, its principal industries are tanneries, woolen mills, and the manufacture of faïence, hats, noodles, and willow toothpicks. A 19th-century traveler, remarking on the quality of the latter in his journal, noted, "I shall advise all my friends in England to take them into use forthwith, in preference to silver, steel or quill."

Coimbra (just three hours' drive from Lisbon on the throughway) is built on the banks and bluffs of the Mondego River, the only major stream that rises and empties within the country. (For this reason, the sentimental and chauvinistic Portuguese forgive it its habit of flooding the town and damaging many ancient monuments.) Although the Mondego is navigable for some distance from its mouth—by high-prowed boats with a steering oar aft—the upper reaches are principally used for irrigation. (This does not, however, interfere with what sparse river traffic may come that way.) Brushwood dams constructed along the sides increase the force of the current in order to provide the energy to operate waterwheels. Big, primitive, and ingenious wooden paddle-wheels are equipped with earthenware jars which dip up the water, emptying it, at the top of their arc, into hollowed-out tree trunks which then pour it into irrigation ditches. In the summer, seen from the Ponte Santa Clara in

* See page 271.

Coimbra, the Mondego—a mere wet sliver running through a dried-out bed of sand—can hardly be credited as a force for good or evil. But its spring freshets over the centuries have been devastating. On the south side of the bridge, for instance, the Romanesque-Gothic church of the convent of Santa Clara Velha * has been encroached upon, silted up, and practically destroyed by the insidious underground seepage. The walls and roof of this late 13th-century church still stand supported by stout buttresses. There is a rose window on a side façade; fine simple carving on the capitals of the interior columns; and several Renaissance chapels (one particularly elegant one, on the left of the transept, has the most lavish carving). But the floor of the nave has been almost entirely eroded. Its arches stand exposed, like the blanched skeleton of some great beast, and, below, pools of stagnant water lie like malevolent mirrors. It is poetic and sad, suggesting the chilly ghost of a beautiful woman (several, in fact), and one cannot help wishing that Portuguese ingenuity would turn toward shoring up what remains of this magnificent architectural phantom before it vanishes completely.

Because of the menacing water, the nuns were evacuated from Santa Clara Velha in the 17th century and installed on a bluff in Santa Clara Nova, a barracks-like building designed for them by a monk, Frei João Turriano. (Except for the church, the convent is now used as a barracks.) The interior is lavish Baroque, with Doric pilasters and a huge stone coffered roof. There is no emotion to be felt here, just an impression of height, size, and rich grandeur. Fourteen side altars have handsome polychrome bas-relief panels depicting events in the life of St. Francis and the sainted Queen Isabella of Portugal, whose body lies in a casket of silver and rock crystal in front of a splendid gilded retable. Around the chancel are six 18th-century paintings, more courtly than saintly. To the right of the choir at the back of the church

* See page 24.

stands the Gothic tomb which Queen Isabella ordered carved of local Ançã stone during the last years of her life. Her body was placed in this sarcophagus according to her wishes and lay there for 300 years until her canonization apparently called for something more pretentious. The early casket, however, combines grandeur with simplicity as it portrays the beloved Queen in polychrome stone wearing the habit of the Poor Clares, her head resting on a red stone pillow. Polychrome figures of the twelve Apostles are on one side of the sarcophagus, the figures of twelve of her nuns—perhaps her favorites—are on the other; the weight of the great coffer is borne by long-suffering stone lions. Behind the church, a marvelous, subtle, and stylish double Renaissance cloister was added by João V in the 18th century.

Coimbra's royal side was tightly bound into its academic life right from the start. Along with the Sorbonne, Bologna, and Salamanca, it was founded in the 13th century by King Diniz,* Queen Isabella's husband. Originally Lisbon-based, the university was repeatedly shifted back to the austerity of Coimbra as a result of student riots. Finally it put down permanent roots here in 1537, first in the Mosteiro da Santa Cruz, and three years later in a portion of João III's palace, where its most noble halls remain to this day. Henry the Navigator † endowed chairs of theology, natural philosophy, and morals; medicine was one of the earliest disciplines, and in the 18th century Pombal ordered that all dead bodies within three leagues of Coimbra were, if demanded, to be sent to the university's anatomical museum.

In Coimbra, sometimes called the "Portuguese Athens," academic gowns nudge donkeys loaded with produce along the narrow steep streets of the upper town. The origins of many university customs are lost in the past. No record shows exactly when the first *caloiro* (freshman) was forced to walk through a

* See page 22. † See page 44.

double row of older students who were privileged to administer kicks and blows on the unfortunate youth unless by rare chance he walked "under the portfolio" (literally briefcase) or protection of a senior. Tradition requires that students go bareheaded and wear black gowns and capes—both preferably tattered. Coimbra can be boiling hot in late spring and early summer, bitter in winter, and although this garb is unsuited to the prevailing weather, the students—male and female—remain faithful to its discomfort. The only note of color these young scholars carry is a ribbon denoting the discipline to which they are attached—red for law, yellow for medicine, light blue for science, dark blue for letters, purple for pharmacy. At night, curfew, colloquially known as the *cabra* (goat), rings at nine and serves notice to any male undergraduate that it is worth a beating and/or having his head shaved if he is caught outside the perimeter of the *alta*, or upper town, by eager senior patrols; that is, unless the undergraduate is under the protection of a faculty member or "a lady wearing a head scarf or a maid wearing an apron."

The *alta* is the aesthetic heart of Coimbra as well as of the university. One enters the 17th-century Porta Férrea: on the right of the huge square are the impressive double stairs that lead to the arcade known as the Via Latina and into the Sala dos Capelos,* a splendid hall—once part of the Royal Palace—where official university ceremonies are held. Farther along the courtyard is a jewel of a chapel, and beside it the famous 18th-century library—one of the most beautiful interiors in Europe. It consists of three rooms which open one into the other through elaborate portals—like proscenium arches—obviously designed to carry the eye to the back wall where a stately portrait of João V is ostentatiously hung against what appear to be silk damask curtains held back by officious *putti*—actually a triumph of painted

* See page 299.

Coimbra . . . inundated remains of Santa Clara Velha

wood *trompe l'œil.* The portrait rivets attention while the eyes adjust to muted splendor on all sides. João V was a dilettante and a competitive monarch who wanted to be on a par—at least when it came to lavishness—with all other European crowned heads. His brother-in-law, Kaiser Karl VI, had recently built the fabulous Hofbibliothek in Vienna, and although João was hardly a bookish man, he determined to go his relative one better. The three wainscoted rooms in Coimbra have splendid gilded wood carving, particularly around the doors and on the corbels, which, according to the best contemporary authority, Dr. Robert Smith, are said to have been largely designed by Claudio de Laprada; elaborately painted ceilings in the manner of Tiepolo (by Ribeiro and Nunes); and inlaid marble floors. But the tour de force is the lacquer decoration of the two-story bookshelves. Each room is lacquered a different color —two are subtle variations of dark green, the third a light sealing-wax red—all decorated with the greatest lightness of design in exquisite arabesques of gold chinoiserie by Manuel da Silva; balustrades along the upper section, utilitarian lacquered ladders which vanish into decorated slots—all enveloped in glistening splendor. English aesthetes of the 19th century despaired of the "tawdry gilding to annoy the eye when all should be simple, pure, and chaste," but the 20th century takes an opposite stand, viewing this Baroque library as "a sight to dazzle and overwhelm . . . nowhere in all this riot of decoration is it possible to detect a single inch of unnecessary gilding."

The university chapel, practically next door to the library, is of an earlier date, less sophisticated but nonetheless stunning. One enters it through a Manueline door, and immediately is brought face to face with a magnificent scarlet organ dating from the 17th century and still in working order. The nave of the chapel is faced with *azulejos* and according to a book written by Lady Kelly, the wife of a former British ambassador, there

Coimbra . . . library of the university

are 1,400 of them in the choir alone. Like everything else in Coimbra, the chapel has its traditional privilege: when the Bishop officiates at services there, the Rector of the University is entitled to wear his doctor's cap or *borla* whenever the Bishop dons his mitre—a shrewd checkmate on vested pride and power, whether it be academic or heavenly.

On leaving the chapel, a left turn leads up to the Sala dos Capelos, all that remains of the 17th-century Royal Palace. A great, lofty hall with a characteristically Portuguese painted coffered ceiling, it has heavily carved wood stalls along two walls to seat the faculties. These stalls are backed by wide panels of blue-yellow-and-white *azulejos;* where the decorated tiles stop, deep red silk damask begins (a Portuguese notion of simplicity), extending up to meet the ceiling, with an occasional oval aperture from which important personages may look down on ceremonials taking place below. The room has a static quality except at such times as it is in official use. Then it is filled with academics and their attendants in Renaissance dress,* with male guests in "white tie and decorations" accompanied by their equally resplendent ladies, all gathered to attend the awarding of degrees, formalities that follow precedents stemming back to the 15th century. At such moments the scholars, the audience, and the room come alive, fitting together like pieces in an intricate jigsaw puzzle.

An outdoor gallery at the back of the second story of this Sala dos Capelos runs the length of the building and provides a spectacular view of the town as seen from one of its highest elevations. Immediately below, the red tiled roofs of the *alta* fan out and overlap like the prayer rugs of a mosque. Here one gets a splendid look at the Sé Velha, which must have been even more beautiful thirty years ago before all its 16th-century *azule-*

* See page 297.

jos were stripped from the dome and discarded in one of those fateful "restorations" that art historians fear will eventually neutralize antique Portugal into a forced Romanesque format. There is plenty of individual connoisseurship and expertise to be found among Portuguese curators, prelates, and intellectuals, but, as the English authors of *The Selective Traveler in Portugal* point out, losses due to such unenlightened bureaucracy are scarcely less than the damages caused by World War II Luftwaffe raids on English monuments.

The Sé Velha is a crusty edifice, built in the 12th century on the remains of a mosque, by two master architects, Bernard and Robert, in the Auvergnat style of that French province. With its battlemented roof line and austere façade, this is a fortress of faith, a show of strength more than a source of consolation. The main portal is strong Romanesque, its plain rounded arches repeated in a window immediately above. In striking contrast to this austerity, the Porta Especiosa on the north side testifies to mid-16th-century extravagance. Three-tiered, with pilasters, niches, and exquisitely carved stone arabesques, it is sometimes attributed to the genius of the sculptor Chanterene. The interior of this severe old cathedral consists of three naves, clerestory windows, a triforium resting on gutsy columns that were formerly faced with 16th-century *azulejos;* the *Guide Bleu* refers to their existence, adding euphemistically that "they were consequently lost." *Azulejos* of the same period covering the walls met with a similar fate, although a sampling remains as though one "restorer" suffered a pang of restraint. On the right of the nave, a door leads to what must have been a lovely 14th-century cloister with 18th-century "restorations" (read additions) and now staggering under a deadly, over-cleaned pallor resulting from 20th-century "restorations" (read deletions). In spite of such short-sighted attacks of legalized pillaging (or is it nervous neatness?), the interior of the Sé retains one matchless ornament, its gilded, polychrome retable over the High Altar. Carved in the final years of the 15th century by Olivier de Gand and Jean d'Ypres, it compares with and possibly surpasses the beauty of the similar, better-known retable of Bruges. History has been made on this site. St. Anthony of Lisbon (Padua's claim on him is secondhand) said his first Mass here in the Sé. And earlier, when it was still a mosque, on June 15, 1094, Fernando I of Spain armed the Cid—that legendary figure of the Iberian peninsula—with the sword he later was to use driving the Moors from Valencia.

People rarely have a kind word to say for the Sé Nova, a vast Baroque building finished late in the 17th century, which in spite of a somewhat heavy façade has its own style and authority. Inside there is a single nave with a caissoned barrel ceiling, an impressive dome and chancel, and elaborate gilded chapels in the transept. Best of all are squads of life-size polychrome angels carrying flambeaux and looking very sanctimonious, for all their piety. The Sé Nova was a Jesuit structure built as an adjunct to that order's monastery in Coimbra. One day Pombal,* the all-powerful Prime Minister and arch-enemy of the Society of Jesus, passed the church in the company of the Bishop of Coimbra. Adjusting his monocle, Pombal took a contemplative look at the façade, where a statue of St. Ignatius, founder of the Jesuit order, was prominently displayed in a central niche high over the main portal. The Prime Minister's subtleties reckoned with no misunderstanding, and when he remarked to the prelate beside him that "the large window over the door gives a fine light inside the church," the Bishop understood what was required. There was no window there. The following day, however, the controversial statue had been removed and the niche had been transformed into a window.

Immediately across from the Sé Nova is the Machado de Castro Museum, housed in the prettiest imaginable Italianate

* See page 63.

Renaissance palace. The work of the architect Filipe Terzi, designed for a 16th-century bishop, the building with its patio and loggias has an air of gaiety and elegance. It contains marvelous things; in fact, its collection is probably second only to that of the Ancient Art Museum in Lisbon. Much of the richness originated in the treasure of Sé Velha, and in nearby monasteries and convents—Santa Clara, Santa Cruz, the Celas—and the finest objects are the sculpture and the church plate. There are a 12th-century silver-gilt chalice and an abbot's baton of the same period; Queen Isabella's coral reliquary; the 15th-century silver-gilt processional cross from Alcobaça,* which is often compared to the more famous cross in the Toledo cathedral; chalices of many periods beginning with Gothic—all peculiarly Portuguese, especially those of the 19th century with their extravagant use of jewels encrusted in silver gilt.

The sculpture is memorable for its quality and its range, from Romanesque to Baroque. There are, for instance, the great *Cristo Negro*, of the 13th century, who appears to carry the weight of human misery on his shoulders; early stone figures with an innocence that appears almost sophisticated; Chanterene's *Entombment*, which makes a 2,000-year-old grief new; Jean de Rouen's bas-reliefs; a lovely stone Queen Isabella in a white nun's habit; a dashing Manueline angel, like God's noblest squire; a polychrome stone St. Michael, prettier than any lady-in-waiting; and an astonishing series of life-size clay figures of the twelve Apostles—each an individual figure—magnificently modeled by Hodart, a mid-16th-century master.

There are also faïence, furniture, painting—but the impact of the sculpture clouds the eye for other things.

The most compelling church in Coimbra, and one of the finest buildings in Portugal, is the ancient Augustine monastery church of Santa Cruz in the center of the lower town. It was founded

* See page 165.

by Afonso Henriques in the 12th century, the king who attended masses here wearing a coarse monk's habit rather than his royal attire. Almost 400 years later Manuel I commissioned Boytac to renovate the ancient structure. Whether the main portal is by him or by Chanterene is controversial, but the fact that it is a superbly sculpted design cannot be questioned; unfortunately, as it was cut in a soft local stone, it shows undue wear, a result of weather, and weeds have been allowed to grow between the old masonry. In the 18th century a Baroque arch or porch was added, probably in honor of some royal visitor, and although it confuses the façade, it does so in a fashion that is more decorative than detrimental. Inside, the church tends to be narrow (but never cramped) with blue-and-white *azulejos* curving along the walls, gold-tipped columns rising to meet Manueline groining. The magnificent early tombs of Afonso Henriques and his son Sancho I are close to the High Altar, and there's a red organ which is said to have more than 3,000 pipes.

Although it is generally thought that one of the most beautiful pulpits in Europe is that of Santa Croce in Florence, people who admire the Chanterene pulpit of Santa Cruz are reluctant to place it second to any. In a setting of vibrant richness that the church provides, it stands as if it were the only object of beauty within miles. The balance of the carving, the controlled elegance of the decoration, its eloquence and restraint, mark this as a major work of Renaissance sculpture.

At the left of the choir one finds a double Manueline cloister —calm and simple for such an exuberant period—with a Renaissance fountain in the center and *azulejos* along the walls; from its upper story one enters the *côro alto*, where practically all elements of constraint have been discarded. The stalls, carved by an artist known only as Master Machim, are staggering in their 16th-century splendor. Covered with red-and-gold carving, they depict caravels at sea, exotic urban scenes, highlights of the

Coimbra . . . cloister of Santa Cruz

exploits of da Gama, ports with a Hanseatic flavor, monkeys scampering in palm trees, all carved in high relief—a triumph of fantasy mixed with fact.

Not far from Santa Cruz, the church of the Carmo has a charming two-story cloister with Renaissance arches below and square ones above; the Graça church, slightly farther on, has Rococo side chapels where the most snobbish angels carry torches and coats-of-arms. One of the finest early façades in Coimbra is that of the church of São Tiago, built in 1183, which has a grave, noble Romanesque main portal with primitive Visigothic figures carved on its capitals. Surrounded as it is by curious narrow streets of the medieval lower town fanning out from the Praça do Comércio, the church seems aloof to the present, turned in on itself. A flight of stairs that leads up to the next street passes the side door of São Tiago, even simpler than the main entrance but with the same aloofness that so often marks the Romanesque.

While one remains in the Coimbra vicinity, there are four places to attract the confirmed tarrier—a convent, a pilgrimage church, a 16th-century cypress forest, and a Roman dig. The convent of Celas, built by the Bernardine order, provided much of the church treasure now exhibited in the Machado de Castro museum. The convent has a late Renaissance portal and a much touted cloister in which rounded arches are supported by twin columns with illuminated capitals—human and animal heads—that are considered among the finest of their period in Portugal. The proportion of this small cloister is feminine and lovely, but one has an uneasy sense of inept restoration particularly after seeing molds of the cloister columns stored in the chapter house, behind a door by Chanterene; there is a rumor that this was originally a two-storied cloister only recently reduced to a single state.

Between Celas and Coimbra, the small church of Santo

António dos Olivais sits at the top of a toy-like set of monumental pilgrimage stairs. It was here that Santo António entered the Franciscan order and so quite naturally the interior of the church is decorated with *azulejos* recounting anecdotes in his life. The sacristy, which one enters from outside the church on the left, has 18th-century tempera panels pertaining to the saint, all surrounded by painted flowers and set in gold frames—very stylish and touching, too.

Bussaco is north of Coimbra, only slightly off the direct route to Viseu. One goes there to see cypresses, possibly the most famous trees in the world. Botanically, the cypress is known as *Cupressus lusitanicus,* and it is believed that the seeds came from Mexico hundreds of years ago. The trees' lacy foliage belies their immense size—sometimes 125 feet high. They attracted the attention of Pope Urban VIII in 1643, who then issued a Bull threatening "excommunication to anyone who damaged the trees of Bussaco." The Palace Hotel, a former royal hunting palace, is a ghastly 19th-century attempt at Manueline, and as loony a building as one could imagine. Aside from that, it is expensive, with unimaginative food, and a clientele to match.

Conimbriga is in the opposite direction, on the Lisbon road, and has the fascination of honest archeology in progress. It is said that the area which now can be visited is only a tenth of what will eventually be discovered of this impressive outpost of empire. One can see the remains of fortifications from the first century B.C., remnants of the Roman road that went from here to Braga, and the underground sewage system for a sizable community of soldiers. One senses that the generals put out here to pasture felt secure enough to live in luxury. One sees the broken columns of their palaces, their hot-water baths, their gardens and pools—both for swimming and reflecting. But, above all, marvelous mosaic floors remain miraculously unfaded; their varied and inventive designs suggest op art, or Persian miniatures, or complex geometrical designs—with a recurrent use of the swastika. Artifacts and broken torsos of statuary have been labeled and placed in a nearby museum-bar-and-restaurant, where one can enjoy some form of refreshment while buying lovely pieces of Coimbra faïence, copied from old models.

VISEU

In order to get a critical taste of the delights provided by three of our "tarry towns" (Évora, Coimbra, and Braga), one must allow several days' time for what the *Oxford Dictionary* defines as a sojourn; Viseu, however, is tailored to fit something shorter, more like a stay. One of Portugal's show towns, but never an academic center or a prestigious ecclesiastical power or a seat of government, it has less to show than some of the others. This is speaking quantitatively, for Viseu has great character, style, and one of the loveliest squares in Europe. Although the Largo da Sé looks like a stage set, it is infinitely too lively to be anachronistic. It is not grand, which is part of its charm. But it is endowed with an intangible mix of harmony and grace that binds together architecture spanning some 600 years—from the 13th through the 18th centuries. None of it apparently appealed to 19th-century tastes, for Murray's *Guidebook* dispatches Viseu as having "a style of architecture between Teutonic and Tuscan." Only a little more than an hour's drive northeast of Coimbra, set in wooded land and vineyards—the excellent Dão table wine comes from this vicinity—Viseu is a town of around 17,000 people. Visiting sportsmen motoring in the environs are quick to notice fast-running mountain streams that should be filled with trout but no longer are, due to pollution—from sawmills and residue of copper sulphate used in spraying the grapes. Meadows often carpeted with flowers and green vineyards, eucalyptus trees, and rocky gorges extend to the very edges of the town. Peasants come to weekly markets on Tuesday with everything from cross-fox skins to flocks of sheep, ground maize and rye, and cabbages.

The town is dominated by the early Sé, built on an elevated height. With Gothic towers, a stylish 17th-century portal, 18th-century balustrades and ornaments, its granite façade has a look of muted elegance. One enters through a porch from which a door leads directly into the church; but it has always been my special delight to proceed first to the far right of the porch in order to pass through an exquisite Renaissance two-story cloister. With its Ionic columns and arcades faced with blue-and-white *azulejos*, its elegant tricks of light and shadow, it appears to have been inspired by some master chiaroscurist. From here there are two portals into the Sé: one, which is now sealed, is Romanesque, with almost trefoiled arches; the other is a handsome Gothic door which leads directly into the nave. The interior of this provincial cathedral is stunning and sophisticated. Plain Romanesque columns support a vaulted roof with thick, knotted, cable groining and gilded stone bosses. Handsome, squarish pulpits are carved and gilded; choir stalls have a hint of chinoiserie. There is the effect of richness and restraint which Kingston, another 19th-century traveler, admired: "it being but slightly gilt exhibiting far better taste than that which overloads those parts of the sacred edifices with gold leaf." (How sad these attacks of Puritan constraint!)

In the big sacristy, blue-and-yellow *azulejos* on the walls should clash with a painted ceiling (rust red, green, and deep saffron) but instead provide a lesson in how conflicting designs —like musical dissonants—sometimes produce harmony. One climbs a flight of stone stairs in order to reach the *côro alto* with its immense music lecterns—one of which is set upon a bronze pelican, the royal emblem of João II. From here, a door opens onto the upper cloister with rooms behind it in which the treasures of the Sé are exhibited—a remarkable assortment of relics and ornaments (such as 13th-century Limoges enamel caskets), along with stone sculpture and fine polychrome figures. From the windows, and particularly from a colonnaded loggia, one has a superb panoramic view of the countryside, of the square immediately below, and of the church of Misericórdia opposite.

If it were not for its twin towers, this Misericórdia could be mistaken for a palace. Haughtily set on a raised platform surrounded by a balustrade, its white façade has a wealth of 18th-century stone ornament—Baroque curves around doors and windows and bat-winged volutes, all mellowed to a golden hue. From the exterior it gives the appearance of being a spacious church, but the Misericórdia is twice as wide as it is deep, with a disconcerting note of shallowness inside.

It is from the vantage point of its platform, however, that one becomes aware of the subtle graces of the square. There are buildings on all four sides, but one has no sense of being hemmed in. Each structure is unlike its neighbor, thoroughly individualistic but in aesthetic accord. Each set of stairs has a personality of its own. The Portuguese talent for designing stairs with versatility and precision is underlined here on Viseu's Largo da Sé. Round steps encircle the pillory; three-sided stairs lead into the Sé; curving stairs, with just a hint of a landing, rise up to the Misericórdia; two-sided stairs lead into the right wing of the old Seminary, and there are none at all on the austere building to the left, which is now the Grão Vasco Museum.

Vasco Fernandes, an artist who became known as Grão Vasco (the great Vasco), was the master of the 16th-century Viseu school of painting. Although Reynaldo dos Santos objects to what he terms his "naturalism," he praises him as a colorist, and

Viseu . . . the Misericórdia

for his passionate, dramatic sense, calling him "the first great Portuguese master of the Manueline Renaissance." There is a brooding sensuality to his work as well as what a critic terms his "shuddering, tortured spirituality." The compositions are usually busy, with architectural perspective in the background striking a Flemish note even when translated to a more luxuriant landscape. Grão Vasco did his finest works for his home-town cathedral and they now hang in the museum bearing his name, along with lesser works attributed to anonymous followers. Whether he painted the Viseu *St. Peter* or the one that hangs in São João de Tarouca * has been questioned. Both depict the identical concept of the saint as Pope. Seated on a monumental throne, Peter appears sad and grave, a plebeian, aging man loaded with rich vestments, weighed down by the Papacy: he brings to mind the late Pope John XXIII. One must not allow the painting to distract one from the rest of the collected objects —ceramics, furniture, rugs, and remarkable sculpture. One is certain to be moved by stone figures such as that of the 14th-century pregnant Virgin, very sweet and solemn in her polychrome stone robes.

There are three other churches in Viseu that it would be a pity to overlook: São Francisco, with its astonishing hanging staircase and elaborate Baroque interior; São Bento, with a richly painted ceiling and gold *boiseries* which surprisingly omit the ubiquitous salomonic columns; and the church of Carmo, possibly the most lavish of the three, with its *azulejos*, its architecturally painted dome over the apse, its gilded pulpits, pelmets, retable, and four dramatically empty but colossal gold frames.

A bustling, prosperous provincial town, Viseu has its share of narrow streets—particularly the Rua Direita, the Rua da Senhora da Piedade, and the Rua dos Andradas—with handsome houses dating back to the 16th–18th centuries, many of which

* See page 255.

have fascinating door knockers. The town takes pride in two legendary figures: Roderick, the last king of the Goths, who is thought to have been buried in the 8th-century church, São Miguel do Fetal; and the earlier resistance hero of Lusitania, a *guerillero*, called Viriato, who fought off the Roman general Scipio and was slain in treacherous ambush in 139 B.C. (Viriato is to Portugal what Boadicea is to England, or Vercingetorix to France.)

Viseu also glories in at least one legendary defeat. Long ago when prelates were more arrogant and powerful than they are now, a certain Bishop of Viseu, returning from a voyage to a remote part of the diocese, heard a church bell sound the hour as he passed through the village of Ribafeita. Never had he heard a lovelier tone. Over the objections of the village elders, he commandeered the bell, ordering it placed in his coach, and proceeded back to Viseu, where his trophy was hoisted to the bell-tower of the Sé. While this was being done, the haughty Bishop paced the square below, impatient to hear the first note of the sweet voice. But the bell was mute. When the bronze clapper struck its side it seemed to groan. For days, bell-ringers pulled and tugged, but the bell made the same hoarse sound. Disgusted, the Bishop ordered it removed and stored in the barn of a nearby convent. But the villagers of Ribafeita wanted their bell back, even though it might never ring again, and they persuaded the nuns to let them take it away. It was hung at dawn on Sunday, and when the village curate touched the cord ever so tentatively, the bell rang and rang, peeling out a song of triumph and glee.

BRAGA

Some years ago when I proposed to visit Braga for the first time, a worldly Visconde at a dinner party in Lisbon remarked, "Surely, you will find it tacky." He couldn't have been more wrong. But I have reason to be grateful to him for exposing me early to what Eça de Queiroz,* the famous Portuguese novelist, calls "the instinctive Portuguese habit of disparaging our country."

Located in the north about an hour's drive from Oporto, Braga is an ancient city with an illustrious past. The Roman legions knew it as Bracara Augusta and built five major military roads to fan out like spokes from this strategic wheel of empire. Later it was occupied by Germanic tribes, first the Suevi, then the Goths, both of whom became Christianized. In 716, however, the Moors sacked Braga and held it for some 300 years after which it was finally restored to Christian Iberia. The Archbishop of Braga to this day retains the resounding title of Primate of the Spains. This is a town of fountains (a recent visitor counted no less than sixty), of religious monuments (some thirty churches, monasteries, convents, and hospices). According to Sacheverell Sitwell, it is "the artistic capital of northern Portugal," a statement I heartily subscribe to, regardless of the ambivalent *Guide Bleu*, which celebrates Braga as "the Portuguese Rome" and then denigrates it by saying "most of the churches are at present devoid of interest." In one day, I looked at nine of them and my eyes boggled with pleasures.

Tarrying in Braga means looking at churches, primarily, all of which have one common denominator. They all have granite

* *The Sin of Father Amaro*, *The Mandarin*, and *The Maias* by Eça de Queiroz are available in English.

façades and interiors decorated with carved and gilded woodwork, a medium that bespeaks both architecture and sculpture. This is the capital of the land of the golden churches. These gilt interiors, which Robert Smith calls "a tapestry of wood," are probably Portugal's finest and most original contribution to the world's decorative arts.

The Sé, built on Roman foundations, with a plaque on one wall dedicated to Iris Augusta, originally was a Romanesque structure begun in the 11th century. An imposing fortress of a church, it is multi-faceted spiritually as well as architecturally. Braga is one of the rare dioceses permitted by the 16th-century Council of Trent to retain its own liturgy; the Braga rubric, according to a missal of 1494, includes an annual blessing of the new grapes (in August on the Feast of the Transfiguration), a custom which probably stemmed from Burgundy (where it is no longer celebrated) and was brought to Portugal by Geraldus, an 11th-century Archbishop of Braga who was a French Benedictine monk from the Cluny monastery. The influence of this monastic order, and the architecture of its church in Cluny, still to be seen throughout France (in Vézelay or Autun), here in Braga is evidenced by the two towers flanking the façade, the sobriety of the south portal, the carving of the pillars of the transept arches, and the austerity of the three-aisle nave. To these have been added eclectic riches of later date. Jorge da Costa, a 16th-century archbishop, appended the handsome porch with festooned arches onto the west portal. Along the east elevation, there appear a rich Manueline (almost flamboyant) fretwork with spiky obelisks and pinnacles along the roof line; and the adorable stone figure of Nossa Senhora do Leite (the Virgin nursing the Child at Her breast) which Reynaldo dos Santos, the distinguished art historian, calls "the masterpiece of naïve gentleness and grace and one of the most beautiful pieces of Manueline sculpture."

Women who have gazed on this exquisite figure hardly need

the church's injunction, "Before entering arms and breasts must be properly covered," to dress modestly.

Inside, the Sé is dominated by a pair of stupendous Baroque organs—elaborately carved, gilded, and painted—gracious angels in the dubious company of disporting satyrs, mermen, devils, and dolphins. Seen from below, the effect is staggering, even more so when seen close to from a richly carved and gilded *côro alto*, where each choir stall is supported by a sexy caryatid. One should not become so overcome by these convolutions that one overlooks the lovely Nossa Senhora Maria da Braga over the High Altar, commissioned by Archbishop Gonçalo Pereira, father of Nun'Alvares, the mighty Constable of Portugal *; or that worldly prelate's tomb in the detached Capela da Glória. One must purchase a ticket to visit the latter, a small ogival chapel with geometric patterned frescoes on the walls enclosing the Archbishop's great stone sarcophagus carved during his lifetime. This probably accounts for the pious expression of serenity on the face of his recumbent stone image. Unlike custodians in Italy, who encourage tourists to buy tickets for every concession within the churches, the Portuguese leave one alone. This laudable attribute demands a certain connoisseurship on the part of visitors not only to know what they want to see but how to find it; it took me three separate visits to the Sé in Braga to see everything. Easily to be missed, for instance, to the right of the main portal there is the finely carved, gilded copper tomb of a young princeling—the son of João I and his English wife, Philippa of Lancaster. There are also the very early stone tombs of Henry of Burgundy and his Spanish wife, Teresa † (parents of the first Portuguese king, Afonso Henriques), in a chapel to the left, just before the crossing. In a Renaissance cloister on the east side, a small stone Pietà is a particular favorite

* See page 35.
† See page 20.

Braga . . . Nossa Senhora de Leite on apse of the Sé
Braga . . . Pietà in cloister of the Sé

of mine: it tells its story as harshly as today's headlines; the strong peasant body of the dead Christ lies across the Virgin's lap, and She, not gentle in her grief, looks down, shocked, angry, and appalled.

Nor should one miss the treasure of the Sé, which means seeking out a ticket vender. This collection includes objects of rare and eloquent beauty: a 10th-century Byzantine cross decorated with pre-Limoges enamel; a 14th-century rock-crystal cross; a silver chalice said to have been used by São Geraldus; a 10th-century carved ivory casket attributed to the court of Caliph Hisham II; Manueline plate; the gaudy red-and-gold vestments of Archbishop Gaspar da Bragança (one of João V's bastards); a portable red lacquer organ with gold chinoiserie decoration which I have heard give tongue with shrill jubilant sound; gold-and-white *boiseries*, and red-and-gold ones, removed from the Sé walls (in a 1930 "restoration"), that now appear lost and alien seen out of context.

Most granite buildings in Braga are carved—as if the stone were *gesso*—to fit the required Romanesque, Renaissance, Baroque, or Rococo style. The church of Misericórdia not far from the Sé, settled for late Renaissance—slender columns, open cockleshells, and a delicious high-relief encounter between the Virgin and Santa Isabella along with their angelic attendants, all behaving as one might expect in a meeting of fashionable ladies at the latter part of the 16th century. The interior of the Misericórdia has a suitable amount of finely carved and gilded ornament, but here in Braga one tends to become blasé, or blinded, by the wealth of this kind of decoration.

It appears axiomatic that a surfeit of aesthetic feasting stimulates hunger pangs, so it is fortunate that here in Braga there is at the least one good provincial restaurant, Ignacio. Set on an open square among modest buildings, it has an unpretentious air, red-tiled floors, and waitresses who appear old, with hair growing out of moles on their cheeks, but who wait patiently for one to make a choice among the fine Minhotan dishes on the menu.*

Braga, with its many squares and ancient streets, invites one to prowl on foot. There is the omnipresent murmur of fountains, the ringing of church bells. Streets are often lined with fine old granite houses sometimes 200 to 300 years old; sometimes, too, a great house appears sandwiched between two modern bank buildings. Some have plain façades with the armorial shield of the family emblazoned on the side; some are concealed back of wooden jalousies, like the Casa dos Crivos, which looks like a seraglio; a few are immensely elegant and grand, none more so than the Palácio do Mexicano (now called Casa do Raio, because it houses the X-ray department of the hospital) with its façade covered with *azulejos* and decorated in granite with curved and hooded pediments over the windows, balustrades, and flaming urns along the roof.

But with all the rich past, Braga retains its contemporary vitality. It has a burgeoning life outside its antiquities. A town of some 40,000 persons, it is a thriving center of small industry (firearms, cutlery, and felt hats) and of agriculture. The pastoral note is particularly charming around the tiny Capela da São Bentinho (diminutive for Bento), where peasants bring their offerings—mostly eggs and live poultry—in thanksgiving for the Saint's favors. (These are sold by the church at a weekly farm market held on Tuesday in a Braga square, and it has been noted that the Saint's indulgences affect the rise and fall of farm prices.)

Not all of Braga's churches are great, or even worth noticing, but many are provocative. There is the small Capela dos Coimbras, built in 1525, which looks like a little Manueline fortress, with *azulejos* on the interior walls and a nearly life-size entomb-

* See page 133.

ment of painted stone. More of an altar jewel than architecture, it is attributed to Chanterene. The hospice of São Marcos looks more like a palace than a hospital and was established in the 16th century by Archbishop Diogo de Sousa (prelates embellished Braga as assiduously as kings did Lisbon). Later, in the 18th century, it was given the new and very stylish façade that we see today, by the architect Carlos Luís Ferreira Amarante, along with twelve splendid granite statues by Machado de Castro, the famous sculptor of that period. The church of Santa Cruz dates from the 17th century, and its decoration looks as though it had been squeezed from a sophisticated pastry cook's frosting bag in a style that combines Renaissance with Baroque. The interior, on the other hand, is stunning, bold enough to deny any exterior fussiness. Subtle grisaille designs painted on the reticulated barrel ceiling are repeated between big granite windows that run the length of the church on both sides, flooding it with light. Pelmets, twin pulpits, a huge organ are decorated with bold scrolls and arabesques of carved and gilded wood from which angels peer coyly; the chancel arch and the High Altar are bound up in similar boiseries—gaudy but grandiose.

The Portuguese have almost consistently exhibited a talent for making excessive decoration both theatrical and plausible without being corny. Their churches tend to be stage sets for joyous devotion. São Vicente, for instance, with its controlled and extravagant façade—granite swags of fruit, flowers, tassels, angels' heads (enough to make Grinling Gibbons turn apprentice), and a stately saint in a niche on top. On one wall, carved in beautiful lettering, is the charming conceit categorically stating that this 17th-century church retains full Lateran privileges, to be paid for with two pounds of beeswax delivered to Rome annually. As for the interior, it is all gold-and-white carved wood, marvelously gay as well as respectful.

We have all been taught not to judge a package by its wrapping, but if one didn't know what there was on the interior, one might forgo the church of São Vitor. It would be a great pity for it lifts the heart. It is both sumptuous and restrained, a difficult balance to attain. There are blue-and-white *azulejos* soaring up to the granite barrel ceiling. Except for its spiraling, vine-covered salomonic columns, the carved and gilded altar is more Renaissance than Baroque. The chancel arch is like an imperial diadem of gold, and the window pelmets are coronets. There are carved and gilded side altars, a delicious organ, and everywhere red or white accents. Kubler and Soria, authors of the authoritative book *Art and Architecture in Spain and Portugal*, remark on the effectiveness of such amazingly diverse ornaments: "Gilding and polychromy of altar linings and church walls, *azulejos* or colored marble [combined] result in harmony."

The Portuguese are more relaxed about religion than their Spanish neighbors. They managed to resist many of the excesses of the Inquisition, possibly because "only the rich can afford to be tolerant" and the Portuguese were once very, very rich. But they are no less devout or less addicted to making pilgrimages to Fatima, to Lamego, but particularly to Bom Jesus do Monte just outside Braga. The site of this sanctuary dates back to the 15th century, but the visual drama of Bom Jesus lies in its Baroque double staircase, the last part of which was designed late in the 18th century by Amarante, who also designed the church on top. Monumental granite stairs, interrupted by landings, soar more than 1,300 feet up the mountainside; running along and between them are gardens, fountains, grottos, chapels, obelisks, and figures depicting the Five Senses and the Virtues. Not as fanciful as similar stairs at *Nossa Senhora dos Remédios* in Lamego,* those of Bom Jesus admittedly are more static, but grander. Penitents often climb all the way to the summit on their knees, which accounts for a charming though ubiquitous tale. A woman who

* See page 255.

had embarked on such an exercise in mortification caught her heel in the hem of her dress. Having great difficulty untangling herself, she looked about for help and, catching the eye of a fellow penitent, she sought his assistance. "Senhor, would you kindly lift my skirt?" she asked. He answered sourly, "Senhora, it is for doing *that* that I am doing *this*," and he left her to her predicament.

Art historians are forever in conflict over the terms Baroque and Rococo as applied in Portugal. One reason is that the Baroque style continued to flourish here for about eighty years longer than it did in the rest of Europe. Kubler and Soria bracket Portuguese Baroque between 1590 and 1710 and describe it as "collected, self-confident, realistic, dignified, measured, neither nervous, nor tortured, nor precious . . . light tends to fuse everything in greater unity." Perhaps another reason is that decorations carved in granite often stopped short of the excesses of true Rococo or shellwork. But when the Portuguese set out to use the Rococo idiom precisely, they pulled out all the stops. This is illustrated by the chapel of Santa Maria Madalena just outside Braga at the summit of isolated mountains, the Serra de Falperra, known until the first quarter of the 18th century as a refuge for brigands. In 1753, however, Archbishop Moura Telles (another of the prelates to adorn the region) commissioned the construction of the small church and its adjoining convent buildings. Santa Maria da Madalena is all Rococo, slathered with granite shells, flutings, swirls, and swags, with just enough plain whitewashed surface to show off the decoration. The interior is replete with swags and urns—all gilded with accents of red, green, or white—over the High Altar, the side altars, overdoors, and window pelmets. There are simple iron balconies under each window, with gauze curtains that tend to blow in the faintest breeze, suggesting the approach of some beautiful ghostly novice.

Braga . . . detail of stairs at Bom Jesus

Two more places in the environs of Braga should be visited and all too often are overlooked: one is a monastery, the other a Byzantine church. In literary terms, one is a tragedy, the other an enigma. The church of São Frutuoso is the only Byzantine Romanesque relic of the 7th century existing in Portugal. Its construction preceded the Moors, but during the Muslim occupation it was naturally allowed to deteriorate, so that it had to be largely rebuilt in the 11th century. One suspects more recent restorations may have occurred, for the observant authors of *The Selective Traveler in Portugal* point out that "a confusing feature is a heap of eight marble pillars just like those within, lying piled up outside, overgrown with weeds."

Built in the form of a Greek cross, São Frutuoso consists of three stone cubes meeting at the dome. Like many early Byzantine churches, it is small, austere, almost secretive, as if trying to be inconspicuous. One enters directly from a Franciscan convent church built in the 18th century, which one tends to overlook *en route* to the astonishing ancient sanctuary. São Frutuoso is very white inside and out. As Reynaldo dos Santos points out, it is in the style of the mausoleum of Galla Placidia in Ravenna, except that here the emphasis is on purity, a dual sense of sanctity, and assertive Christianity. (One gets the feeling that it would be easier, as well as more appropriate, to kneel rather than to remain standing.) The bands of geometric stone carving, of stylized lilies and acanthus leaves, bespeak an eclectic heritage—Byzantine, Visigothic, and Mozarab.

It is only when one steps back (or, more accurately, forward, in time at least) into the 18th-century Franciscan church that the eye is jolted by overblown riches; the painted ceiling, the carved and gilded festoons faintly touched with red, the handsome altar stalls—said to have been removed from the Sé in Braga in the middle 18th century—all these seem glorious but a bit excessive. Such glossy aspects of the Christian faith provide delicious visual memories, but São Frutuoso leaves a mark on the spirit.

Much that is characteristically Portuguese is revealed during a visit to the great, abandoned monastery of Tibães, once the headquarters of the Portuguese branch of the Benedictine order. The short-sighted policy of the Ancient Monuments Commission; the fallibility of *morgado* or primogeniture; the poverty of the clergy; the courteous interest of the peasant—all are evident to those who explore this crumbling property. Set on an elevation with a sweeping view of the surrounding country, the future of Tibães falls among three stools. These are the Church, which still holds services there; the Ancient Monuments Commission, which has claims on a cloister; and private owners. In the 19th century, when religious orders were banned in Portugal, the dormitories of this monastery, along with its rich farms, passed into secular hands. The present owner, an old lady, lives in Braga and has little concern about the property except for the revenues it pays.

The mother of the priest, as shabbily dressed as the poorest peasant, and in all probability almost illiterate, showed me around the church, the chapter house, and the sacristy, taking delight in my obvious interest. The beauty to be found in this great 17th-century convent church of São Martinho is equaled only by a shocking neglect of national treasure. Half of the great proscenium arch, majestically carved and gilded, which was designed to adorn the transept, is missing. There remain the High Altar, six side altars, a pair of pulpits, window pelmets, an organ case—dazzling examples of the most splendid Rococo-Baroque gilded woodwork in all Portugal. (Dr. Robert Smith, in his new and immensely authoritative book, *The Art of Portugal*, attributes the over-all interior design to André Soares and dates it 1628–1661, and the magnificent carved choir stalls to a genius known only as Sousa.) A richly gilded balustrade surrounds the *côro alto,* where a great gold-and-white frame seems from the nave to contain a sunburst more lavish than any designed for France's lavish Sun King. Only when one climbs to this monks' choir with its elaborate stalls, carved with the head of kings, peasants, animals, and half-naked caryatids, does one see the splendid crucifix for which the great sun provides a worthy nimbus. Nothing in Portugal matches the masculine extravagance of monastic Tibães, the male prototype of the gilded female finery adapted by the Poor Clares.*

There is overwhelming sadness in this neglected monastery—in the chapter house with *azulejos* and a ceiling painted in a geometric design, in the sacristy with fine polychrome figures—and one wonders what vestments or church plate lie in the huge carved-chest drawers. There are four cloisters with rounded arches, lovely *azulejos* on the walls, and fountains in the center. There are miles of empty corridors—indeed, one has to watch one's step so as not to put a foot through a rotted floorboard. And equally long and sad stretches of painted coffered ceiling are left to the mercy of leaking roofs. As things stand, Tibães will not survive much longer. But it could be saved if Church, state, and private ownership would act as one. Otherwise it is doomed to crumble or be torn down. Some of the *boiseries* will find their way into museums, but the guts of the place, the integral whole, once it is dispersed, will vanish.

Two boys who were valiantly herding some lyre-horned Minhotan cattle through the arch leading into the farm courtyard offered themselves as guides to the abandoned gardens at the back. They and their families were employed to work the farm for the old lady in Braga; they were the ones who told me about her. They escorted me with gallantry around manure piles, farm implements, snotty baby brothers; they tied two fiercely barking watchdogs to iron rings, and led me out to what once must have

* See page 284.

Tibaes . . . monastery cloister

been grandiose gardens along a flight of steps going down the mountain. One could imagine what they had been like when water ran down from the aqueduct, filling the ponds and overflowing into fountains below. One caught an occasional glimpse of a carved stone figure and it was not hard to believe that these Benedictine gardens had inspired those of Bom Jesus. Even when they grow wild, gardens retain a living beauty.

CHAPTER V

Food and Drink ...and Especially Port

FOOD

PATRIOTISM IS based on a love of the good things we ate in our childhood," a Chinese friend recently explained. Few people feel more deeply about their native land, their childhood, or their food and drink, than the Portuguese. One need only watch the way they sit down at table to recognize that to them this is an engrossing matter, literally and metaphorically. They have little of the strictly sensual or intellectual approach to food that characterizes the French gourmet. This, in fact, would be quite unsuitable. The best of Portuguese food is provincial, indigenous, eccentric, and proud—a reflection of the chauvinism of this complex people. It takes no sides, assumes no airs, makes no concessions or bows to Brillat-Savarin—and usually tastes wonderful.

Like the French, the Portuguese complain of their livers and pay lip service to diets with utter disregard for such specifics as cholesterol and calories. Potatoes not only appear at every meal except breakfast but are often prepared in diverse fashion to accompany both the fish and meat courses; in rice-growing regions, rice is served as well. Desserts which lean heavily on sugar and egg yolks are the richest and sweetest to be savored outside a Turkish harem; most of them originated in nunneries. It is not uncommon to be offered two sweets, and to refuse a proffered dish is an affront of sorts.

Generally speaking, the Portuguese most enjoy eating when surrounded by children and grandchildren, as if their taste buds quicken as they watch the fledglings ingesting patriotism with every succulent morsel. This holds true among all classes—peasant, bourgeois, or aristocrat. Eating hours are more like those observed in Italy than those of Spain. Between one and three, and eight and ten at night, the country as a whole sits down to five or more courses—and a period of relaxation. (Peasants excluded, for although they take a siesta in the fields, their meals are simpler, scanter, and timed to the sun's rising and setting.)

The fish and shellfish of Portugal are truly magnificent in quality, quantity, and variety. There are lampreys, trout, and salmon in the rivers. Almost every species of Atlantic fish is caught along the coastal waters—tuna, sardines, swordfish, sea bass, sole, *cherne* (a kind of turbot) and *imperadors* (a pink-scaled fish with a grotesque head and a succulent flavor). There are crabs, *lagostas*, *lagostinas*, shrimp, prawns, edible barnacles, oysters, clams, squid, and cockles. All these taste fresh from the sea and rarely have been refrigerated for more than six hours from catch to table. In spite of this lavish river and ocean harvest at the nation's front door, the national dish of Portugal is *bacalhau* (salt cod) and the recipes for preparing it run into the hundreds. Each year Portuguese fishermen make the long, often dangerous voyage to the codfish feeding grounds along the

Newfoundland banks, which their ancestors were the first to sight in 1490. This underlines a quirk in the national character—given a problem involving the sea and ships, the Portuguese run to it compulsively as if trying to relive the bygone days of the discoveries.

The country is blessed with most of the raw materials that contribute to the delights of the table. Monks in 14th-century monasteries taught the peasants the art of growing superb fruit—apples, oranges, pears, lemons, peaches, apricots, melons, plums, figs, and grapes. In season, stalls in village markets or in fashionable food shops (like Lisbon's Martins & Coster) are piled with fruit that looks as if it came from a royal hothouse—instead, it is the simple produce of the land, tasting of the out-doors, of rain and sun, and of being picked only when *maturo*. Vegetables are garden fresh, seasonal, and rarely overcooked. Beef generally is not as good as the top American grades. Smoked hams, known as *presunto*, are at least the peers of Italian *prosciutto*. There are partridge and quail in season; chicken, ducks, and turkey have a taste no longer to be found in poultry nourished on chemical foodstuff. There are at least three reliable and great cheeses: quiejo da Serra, quiejo da Serpa, quiejo da Azeitão. It is sad, in view of this, that far too many hotels, *estalagems*, and *pousadas* persist in offering the visitor Flamengo cheese, which is no more than a fair replica of Dutch Gouda, but which they believe is suited to the tourist palate.

Although the two great Lisbon restaurants, Aviz and Tavares, are never too grand to serve grilled sardines or *bacalhau* and include other Portuguese specialties on every menu, they are the exceptions to an unfortunate rule which assumes that visitors have timid tastes. Many establishments offer a relentless and mediocre fare of fried fillets of sole, roast veal, or stringy beef, with the ubiquitous potatoes, and caramel custard. It appears as though the nation's dieticians are torn between superiority and inferiority—wavering hopelessly between two extremes. Is the newcomer *worthy* of the local specialties, and/or are the specialties *sophisticated* enough for the visitor? As a result, they inhibit the traveler's exposure to the country's disarming and unique cuisine, much of which combines the most surprising tastes and textures. There is, for instance, a spicy casserole of pork and cockles, called *porco com amêijoas;* or baked sole and bananas, *linguada com bananas;* or an equivalent of jellied meat loaf with green peppers, *pudim de carne fria;* or delicate waffles shaped like rose windows and served with segments of fresh orange, *formas com laranja;* or duck with nutmeg sauce, *pato a moda d'el Rey;* or tiny tarts of cream cheese and almond paste, the famous *queijadas da Sintra.* Every town has its local pastry specialty, mouth-watering and enough to appease any sweet tooth. And in town after town, at places like Gião's in Évora, Ignacio's in Braga, the Comercial in Oporto, Pinto d'Oro in Coimbra, the Casa dos Frangos in Colares—all of them impeccably clean, family restaurants. The china may be coarse, the service haphazard, but the food is different, digestible, and delectable.

DRINK: NOTES ON TABLE WINE

Considering its size, Portugal produces a greater variety of wine than any other country. According to Alexis Lichine, "Around 240,000 people are permanently engaged in this branch of agriculture, while some 1¼ million depend directly or indirectly on the wine trade for their living." The pity of it is that outside the country little is known concerning the merit of

Fishermen's boats in the main canal at Aveiro

GATO PRETO
CAFE

wines which one expert remarked "have a special flavor born of the mountain and the sea, and the hot southern sun." The Portuguese wine industry—Port excluded until later—might well hire a super-salesman to promote the full-bodied reds and the dry whites (as opposed to the *rosés*) along the international drinking circuit, simultaneously encouraging wine producers to standardize and to properly age the wines they plan to export. If the tourist bureau, for instance, supplied pocket wine-guides to suggest what to drink and where—naming estate, year, and other relevant data—it might step on some toes at the beginning but eventually would bring benefits to the entire industry.

Although by ordinary price standards no Portuguese wine is costly, there are grave uncertainties as to the standard of wine one drinks while traveling about. My rule of thumb, not necessarily an infallible one, is to drink the *vinho do casa* rather than choose from the wine card; generally speaking, advice proffered at provincial inns tends to be more pretentious (or prejudiced) than wise. One of the most reliable labels, however, one likely to be found almost everywhere, is Grão Vasco, which comes in *tinto* and *branco* (red and white). H. Warner Allen, an Englishman knowledgeable about Portuguese wines, writes of the Dão *tintos* generically, "They are nice to drink when they are young and there may be a temptation to let the Dão region prosper on the sale of ordinary table wines without sufficient attention to their potentials as a fine vintage wine . . . [but] they certainly age well." My particular favorite among the various Dão's is a Reserva 1954, Caves Alianca—which in smoothness, body, and quality stands up to many French wines and costs half the price.

Dão is only one of at least seven major wine regions on which we shall cast our eye—once over lightly. The *rosés* are the best-known Portuguese wines, and those bearing the Mateus * label are outstanding. The *vinhos verdes* of the Minho province are a

* See page 266.

curiosity—wines best described as eager, zestful, and very slightly *pétillant*. They come in red and white, and the white is to me preferable. The best of these *vinhos verdes* resemble a naïve Vouvray, and the best one I ever tasted was a Casa de Vilacelinho, *engarrafado na origem*. At their worst they are harsh and acid. But between these extremes one finds an interesting, exhilarating drink, especially for a hot day. Aromatic white wines are produced from the grapes growing along the slopes of the lovely old fortified town of Obidos; the best of them have been compared to Orvieto's "potable gold." Another golden wine is produced in the environs of Alcobaça and surely traces its origins back to the Cistercian monks who farmed the monastery lands as early as the 15th century. There is a kind of Portuguese hock produced in Bucelas which goes superbly with fish. (In the wine cellars of that region, anchovies are served "to cleanse the palate" at wine tastings.) As for the famous red wines of Colares, they are difficult to obtain but worth the effort for a truly fine bottle, the kind that Beckford savored in the 18th century when dining with his prestigious acquaintance the Marquês of Marialva. As for the grapes of the Douro—grown on tenacious vines that send their roots into schistous soil and welcome cold winds and blazing heat—they are endowed with a twofold goodness. About one fourth of them are used for making Port (see next section); the rest is made into table wine, generically known as *consumo*. Some of these *consumos* when properly aged acquire a bouquet and grace comparable to an Ermitage: I have been lucky enough to sample a superb one recently, a Ferreira Reserva 1941.

André Simon, the distinguished wine authority, has often said, "Most people love sweet wine, although very few care to say so." For me the Muscatel of Azeitão is irresistible, a perfect dessert wine made with muscat grapes, fortified with brandy, with some fresh muscat grape skins added. This unorthodox procedure of adding the skins gives the wine a bouquet and aroma of fresh fruit which to me is exquisite. I inevitably take a bottle in the car when motoring—to ward off bad temper or fatigue.

The wine steward of the Aviz restaurant prepared the following lists of wines which he recommends (all of which I have enjoyed). The descriptions are his.

White Wines

BUCELAS GARRAFEIRA 1939: full-bodied, charming bouquet.
DÃO TERRAS ALTAS: soft, aromatic.
COLARES T. RODRIQUES: light and dry.
QUINTA DA CARUNCHOSA: light and dry.
COSTA TALIA: fine, light, dry; from Ribatejo.
RESERVA PARTICULAR C. R. FERREIRA: mellow, rich, aromatic.
VINHOS VERDES: The white ones have a low alcoholic content, are rich in malic and lactic acid, fresh, light, and naturally sparkling. Alvarinho Cepa Velha has special characteristics derived from the Alvarinho grape. Quinta de São Claudio is light, dry, fresh.

Red Wines

BARCA VELHA: a great wine of magnificent quality, not very full-bodied but fine with a suave bouquet.
CAVES DE SÃO JOÃO 1952: soft, noted for finesse.
RESERVA PARTICULAR ALIANÇA: soft, noted for finesse.
RESERVA PALMELA 1959: light claret, pronounced flavor.
DÃO TERRAS ALTAS: full in body, velvety.
DÃO ALIANÇA RESERVA 1954: ruby-red, very smooth, strong bouquet.

PORT WINE

"Do you believe that there would ever have been an American Revolution but for those three bottles of vintage Port the English Establishment drank at night?" My Portuguese acquaintance could barely conceal the sly look on his face as he asked the question. For centuries, politics and Port have been enthusiastic bedfellows. Bedeviled by dogma, cant, and mumbo-jumbo imposed by the English gentry, Port survives with a surprising vitality which often seems far stronger than empire. Seen in the framework of world wine, Port is a character, and a likable one at that—even on first exposure, rather like vanilla ice cream. Along with its broad range of subtle variations, it has a firm restorative potency which makes it equally at ease in the sickroom or the banquet hall. And probably more than any other wine, Port, with its vast lore and 300-year history, appeals to the minds of men as well as to their taste buds.

Library shelves are lined with Port histories, books concerned with its intricate viticulture, blending, and aging, its status and ceremony. What I propose to do here, however, is cast a speculative and appreciative eye, lightly, on pertinent facts and fantasies, leaving the reader to draw his own drafts.

"Claret would be Port if it could," said Richard Bentley, the distinguished 18th-century Master of Trinity College, Cambridge. It cannot be for one specific reason. Port can be produced only from grapes grown within the Douro District (not the whole of the Douro province). According to the Instituto do Vinho do Porto, the Supreme Court of portdom, this consists of a narrow, precipitous stretch of country—from twenty to forty miles wide—running along the Douro River on both sides for about sixty miles north and east of Regua. Even within this staked-out territory, strict regulations exist. "No vineyard may be reconstituted or new one planted except on a hillside at an altitude of less than 600 meters; on schistous soil; where the vines will be suitably sheltered to insure the production of high grade wine." In less specialized language, this means that the best grapes grow where practically nothing else will—in flaky, crystalline soil, geologically defined as schist which is possessed of a high mineral content. The finest wine is made from grapes grown almost precisely halfway up the slopes—wine made from the grapes at the top is too thin; from those at the bottom, too coarse.

The first Port wine was exported to England in the first part of the 17th century, somewhat accidentally, it would seem. A Liverpool wine merchant sent two of his sons to Portugal in order to learn something of viticulture. During the course of what would appear to have been a pleasurable educational progress, these lads spent several days in a monastery in the Douro District where they drank a wine much to their liking. Diligently they bought what they could of it to ship to England, wisely adding a dollop of brandy to fortify the wine against the rigors of the journey. These young men had hit on a good thing, it would seem, and in 1703 an Englishman, John Methuen, was empowered by his government to sign a treaty with Portugal which would allow Port wine to enter England at a much lower tariff than the duty charged on French wine "in exchange for free entry of English woolens into Portugal." Ever shrewd, England built up her exports while simultaneously damaging the economy of France, a hereditary rival. "In the wines of Portugal we drink to the success of our armies and the confusion of the enemy" was a popular saying, and most Englishmen knew whose confusion was intended.

Like all international treaties, the Methuen agreement was

flawed, and with time deteriorated until it became little more than a prop for a profitable British monopoly. But in 1756, Sebastião José de Carvalho e Melo, Marquês de Pombal and Prime Minister of Portugal, upset the alien apple cart. Although at the time his reforms enraged the English shippers, most of them are still enforced. The demarcation of the Douro District was spelled out for the first time by an august body consisting of one taster, twelve deputies, and twelve councilors, chosen among "intelligent men of the Trade," and all of them Portuguese subjects—which was empowered to act as a watchdog over viticulture and wine-making. To disobey their edicts was to risk heavy fines or imprisonment, and one of their most important rules forbade the use of manure in vineyards. Such heavy fertilizing promotes quantity, and the oldest rule-of-thumb among wine-growers is that "quantity is the enemy of quality." Some farmers today grow lupin and beans between the vines, a practice which purists believe makes the soil unduly rich; some use *marc* left over from the last pressing as a restorative for the schist; but mostly they settle for fallen vine leaves dug in around the roots.

It was Pombal's new vigilantes who made it illegal to blend white grapes with red, and forbade the use of elderberries to darken the wine. By some mysterious osmosis, the British drinking public had convinced itself that good Port must be "dark and rich . . . black as ink" and to indulge this fallacy various methods of adulteration were indulged in by unethical vintners when elderberry juice was banned. Such "nefarious practices" went to extreme lengths, according to a 19th-century author of adventure stories, W. H. G. Kingston, whose family was connected with the Port trade. In *Lusitanian Sketches*, Kingston writes of an eccentric vintner who became obsessed by twin theories. The first was that the violent fermentation of a vinous fluid extracted the color from any substance steeped in it, just as it did from the skin of the grape; and coupled with this, he theorized that the darkness of the Negro race was caused by a black substance in the epidermis. At this point Kingston adds, "I'll say no more." Fortunately for us, however, he proceeds to recount certain events which were said to have occurred. In June a ship arrived carrying slaves who were to be exchanged for wine from this racist Douro grower. Subsequently the activities around his vineyard were shrouded in titillating mystery. It was reported, however, that following the first harvest the blacks all wore high socks over long, tight-fitting trousers; after the second harvest, gloves were added. Three years thereafter the "quality of his wine improved . . . it appeared to have more body and a darker color." But after the fourth year these benefits faded, and, coincidentally, the blacks seemed to have disappeared, although there was said to be "a very fine set of perfectly white men around those parts who could not speak Portuguese."

In spite of such apocryphal tales, along with talk of perfidious influence and ineffectiveness, the Alto Douro Wine Company and its heirs protected their product and its markets with admirable efficiency. So much so that in 1932, when Dr. Oliveira Salazar took over the reins of government as Prime Minister, the Port trade was practically the only stable institution in that country.

The climate of the Douro is dry and violent. It tends to be blazing hot in summer, bone-cold in winter. But it suits the grapes that grow there. According to oenologists (wine scientists), the ideal weather for a fine Port year is a wet winter and an early spring: "a fine May to set the fruit; a hot summer; a little rain in August to swell the fruit; and a dry harvest." These textbook specifics produce high-quality wine, but so will a combination of less advantageous conditions. Viticulture is more unpredictable than most agricultural efforts, which may have something to do with its fascination. This upper Douro valley is

Lisbon . . . flower market

an enchanted countryside, sometimes dour, sometimes smiling, always grand. One looks down into its deep, mysterious, fierce gorges. One glimpses the ribbon of the river as it meanders along until it takes a sudden notion to hurry and then races and boils through the rapids. On every side, slopes laid out in a pattern of steep terraces rise in landscaped grandeur; running parallel one to the other, curving to fit the mountain contours, their retaining walls—mostly of unmortared stone—have a Buddhist-Gothic look. All this prompts total recall for those who have looked upon it—beauty harnessed to enormous effort, testifying to man's dogged labors and the persistence of the vine itself.

There was a time when it was feared that all the vineyards of Europe would be destroyed by the scourge of phylloxera, a plant louse from America which struck the Continent in the 1860's. Within less than twenty years, in spite of spraying and other conventional protective measures, it had written the swan song of French and Portuguese pre-phylloxera vintages, destroying close to nine tenths of the vineyards. With their inventive daring harnessed to English initiative, the Portuguese reacted more quickly than the French in accepting the need for drastic action if grapes were to flourish or even survive. American stock appeared to have developed a resistance to its native louse, and the Port wine-growers were the first to try grafting their Portuguese vines onto these immune American roots. (As insurance against any possible return of phylloxera, this technique still is used on all new planting.) "It is the soil, rather than the kind of vine which decides the quality of the grape," Rupert Croft-Cooke writes, "and, although at first the American influence may have made the wines a little less full-bodied, there is no reason to think that today they are much different from the wines of 1860."

Even the hardest heart sinks at the sight of the "mortuaries," as the terraces abandoned since the phylloxera plague are called

—crumbling ruins along the hillsides, testifying to man's effort and his despair. Rather than salvage these old terraces—deserted because of a mixture of superstition and growing concern for labor conditions—new ones have been planted, generally on north-facing slopes to spare the men the extremes of heat that occur when working the southern exposure. On the big holdings, such as A. J. da Silva's great Quinta do Noval, the modern terraces are supported by retaining walls engineered of concrete and calculated to a fine point of strain and stress. They have a dramatically up-to-date look of spaciousness with row after row of vines growing on each level. But as one of the cognoscenti said, "One of the most endearing things about the Douro is the harvest of the little vineyard, a triumph for the man who owns only a few acres, an achievement of the peasant-proprietor." This is the man who built the walls, who blasted the rock with dynamite so that the newly planted vines would be able to put their roots down far enough to find sustenance. In the spring he loosened the soil to aerate the vines, sprayed, weeded, and tied the new growth up for support. He saw that they did not grow much over three feet from the ground so that the grapes would benefit from the reflected heat radiated off sun-hot schist. By August he would make a tentative deal with a shipper with whom he chose to do business, and then the harvest was on, and it was time to start picking.

What makes all this so satisfactory, as a Douro-watcher told me, is that "it's a matter of individuals doing business with individuals in their individual way." Quality is what the vintner aims for and what his shipper demands. Quantity is a word scorned by the Port trade. According to Cockburn, one of the most distinguished firms among the Port aristocracy, a thousand vines can produce anywhere from one hogshead to twelve hogsheads; while the finest vines rarely yield more than four—the equivalent of 276 gallons per thousand vines.

Before the harvest gets under way, the Instituto do Vinho do Porto sets a minimum price to be paid the grower, and decides precisely how much Port can be made—usually 60,000 to 70,000 pipes. (A pipe equals two hogsheads.) Generally speaking, this will amount to a quarter of the total harvest. The surplus grapes will be either distilled into brandy or fermented out into beverage wine, referred to generically by Port men as *consumo*, some of which turns into such proud table wine as Evel.

As the precise moment for the harvest approaches, so do the itinerant vintagers, who appear as if summoned. Women cut the grapes with the help of old men and children. They discard the imperfect fruit, chatter, laugh, and consume pounds of grapes. Simultaneously they pick, placing the choice bunches in small baskets later emptied into tall hampers capable of holding 130 pounds. Lines of men stand eager to hoist these loads onto their shoulders and set off at a brisk jogging gait. Their destination is the *adega*, or winery, where the presses stand; should these be too far away, the men transfer the grapes to ox-drawn carts. The Douro oxen pull with their heads; yoked in pairs by great, round leather turbans, they move in reflective harmony like two medieval potentates. So faithful are these beasts who work a lifetime together that when one dies, the survivor can rarely be trained to pull with a new yoke-mate.

When the grapes reach the *lagares*, or wine presses, they are immediately thrown into the granite troughs—approximately three feet deep and fifteen by eighteen feet over all. The big *quintas* will have many *lagares* side by side, while the small grower has need of only two; but the process remains the same. The grapes are piled higher in the center of each *lagar* so that their weight starts crushing the fruit at the bottom. This *lágrima* is deftly run off to prevent fermentation from starting before all the grapes are in, but is tipped back into the must after treading has begun. It starts when a team of barefoot men in shorts leaps

Douro province . . . vineyards running up the hillside

into the trough, stamping to a crisp one-two count called by the leader. This first work of cutting the grapes is grueling—the fruit is cold, surprisingly hard, like marbles—but within a couple of hours the preliminary process is terminated. The leader gives another different signal and music strikes up. Now the treaders find their own pace, improvise their own movements, twining in a serpentine satyr's pattern as they continue to tread the must. The teams work for four-hour shifts with two-hour rests between and invigorating tots of *bagaceira* or *marc*. Generalizations are particularly dangerous in dealing with wine, but after twenty-four hours of treading, the must has usually reached a point of fermentation that demands the concentrated attention of the overseer—whether it happens to be the grower, his wine-maker, or the shipper's representative. This moment is crucial. A saccharometer provides a scientific yardstick as to precisely how much sugar remains in the must; equally important, however, as a more subtle subjective gauge, is the overseer's experience. Combining these two insights, he will decide at what moment to stop fermentation. This is done by running the grape juice or raw wine into a container or *tonel*, where it is slugged (literally) with the addition of twenty percent of its volume of brandy. (Fermentation of wine ceases when only sixteen percent alcohol is added.) Recently, due to costs and labor shortages even in Portugal, much of the treading is being done mechanically, at least on many of the big properties. Although everyone agrees that no invention could improve on the human foot for this particular job, auto-vinification provides a more hygienic and efficient method in the light of contemporary labor shortages.

In the language of Port, this is "harvest home." In the late autumn of the same year, the raw wine is "racked off its lees"—shop talk for agitating the *tonels* and drawing the clean wine into a Port cask or pipe, or back into its cleaned-out *tonel*. This process is usually repeated every four months when the wine is

A country chapel near Caminha

young, for, as the wine masters say, "Port is a living thing and throws down a deposit," which in casks is called the lees, and in bottles the crust. Now the young Port is ready to start its travels, first to Oporto, or more exactly to Vila Nova de Gaia, immediately across the river, where the wine firms have their warehouses, or lodges, as the ground-floor storage space is called. Until fairly recently the young wine traveled hazardously aboard the *barcos rabelos*, oversize sailing gondolas with a high poop aft and a steering oar with which to negotiate the rapids. Some shippers have kept one of these romantic craft in their lodges as a collector's item now that most of the wine comes down by train or even truck.

There is magic to be found in the Port lodges of Gaia, as the town is colloquially called. These are cool, dark, slightly hushed places with a sweet smell of wood and wine, where cellarmen patter around on rope-soled shoes among avenues of pipes stacked in three or four tiers; one of the men's fringe benefits is four drinks of *consumo* during the course of each work day. For the visitor it is an intoxicating experience to stand beside one of the huge wooden blending vats capable of holding more than 150,000 bottles of wine. These are triumphs of the cooper's art, a craft that is slowly dying out except here in the wine lodges. To listen to the English, they taught the Portuguese how to make casks, or so a famous letter written by a wine merchant in 1704 suggests: "Ye English cupers are a drunken lott," he wrote, "but ye natives now know how to make casks." What seems to have been overlooked in this attribution is that the first coopers were shipwrights, and Portuguese shipbuilding was well ahead of that of their English cousins back in Henry the Navigator's day.

The Port trade prefers its casks made of memel oak, but also uses Italian and native chestnut for their vats; American oak is considered unsuitable, as it tends to leave a residual woody taste. When asked why the Sherry firms use it, a shipper gave me a crisp retort: "You probably wouldn't taste it in Sherry." In any case, refunds are offered for the return of old casks, which by law must be broken up, cleaned, and remade at Gaia; new ones are seasoned with ammonia under steam pressure, then filled with cheap wine and left to stand for months before they are deemed fit for Port.

Having diligently tried to follow the wine from the Douro District this far, we come on the trickiest part of our investigation, and closer to the happy moment when we may begin to drink it. Ernest Cockburn often quoted the didactic statement made by one of his acquaintances: "Any time you are not drinking Port is a waste of time." But we must waste a bit more time in order to get our bearings.

Although there are several kinds of Port—to be defined later—all Port is blended or bred, as the experts prefer to call it. To be successful, these must be marriages of affinity and never of convenience or profit. The palate memory, which is the expertise of the tasting room—its computer, in fact—is a subtle *tour de force* based on the most refined combination of sight, smell, and taste. It is impossible to explain; we must simply accept that it works, that some men can do it, and that only one woman ever has.

If the year has been exceptional, a shipper may set aside approximately ten percent of his best wine to make Vintage Port. Others may decide to do likewise; a vintage is most often declared by agreement among all the shippers. Three or four such vintages may be declared in a decade, hardly more. A Vintage Port is one of several specific things; it is a blend of wines of the same year; it spends two years, sometimes three, in a cask at Gaia and is shipped to England, or other countries, and bottled on arrival; it takes a minimum of ten years in the bottle to mature and is likely to reach its peak at twenty-five; it is supremely good, and it refuses to conform to the exigencies of contemporary life.

Because Vintage Port "throws a crust" in the bottle, it likes to lie quietly on its side from the day it is put in its glass container almost to the morning it is decanted. (It resents the hop-skip-and-jump of today's transient existence.) It should be decanted ten hours before being served, and as it tends to change in twenty-four, preferably there should be none left in the bottle. (This last does not qualify as objectionable in this writer's opinion.) But, oh, the problem of decanting! Geoffrey Tait, the prestigious Port essayist, says, "To be perfectly certain of getting the best out of Vintage Port . . . every bottle should have the neck cracked-off with hot iron-tweezers." This process requires heating a pair of specially devised tongs or neck-crackers, holding them to the neck of the bottle for a minute (while it's lying on its side, mind you), and then, according to Croft-Cooke, one may remove the tweezers and "with a cloth dipped in cold water take the top of the neck and you will find that it comes away cleanly."

Next in status is Crusted Port, a blend of several years, which has spent somewhat longer in the cask but otherwise is treated in the same fashion as its Vintage relations: it is expected to rest seven or eight years in the bottle; it has a shorter life expectancy; costs less; and because it, too, throws a crust, it is almost as hard to handle in today's do-it-yourself household.

Wood Port, however, although it never achieves the splendor of a great Vintage, can reach great heights. (Also one can pull its cork in the conventional manner.) It spends its life in a cask, where it is repeatedly blended and refreshed—sometimes with a bright young wine or a wise old one—in order for it to follow its maker's "mark" or standard. Like the rest of us, with time it fades—going from Ruby to Tawny—but, unlike the rest of us, it improves in this process. (The bottle, as far as Wood Port is concerned, is simply the container in which it travels from Vila Nova de Gaia, where it is bottled, to you or to me.) There is even a vintage (note the lower case) Tawny, several bottles of

Cooperage in a Port wine factory

which were made available to me by Fernando Von Zeller of A. J. da Silva: this is a wine that has been refreshed repeatedly but only with wines of the same year. I plan to have a glass right now!

White Port, which is made of white grapes, makes a fine apéritif—it is dryer, more of the sugar was allowed to ferment out of the must—and enjoys being chilled.

As for the jiggery-pokery—as an English friend calls it—of pouring Port: one takes the decanter in one's right hand and automatically passes it to the left. After all, it is hardly customary to play backhand shots at the dinner table. Port is perfect dessert wine and one glass rarely suffices. Yes, the decanter's coming round again.

There's a charming rhyme. It goes like this and suits us for an *envoi:*

> I must have one at eleven,
> It's a duty that must be done.
> If I don't have one at eleven,
> I must have eleven at one.

CHAPTER VI

A Monastery, Two Abbeys, and a Fortress-Church

TO KNOW what made the Portuguese what they were over the centuries and still are today, to assess their complex responses whether they be political, emotional, or spiritual, one does well to look at (and into) four of their extraordinary monuments, the Convento dos Jerónimos de Belém, the abbeys of Alcobaça and of Batalha, and the Convento do Cristo at Tomar. The most ancient of these dates from the 12th century, the newest from the 16th century, and all four express something characteristic of the Portuguese, a facet of a great people. These beautiful piles of stone spell out the national fiber even more explicitly than does the epic verse of the Renaissance poet Camões—its individual strands of courage, pride, tenacity, piety, and passion for riches. These are people historically determined to keep their word. They are non-violent and view their actions as consistently defensive. With their typical mix of arrogance and humility, they see themselves endowed with a "*talant de bien fere*," the motto of their most celebrated son, Henry the Navigator.

It is often said that the Jerónimos was "built with pepper." More precisely, this 16th-century monastery-church was built with the revenues from many spices, including pepper. As a result of Vasco da Gama's successful voyage to Calicut, spice, which next to gold was the most prized medieval or Renaissance cargo, now entered Europe through the port of Lisbon, where it sold at a net profit of some sixty times its cost. The Jerónimos is younger than the other edifices with which we are concerned, but it is in Lisbon and, as such, is the most obvious one for almost every traveler to visit. The cornerstone of the great church was laid in 1502 by the opulent Manuel I, a ruler who converted much of the seemingly inexhaustible Crown wealth into building. During his twenty-six-year reign he is credited with nearly a hundred architectural projects both spiritual and secular—monasteries, fortresses, aqueducts, churches, bridges, and palaces. His best architects, Boytac, the two de Arruda brothers, and Fernandes, developed a highly inventive, indigenous decorative form which bears the sovereign's name and is known as Manueline. Sacheverell Sitwell describes it as "an *art nouveau* more extreme than anything that came later in the age of the Baroque."

Manueline is all that and more. It is a complex, aggressive style made up of a concentration of elaborate decoration imposed onto vast, bare surfaces. It is deeply concerned with the play of light and shadow on portals and façades—as might be expected in a land where light is strident—and with the interplay and sifting of these same elements through stone screens in cloisters and church windows. Manueline is assertive, and because it is unfamiliar, it often seems to affront the eye with its unrestrained, powerful exuberance—acting on the retina like the proverbial bull in a china shop. It is basically naturalistic in design, intent on the symbolism of the sea and sailing ships. Its arches are rarely pointed—more likely to be round, or trefoiled, or geminated, lined with wavy curves, or patterned angles, or cusps that appear like a fringe of inverted pinnacles. Although it grows on a Gothic base, it has overtones of the Far East, of Moors, and the Renaissance. It sings of Venice and Marrakech in a flamboyant manner, but Africa predominates when one recalls that all four of the major Manueline architects visited the "Afrique shores," according to Reynaldo dos Santos, the elder statesman of Portuguese art historians.

Although Diogo Boytac was born in France in the second half of the 15th century (he died in 1525, Manuel reigned from 1495 to 1521), he did not attempt to import France to Portugal. Instead he felt the heartbeat of his adopted land and translated it into an architectural idiom that expressed the dynamism of the times in which he lived. Like most creative surges reflecting a national vitality, this one was something more than contagious; the explosive, assertive ferment of the age was reflected almost simultaneously by other architects—especially Mateus Fernandes and Diogo and Francisco de Arruda. A whole new iconography of ornament ensued—ropes, anchors, ships' sails, armillary spheres, coral roots, barnacles, and the Cross of the Order of Christ, which the daring caravels bore on their sails. Of all these Manueline builders, Boytac probably was the most gifted as well as the most prolific. Already in demand in the reign of Manuel I's royal predecessor, João II, he had been commissioned by that monarch to build the convent-church of Jesus in Setúbal * "for the King's nurse."

* See page 223.

THE CONVENTO DOS JERÓNIMOS DE BELÉM

A man of such architectural distinction was the obvious choice to direct Manuel's most grandiose project, the Mosteiro dos Jerónimos. It became Boytac's primary concern for the next fifteen years, until he was relieved by Manuel in order to assume another royal assignment—at the Batalha abbey—and he appointed as his successors Mateus Fernandes and João de Castilho. By this time, however, the project for the monks of St. Jerome was well set in Boytac's mold. This elaborate ecclesiastical compound, with its great church of Santa Maria da Belém, was built on the site of a small seamen's home and chapel founded by Henry the Navigator, located in an outlying region of Lisbon known as Belém (Portuguese for Bethlehem), not far from the banks of the Tagus River. Today with its majestic limestone façade mellowed to silver-gray, it soars toward heaven in a noble and poetic testament of stone.

The south façade of Santa Maria de Belém has a kind of eloquence ringing out in many tones of voice, all of them impressive. These voices are possessed of surprising subtlety as well as strength, particularly in view of the size of the structure, the largest monument in Lisbon. With its robust frame, stern buttresses, and the insistent bareness of large masses of masonry, it promises fortitude and strength. Two immensely tall, slim, recessed windows—bordered with three stone bands carved in different geometric designs and flanked by girded unicorn horns—convey a sense of elegance held in restraint. Fretwork around the roof—a diadem of coral roots studded with crowns and pinnacles—lays stress on power and majesty. The great stone portal overlooking the Tagus is a triumph of opulent piety. A kind of late Gothic outdoor retable, it rises to the full height of the façade, populated with saints in canopied niches all festooned with underwater vegetation. Any single statue, especially the enchanting Virgin directly above the portal arch, is a splendid example of 16th-century sculpture; as for the concept as a whole, it is full of stylish spontaneity. (From this portal it is customary to bless the fishing fleet before it sets out each year in search of cod off the distant banks of Newfoundland.)

The vast interior of the Jerónimos—the church is over 300 feet long—is overwhelming. Justly called one of "the most beautiful places of worship in the world," it has a pervasive mystique. One is numbed by a sense of unlimited height, of freedom of space. The great stone roof seems to float overhead. Six octagonal columns of unusual slimness, covered with shallowly carved arabesques and leaves, support the fan traceries of the ceiling, and appear like stately trees growing into a stone sky. Everything accentuates the sense of loftiness: the north wall, for instance, a great plain expanse of stone, almost cliff-like, with small windows set far up; a row of ten low stone confessionals flush with the floor; very tall, narrow, and conspicuously empty niches. The loftiness is semi-sacred, semi-pagan.

Having entered through the south portal, one is propelled almost to the center of the three-aisle nave. Instinctively, as in any church, one moves toward the chancel and by the time the transept is reached one is due for further amazement. Extending some ninety-five feet across, this transept is more than sixty feet wide and has a barrel-vaulted ceiling even higher than the lofty nave. Walter Crum Watson, whose book *Portuguese Architecture* still remains after sixty years a major research source, claims that this apparently unsupported vault was "the largest attempted since the days of the Romans." To appraise the skill and daring involved, one must consider that this 100-foot-high vault has no buttresses; the great superstructure rests on outside walls and inside piers less than six feet thick. Small wonder that it excites Watson's astonished praise.

There are thirteen royal tombs in the transept chapels and within the apse, including that of Manuel I, whose great marble sarcophagus is supported by elephants—beasts he dearly loved as symbols of exotic richness and power. The 17th-century painted panels of the altar retable are almost invisible in the muted light, which hardly matters—in the Jerónimos it is the stones that count. Everywhere the eye turns, it becomes aware of a magic masonry. The square sacristy, entered off the right of the transept, virtually takes one's breath away: the vault of this beautifully proportioned room springs out of a round shaft in the center—a great stone date palm covered with arabesques.

Returning to the body of the church and moving west, one glimpses the 16th-century stalls of the *côro alto*, which appear singularly severe for Portugal. Beneath the gallery of this upper choir are found two pretentiously carved, fake-Manueline stone caskets—the tombs of the great explorer Vasco da Gama and his contemporary, the equally renowned poet Camões. At the time of his death, Camões was in poor political repute with the Crown, and his earthly remains have apparently disappeared. Mock-carving by an unimaginative 19th-century sculptor seems exactly right for an empty tomb, a twist of fate that this great Portuguese epic writer would have most enjoyed—genius can laugh at such historic afterthoughts.

The *Guide Bleu*, referring to the Jerónimos, caustically remarks that "the 19th century brought to this work . . . its archeological ignorance and lack of understanding of the Manueline style." This philistine approach is apparent not only in these two tombs but (more blatantly reprehensive) in the near-disfigurement of the superb west portal carved by Nicolau de Chanterene in 1517, which is now partially obscured by a 19th-

Lisbon . . . vaulting in the church of Santa Maria de Belém in Mosteiro dos Jerónimos

century gallery leading to a bastard structure that houses the Ethnological Museum. Chanterene, with his lyric sense of composition, of elegance and sensitivity, is credited with bringing the Renaissance to Portugal, and this portal is thought to be one of his earliest works in his adopted land. On either side of the (ogee) arch which frames the west entry to the church, he placed his principal statues, surrounding them with what could easily have become Gothic confusion in less skillful hands. With Chanterene's mastery of stonework, however, confusion is transformed into a statement of richness appropriate to the dignity and exalted position of the kneeling figures of King Manuel I and his Queen, alongside their patron saints, Jerome the scholar and John the Baptist.

Passing through this splendid doorway and bearing right (the Portuguese are determined that visitors must make their own voyages of discovery), one ultimately arrives at the famous two-storied cloister. A wondrous concept, designed by Boytac and ultimately completed by João de Castilho, this has been called "one of the most original works of architecture in the world." A square of some 185 feet on either side, with flowers blazing in the central garden, it has cut-off corners that give it the air of an octagon and provide space for the magnificent lion-man fountain spouting water in the corner outside the monks' refectory. This cloister is infinitely more royal than monastic and it is not surprising that King Manuel enjoyed retreats within its walls, where a special apartment had been decorated for his use. Lovely fan tracery decorates the vaulted ceilings of its elegant sheltered promenades. Buttresses supporting the garden side of rounded arches are encased in carving, which makes them seem more decorative than functional. Recessed deep within these stalwart arches, a second row of geminated arches appears fragile as *papier-mâché* decoration for a gala fête rather than 400-year-old masonry.

The lovely face of the Jerónimos retains an enduring capacity to bemuse and enchant all those who come its way—it is impossible ever to take it for granted.

THE MOSTEIRO DE ALCOBAÇA

Three hundred and fifty years before the cornerstone of the Jerónimos was laid, Afonso Henriques, the first Portuguese king, in about 1152, founded a Cistercian monastery in a valley between the Alcoa and Baça rivers. Today this softly rolling, rich and fertile region produces the finest peaches and other fruit, including grapes * from which an excellent white wine is made. But in the middle of the 12th century the countryside was a mere tangle of thickets, and barren stretches alternating with useless swamp. On the eve of the battle of Santarém, the King promised that were he to be victorious against the powerful Moorish garrison, he would build a conventual church in thanksgiving to the Virgin. Once victory was in his grasp, Afonso Henriques directed a letter to be written to Bernard de Clairvaux (later St. Bernard) requesting an abbot of the highest competence to head a major Cistercian community in which he planned to invest great secular power. This was to become known as the abbey of Alcobaça, celebrated for a variety of reasons including austerity, power, gluttony, agronomy, and wealth. But not all of these at one and the same time.

Bernard chose as the first abbot of Alcobaça a monk called Ranulph, who, according to custom, brought with him to Portu-

* See page 139.

gal the plan of the parent house at Clairvaux in France. These monks prided themselves on being developers as well as ascetics. They set out to improve the land, to clear and irrigate, to form *granjas* (precursors of our granges), where they taught farm skills, provided seed for suitable crops, directed the proper fertilizing of fields, the pruning of fruit. They must have camped out, literally, for the first fifty years, as it took that long for the church to be completed and three years more for the rest of the enclave—living quarters, kilns, barns, and stables. When all were complete, Alcobaça, of all Cistercian monasteries, came closest to Clairvaux.

Rigid self-abnegation was a rule of the order and this extended to the architecture as well. Simplicity was stressed, even a studied plainness. Renunciation of the world was made apparent to every wandering eye. Only crosses of wood, candlesticks of iron, were allowed; all needless ornament—including stained-glass windows, pinnacles, and towers—was forbidden. That was the way it started at Alcobaça.

The monastery was a teaching center as early as 1269; the monks of Alcobaça helped King Diniz found the nation's university (today located at Coimbra *) by donating books and money, although, according to an early manuscript, they "only acknowledged the King insofar as to give him a pair of shoes or boots when he chanced to come to Alcobaça." Their community now consisted of 999 monks and Mass was said without intermission throughout the year. By now the abbot had been given jurisdiction over all Cistercian houses in Portugal—some 111 of them. He was superior of the Order of Christ, and governor-general of thirteen towns, three seaports, and two fortified castles. Besides that he was Chief Almoner and King's Councilor; his enmity was as dangerous as that of the monarchs. Obviously, exposure to so much power tended to erode self-abnegation.

*See page 99.

Lisbon . . . cloister in Mosteiro dos Jerónimos

One is not, therefore, unduly startled by the façade of the church of Santa Maria de Alcobaça as it appears today. Unlike the Jerónimos, where the stones silvered with age, the patina of Alcobaça is sun-kissed to a muted gold like the skin of the local peaches. Late in the 17th century the outward signs of Cistercian severity disappeared in a burst of towers, pinnacles, obelisks, figures of saints and virtues that sprouted over the 600-year-old building. Only the rose window and the plain Gothic portal testify to its original austerity. What is surprising in view of these disparities is that two such divergent states of mind contrive such visual amiability.

A large platform extends out in front of the main portal—like an outdoor reception room, which indeed it was when William Beckford, the young English aesthete, visited the monastery in early June 1794. He was accompanied by a pair of high-ranking, sybaritic prelates, the Grand Prior of Aviz and the Prior of St. Vincent's, and he noted in his diary, "The first sight of this regal monastery is very imposing; and the picturesque, well-wooded and well-watered village out of the quiet bosom of which it appears to rise, relieves the mind from a sense of oppression the huge, domineering bulk of the conventual buildings inspire." He goes on to explain that a broad hint from the Secretary of State had advised "these magnificent monks" to expect important visitors and that therefore they were greeted by a tremendous ringing of bells as soon as their party was spotted. "Fathers, friars and subordinates, at least four hundred strong," Beckford says, "were drawn up in grand spiritual array on the vast platform before the monastery to bid us welcome. At their head, the abbot himself in his costume of High Almoner. . . ."

Alcobaça is the largest, longest church in Portugal, its dimensions more grandiose than those of Clairvaux, the monastery on which it was modeled. Rows of great clustered columns rise up sixty-six feet on two sides of the nave, forming three aisles. The nobility of their over-all proportions seems to slim down the bulk and defy ornament. Naked austerity and whiteness generates an astonishing emotional response. Today, again bare of all the extravagances so much admired by Beckford (gilded wood carving and other ornate church furnishings), Alcobaça has almost returned to its original state of grace. But not quite. The Portuguese restorers stripped away everything, including the functional monks' stalls, the organs, and lastly the monks, who were expelled in 1834. Some of the life of the church was bound to go with them, but its spirituality remains to this day strong enough to bring an agnostic to his knees. Here one feels engulfed in the womb of Christian faith.

No wonder that King Pedro I * brought the body of his murdered Inés to lie at Alcobaça *a fin do mundo* (until the end of the world) and that he ordered his own body placed in the same church, directing that the caskets be placed so that the two lovers would rise face to face on the Day of Judgment. The superb stone sarcophagi now lie on either side of the transept at the crossing: elaborately carved in high relief—of a local limestone which is soft and easy to cut when just quarried but hardens with time to a marble-like consistency—they are worked with the intricacy and skill usually reserved only for fine ivory objects. Watson says, "Nothing can exceed the delicacy and beauty of the figure sculpture, the drapery is all good, and the smallest heads and hands are worked with a care that cannot be surpassed." Six angels-in-waiting on each tomb seem gently to be laying the body to rest, straightening, smoothing, and fussing over the robes. Each casket is supported on the back of strange animal figures with human heads. Professor Elie Lambert, of the Sorbonne, considers these sarcophagi "the most celebrated Gothic sculpture in Europe." Rejecting the theory of their French origin, he attributes them to a Portuguese sculptor

* See page 32.

of great talent whose name unfortunately has long since been forgotten.

Both tombs were gravely damaged by Napoleon's troops during the Peninsular War. According to Sir H. Maxwell, an officer on the Duke of Wellington's staff and the author of a biography of the Iron Duke, the caskets were forced open, "the embalmed Kings and Queens were taken out of their tombs and I saw them lying there in as great preservation as the day they were interred." (Others claim the bones were ruthlessly scattered.) In any case, Maxwell goes on to describe the looting and burning of the abbey's treasure, adding, "An orderly-book found near the place showed that regular parties had been ordered for the purpose." The soldiers hacked at the carving on the tombs, which without this Gallic savagery might have come down to us intact.

Except for two doors at the right of the ambulatory, the exuberance of Manueline never touched the aloof serenity of Alcobaça; but these overdoors are richly carved with coral-root, magnolia cones, and sea anemones, typical signature of the late Manueline, the stylish work of João de Castilho. Passing through one of these, one enters a pretentious sacristy which, according to Beckford's taste, was "gorgeous and glistening . . . worthy of Versailles itself, adorned with furbelows of gilt bronze, flaunting over-panels of jasper and porphyry." At the far end of this room there is a circular reliquary chapel which has a veritable crush-hour conglomeration of polychrome saints, agitated cherubs, reliquary busts, each carved with the lifelike individuality of portrait sculpture.

Alcobaça boasts of "the largest Gothic sleeping quarters in existence"; its refectory is without doubt the plainest and the most elegant, with a recessed colonnade leading up to where a reader led the monks and lay brothers in "graces, prayers and lofty thoughts." But it is Alcobaça's kitchen that is most cele-

Alcobaça . . . façade

"the most distinguished temple of gluttony in all Europe."

brated and appears to have been at the time [illegible] visit. He describes it as "the most distinguished temptation of gluttony in all Europe," and one might well believe that for once Beckford was not exaggerating. He writes: "My eyes never beheld in any modern convent of France, Italy or Germany, such an enormous space dedicated to culinary purposes. . . . Through the center of the immense and nobly-groined hall, not less than sixty feet in diameter, ran a brisk rivulet." The Alcoa River was thus diverted expressly for the utilitarian purposes of keeping fish alive till needed for the cook pot, and for washing dishes and kitchen utensils. Monumental chimneys covered in white-and-blue glazed tiles provide space adequate for roasting six or seven oxen simultaneously. Beckford says, "On one side, loads of game and venison were heaped up; on the other, vegetables, fruit in endless variety . . . a numerous tribe of lay brothers and their attendants were rolling out and puffing up [pastry] into an hundred different shapes, singing all the while as blithely as larks in a corn-field." Later he was taken to his quarters, which he describes as having bare walls, adding that "the ceiling was gilt and painted, the floor spread with Persian carpets of the finest texture, and the tables in rich velvet petticoats, decked out with superb ewers and basins of chased silver, and towels bordered with point-lace of curious antique pattern—a strange mixture of simplicity and magnificence." He ate potted lampreys, "strange messes from Brazil," sharks'-fin soup, and other rarities, and was especially delighted when the Lord Abbot requested of his chef the recipe for *omelette à la provençale.* Beckford, it appears, never moved without a complete retinue of servants and his own bedstead. His account of this visit (and one to Batalha) were published some forty years after they took place, when Beckford was an old man; a year after the book appeared, the monks were expelled from Portugal.

The great nave of Alcobaça is an impressive testimony to Cistercian faith, but perhaps one feels the peace, the cool detachment of the order, most strongly in the spacious 14th-century Cloister of Silence at the left of the chancel. Ogive vaulting, strong, plain groining, and rose windows in the succession of arcades supported by twin columns combine to give a momentary insight into the best of the monastic life. The Portuguese have a saying, "*Quem passa por Alcobaça têm que voltar a Alcobaça*" (Who passes Alcobaça returns to Alcobaça). It is almost impossible to resist the magnetism of its Gothic conviction.

THE MOSTEIRO DE SANTA MARIA DA VITÓRIO DA BATALHA

The abbey of Batalha, as it is generally known, a magnificent conglomeration of buttresses, pinnacles, and fretted spires surging up in a resplendent burst of pride, is probably the greatest 14th-century traffic hazard in the world today. This noble apparition looms up unexpectedly around a curve of the throughway to Coimbra some sixty miles north of Lisbon, set among low hills covered with pine trees, vineyards, and olive groves. Although it appears close enough to touch and can be photographed from the window of a moving car, its grandiose masses are astonishing enough to trigger a reflex on the foot brake. Seeing is not necessarily believing when it comes to Batalha, and cursory acquaintance with this splendid edifice suffices only for the unimaginative and blasé.

Just as Alcobaça was the royal thanksgiving offered by the first Portuguese king, Afonso Henriques, whose Burgundian line ruled for 257 years, so Batalha was begun toward the end of the 14th century by the first king of the Aviz dynasty, João I.* Threatened by the powerful armies of Castile, the young King,

* See page 35.

still in his twenties, along with a contemporary and friend, Nun'Alvares, his newly appointed commander in chief, rounded up a ragtaggle army of Portuguese peasants and soldiers bolstered by 500 English archers, to make their stand on the nearby plains of Aljubarrota. It was a battle where winner took all and João was the underdog. Placing himself and his followers in the hands of the Virgin, he vowed that if his forces triumphed he would "erect a temple and monastery which should surpass the most stupendous throughout Christendom . . . to be built where the battle commenced, or in its neighborhood." The miracle of victory occurred and within two to three years the work on Batalha (The Battle) was under way with Afonso Domingues as architect in charge; he shared his royal master's feelings of dedication, for Domingues too had fought on that glorious occasion. The King by now was married to an English princess, Philippa of Lancaster, daughter of John of Gaunt, and her influence pervades the ancient walls, although the English architectural critic Walter Crum Watson is forced to admit, somewhat ruefully, "the plan is not English but quite national and Portuguese."

Batalha combines a sturdy robustness with a dream-like illusive quality. The lofty, majestic basilica, which Beckford calls a "glorious huddle of buildings," appears to contradict itself—chaste and noble plainness is suddenly interrupted by exuberant and totally unexpected bursts of ornament. "I could hardly believe so considerable and striking a group of richly parapeted walls, roofs, and towers, detached chapels, and insulated spires, formed parts of one and the same edifice," Beckford wrote. "In appearance it was not merely a church or a palace I was looking at, but at some fair city of romance."

Here the limestone façade has aged a softer gold than that of Alcobaça, with time-worn smudges of black, dramatic as kohl-rimmed eyes. Frei Luis de Sousa, a 17th-century Dominican

Alcobaça . . . monastery kitchen

monk, commented on its by then 200-year-old color changes, comparing the stones of Batalha with "a beautiful face exposed to influence of sun and air, yet [it] is scarce ever injured as to lose every trace of its former charms." Sousa was a competent judge of femininity; as a fashionable young noble, he had married a lovely widowed lady of title whose husband had been reported killed some ten years earlier while fighting the Moors in the campaign of 1578. She and Sousa "lived in the greatest harmony" but only for a short time. A merchant from Africa arrived in Lisbon, informed the lady that her husband was a prisoner-of-war, and sought her help in obtaining his release. When the distraught pair proved to their satisfaction that the story was true, Sousa retired to a monastery, she to a nunnery, but they tried by every possible means to effect the freedom of the wronged husband.

Batalha's magnificent west portal, which rises to a height of more than fifty feet, is rich in Gothic carving—with hundreds of figures of popes, saints, kings, angels (the Apostles are restorations)—and surmounted by a deeply recessed, flamboyant stained-glass window. (Batalha is one of the few Portuguese churches where any good stained glass remains.) The façade "is formed out of as simple material as the great pyramid of Egypt," and conveys a similar sense of enduring power. A three-aisle nave (263 feet long, 106 feet wide, and 105 feet high) has arches and moldings which remind the English of Winchester, while the French liken its dignity to Amiens. ("The height is such," an early Dominican noted, "that an athletick [sic] slinger can scarce cast a stone to the vault of the nave.")

The general plan was borrowed from Alcobaça with modifications of that insistent austerity demanded by the early Cistercians. Some of its subtle warmth stems from the remaining stained-glass windows (dating from the 16th century), which cast a glow—faint as threadbare needlework—on otherwise plain walls and the boldly groined ceiling. Originally there were thirty such windows, and an 18th-century visitor noted that at night "the church is almost as luminous as an open square, notwithstanding that the glass is covered with colors." This was before the Peninsular Wars, when Napoleon's armies burned and looted all church furnishings. (An idea of what they destroyed or stole here can be ascertained by reading a partial list of eighty-eight pieces presented to the royal monastery by the Emperor of Constantinople, Emmanuel Paleologus. Included were fifteen statues "cast of silver and very costly and beautiful," twenty-eight chalices "most of them are gilt," two "lofty gilt candlesticks," two gilt torch stands, etc.) The soldiers also amused themselves by taking potshots at stained glass; Beckford, who saw Batalha before this occurred, described the light filtering into the great nave as a splendor of "golden and ruby light which streamed forth from the long series of stained-glass windows . . . casting over every object myriads of glowing mellow shades ever in motion undulating to and fro . . . the white monastic garments of my conductors seemed as it were embroidered with the brightest flowers of paradise."

While the 18th century saw many indulgences among the Cistercians, the Dominican brothers of Batalha clung to their rules of poverty and abstinence. Records show they were allowed four feasts a year which entitled them to two days' double rations; otherwise they permitted themselves one and one-quarter pounds of meat a day, an equal amount of fish, two small loaves of bread, soup and rice, plus fruit and wine. In 1789 when the English architect James Murphy spent thirteen weeks as their guest in order to document specifications and details of the abbey, he remarked that "the piety, hospitality, and simplicity of these Reverend Fathers can scarcely be imagined in these degenerate times . . . it seemed to ascend like an exaltation." Poverty and self-abnegation were not a boast but a way of life here.

What excesses there were were stated in stone, to be seen, enjoyed, and marveled at, then as now. This explains, perhaps, why one is less aware of the monks' absence here in Batalha, where highly ornamented masonry populates the monastery, minimizing the sense of emptiness.

Murphy made one further comment of major importance: "Throughout the whole," he wrote, "are seen a correctness and regularity . . . the result of a well conceived original design . . . immutably adhered to, and executed in regular progression without those alterations and interruptions to which such large buildings are commonly subject." One feels this immediately on stepping into the nave. At the right, in the space that otherwise would have been occupied by three bays, is the regal Founder's Chapel. This sixty-five-foot square chamber with a *pavillon* formed by an octagonal lantern tower resting on pillars—fretted, pinnacled, and crocheted like an inverted crown—contains the tombs of João I and Queen Philippa along with four of their five sons. Camões, the literary voice of the Portuguese Renaissance, refers to them as "*inclita geracão, altos Infantes*"—"the most illustrious generation of Princes," as indeed they were. Their tombs seem designed to impress in the most correct Gothic idiom; only Henry the Navigator's sarcophagus, carved in his lifetime and probably to his precise instructions, conveys any feeling of the man. (The crown he wears reminds one that among his many titles, he was also King of Cyprus.) The *mise-en-scène* is immensely grand, noble, and chill, with every armorial device succinctly carved. The Queen was the first to die, and small wonder that this pantheon of which she was the earliest tenant appears wholly English or, again in Beckford's words, has "a Plantagenet cast." João (one of the earliest foreign monarchs to receive England's chivalric Order of the Garter) lies fondly hand-in-hand with his Philippa in the center of the chapel, their stone images very proper and well mannered in this

Batalha . . . west front of church

last affectionate gesture. One sighs, however, for the eloquent passion and beauty of the sepulchers of Pedro and Inés at Alcobaça; the impact of illicit love and star-crossed lovers on worldly memory inevitably overwhelms the virtues and serenity of lasting marriage.

Returning to the lofty nave and walking toward the transept —enfolded as it were in a straightforward Gothic statement—it is well to collect one's thoughts and prepare for aesthetic surprise. Batalha marks the crossroads of Portuguese architecture. Here we encounter the earliest flowering of Manueline—it had just budded at the church of Jesus in Setúbal,* but at Batalha it establishes itself once and for all, according to dos Santos, as "a hybrid of the Gothic family." This resplendent offshoot, obsessed with oceanic lore and seascapes carved in stone, bursts upon us on entering the Royal Cloister (just off to the left of the transept before the crossing). Today this most beautiful cloister appears not exactly as Afonso Domingues designed it when he was chief architect of the monastery. Quite naturally he thought of it in purest Gothic terms—serene, reflective, suggesting the rustle of cassocks, sandaled feet, and rosaries. But to the eyes of Manuel I, about a hundred years later, these beautiful arches, for all their meditative beauty, appeared plain and bare. It is thought that the new King summoned Boytac † to add ornamental (and functional) stone screens to keep out the sun and rain, filter the light, create patterns of shadow play, and produce a dazzling ornamental effect.

At first sight these Oriental-Gothic cloisters call up visions of the Taj Mahal with its eloquent marble screens. But this is no seraglio, no tomb for a Mogul's favorite. The design here is bold, male, ocean-oriented. One can identify three variations on a recurrent theme of coral root, seaweed, armillary spheres, and

* See page 223.

† Walter Crum Watson alone believed Boytac to have been born in the town of Boutaca near Batalha.

the Cross of the Order of Christ. These monastic *moucherabis*, or Moorish screens, probably originated in Boytac's imagination during the campaign against the Infidels in Africa; captive Moors may well have worked on Batalha. The designs are immensely intricate and many appear as if lifted from Moorish-embroidered fabric; this intricacy fooled a 19th-century Portuguese queen who claimed the carving must be plaster and ordered it tested with a hammer. Although Beckford was at times scornful of Batalha (as we will note), he marveled at the wealth of carving and was deeply impressed by "the admirable order in which every minutest nook and corner of this truly regal monastery is preserved: not a weed in any crevice, not a lichen on any stone." He mentions the delicious fragrance wafted from the gardens, which were, and often still are, "be-rosemaried and be-lavendered."

Keeping to the east of the Royal Cloister, one quickly comes to the extraordinary chapter house, an architectural phenomenon. (Since 1921 it has contained the tombs of Portugal's two Unknown Soldiers—one killed in France, the other in the African campaign of World War I.) This astonishing sixty-two-feet-square chamber contains the boldest example of Gothic vaulting to be found anywhere. According to Watson, there is no other room of its size to have been vaulted without supporting columns, "and probably none where the outside buttresses, with their small projection, look so unequal to the work they have to do." This engineering feat was not easily accomplished; the roof fell twice, injuring and killing many construction men. Finally the King, refusing "to hazard any more lives of his workmen in striking the centers . . . ordered from different prisons of the kingdom such men as were sentenced to captial punishment in order that, if disaster happened a third time, none would suffer but those who had forfeited their lives to the offended laws of their country." This time the vaulting held, with the dazzling result we now marvel at and which Beckford called "bold unembarrassed space . . . unsupported by console or column . . . it seems suspended by magic." When it comes to relating how this was accomplished, Beckford lapses into blatant euphemism: "Perseverance," he says, "and the animating encouragement of the sovereign founder" sufficed.

Batalha once had three cloisters, one of which was destroyed by fire and then (literally) swept away, but in addition to the Royal Cloister there remains a second cloister. Built by Afonso V, a grandson of João, in 1481, it provides an example of a smaller, simpler version of the Royal Cloister as it may have appeared before Boytac added his glorious screens. To reach it one passes an elaborately carved and scalloped fountain where the monks washed before entering their great refectory (souvenirs are now sold there); from this fountain there is a fine view of buttresses on the south, of pinnacled parapets and twin-belted spires. Then, passing through a gallery alongside the monks' wine bins, one enters the Cloister of Afonso V, austere and classic. Its simplicity clears the eye of extravagant feasting, and just in time. There is one more astonishment left at Batalha, the famous Capelas Imperfeitas or Unfinished Chapels. To enter them it is necessary to leave the monastery buildings (from the east corner of the Cloister of Afonso) and re-enter through a door just north of the apse.

João's heir, Duarte, was the son who was *not* buried among his family in the Founder's Chapel; instead, he planned an even more imposing, octagonal edifice—a super-chapel twice the size of the one his father had built—to be his resting place and that of his descendants. As architect he chose Ouguete, who worked on the Founder's Chapel and is said by some authorities to have been of English origin, while others claim him as French. The plans called for seven radiating bays, the vaults of which were probably still incomplete three years later when Duarte died.

Batalha . . . stone screen of cloister of Santa Maria da Vitório

During the next two reigns the project was abandoned, until fifty-seven years after Duarte's death, when Manuel I came to the throne. An obsessive builder, he ordered work resumed on the Unfinished Chapels according to new designs furnished by Mateus Fernandes.

Not even the richness of the Royal Cloister foretells the grandeur of Fernandes' creation. His extravagantly decorated arched portal (fifty feet high and twenty-five feet wide) is overpoweringly compelling, and few can resist falling victim of its fascination—except Beckford, who disdained "Dom Emanuel's scallops and twistifications," although he admitted the effect was "exuberantly light and fantastic in the detail." Nowhere in Portugal can one find richer or more abundant architectural sculpture. Shaped rather like a monumental beehive, covered with lacy niches, carved foliage, and stalactites, it has the words of Diniz' royal device, "*léaute faray ta yaserey*," repeated more than 200 times—like an echo captured in stone. The elaborate bosses and ornamented ribs carved on the chapel vaults, the escutcheons of royal personages, the fretted parapets all are credited to Mateus Fernandes. He built the lower portion of the great piers which were meant eventually to support a vaulted roof, covered their front surface with oceanic vegetation and the initials of his royal patron, Manuel, and backed them with clusters of small columns belted with crowns. About the time all this was happening, Manuel lost interest in Batalha to concentrate on the Jerónimos, where he had decided to be buried. He had already left behind what Watson calls "the *chef d'œuvre* of the Manueline style."

His successor on the throne, João III, showed only desultory interest in the great complex of chapels—his architectural concern was a Palladian cloister under construction at the Convento do Cristo at Tomar—but not withstanding he commanded João de Castilho to begin a Renaissance loggia over the portal of

Batalha . . . Mosteiro de Santa Maria da Vitório, fountain in cloister

Batalha's Unfinished Chapels. This, too, remained unfinished, ending the cycle of Gothic to Manueline to Renaissance which has made these chapels a treasure house of stone ornament. Standing beneath Fernandes' great portal, one believes that this arch was predestined to remain triumphantly open to the heavens, for the swallows to dive and circle in this glorious aviary, repeating its stone arabesques in the swooping patterns of their graceful flight.

THE CONVENTO DO CRISTO

Architectural experts and art historians rarely reach a consensus concerning Portuguese dates, attributions, or the status of a monument, except when it comes to the Convento do Cristo, which is the outstanding exception to the rule of contention. Everyone agrees that this fortress-church-monastery is one of Europe's unique and impressive sights. Located at Tomar, a town of some 12,000 people set in the broad, fertile valley of the Nabão River about eighty miles north of Lisbon, it remained scarcely known until recently because of the difficulty of getting there. As late as 1926, Sacheverell Sitwell described the road from Leiria to Tomar—a matter of some twenty-five miles—as "execrable," adding that, having driven over it, he arrived "shaken and exhausted." Fortunately, this is no longer the case. Now one can make the journey in a long, single-day round trip from Lisbon.

A stronghold of temporal power and an axis of chivalric piety, the Convento do Cristo combines solemnity and exuberance with its multi-faceted past. Dating back to 1160, the earliest portion of the edifice was constructed for Gualdim Pais, Grand

Master of the Templar Knights of Portugal. Thirty years later the stronghold repulsed a fierce Moorish attack, thereby earning the appreciation of a long line of Portuguese kings. The Templars, one of the three great militant orders founded in the 12th century, were first known as "The Poor Knights of Christ and the Temple of Solomon." Originally under oath to the Patriarch of Jerusalem, they guarded the public roads and protected pilgrims who flocked to the Holy Land in the wake of the First Crusade. The King of Jerusalem, Baldwin I, ceded them a portion of his palace, close to the great mosque of Omar (also known as the Temple of Solomon). It was from this temple in Jerusalem that they took their first name; and its design remained the architectural image for some of their finest sanctuaries.

Far from being exclusive, this order sought out excommunicated knights, clearing them for heaven, as it were, by a special rite of absolution. From an unruly rabble of "rogues, impious men, robbers, and committers of sacrilege, murderers, perjurers and adulterers," they formed a disciplined military order which grew to infinite prestige and power. Knights, chaplains, squires, and servants all lived according to a stringent set of rules bracketed by unique privileges. Chastity was required of those members entitled to wear white robes, although Rule 70 of the Templar's Code cautioned all members against association with women. Even a maternal kiss was suspect. ("*Perileuse chose est compagnie de feme, que le diable ancien par compagnie de feme a degete pluisors dou droit sentiers de paradis*," the French branch was warned.) Templars were also forbidden to confess to any priest except one of their own, and these were "declared to have more power to absolve than an archbishop." Within less than twenty-five years such dispensations earned them the enmity of priests and bishops in general; but the arrogant Templars, secure in Papal prestige, ignored any necessity to improve public relations. They had become the most influential power in European politics. Vast wealth at their command stemmed from extensive territorial possessions and their prowess as international financiers. Such blatant power was risky at any period of history, and disaster struck the Templars in 14th-century France, where the King's finances were in parlous state. Philip IV was royally broke, having exhausted most means of raising money. He had debased the nation's currency, raised taxes, fleeced the Jewish moneylenders and Lombard bankers; only one trump remained to be played. Pope Clement V was virtually Philip's captive in Avignon. By pressuring him to suppress the Templars on charges of heresy and other grievous offenses, the King was enabled to confiscate their wealth, thereby replenishing his depleted coffers.

Having made few efforts to win supporters to their side, the Templars found that most other monarchs went along with Papal policy against them. Loyalty and a sense of gratitude, however, run strong among the Portuguese. King Diniz, grateful for past services at Tomar and alert to a potential for future assistance from this company of knights, made token gestures of suppression and confiscation. He then requested a Papal Bull authorizing him to form a new military order to be called the Knights of Christ. Surreptitiously, word went out that ex-Templars would be welcomed; their confiscated wealth and privilege, as far as Portugal was concerned, were transferred to this new account. Diniz made two conditions: he insisted that the succession of Grand Master now pass through royal hands, and that the new headquarters remain temporarily inconspicuous in the remote Algarve town of Castro Marim. Within less than fifty years, however, the Knights of Christ had moved back to Tomar.

Among the princes who bore the title of Grand Master, none did more to heighten the prestige or wealth of the Order of Christ than Henry the Navigator. His caravels carried the Red

Batalha . . . unfinished chapels

Cross of Christ painted on their sails as they set off on their long voyages of discovery. And wherever they claimed land, they were empowered by Papal authority to claim spiritual jurisdiction—"as if they were in Tomar itself."

The Convento do Cristo is a staggering sight as it sits dominating the crest of a hill. Its massive bulk is crowned by a pierced and fretted parapet running along the endless roof line—like a starched lace ruff, stiff with square crosses and armillary spheres repeated with hypnotic insistence. Gardens and tall trees line the slopes with verdant majesty. Passing along the base of ancient barracks and towers, and driving through an ogival door into the shaded, beflowered courtyard, one has an uneasy sense of trespassing. Here one is in the presence of austerity, of richness, of power, and of grace. The rugged polygon of the 12th-century church—militant and severe, with shut-in buttresses and no trace of ornament—is as stern as an interdiction. To reach it one mounts an elegant stone stairway, unornamented except for stone orbs marking the landings, to a spacious terrace built for Manuel I.

Finding one's way through the endless passages, seven cloisters, two chapter houses, and a church-within-a-church is complex. (After six visits I still get lost.) Guides show what they feel up to, rarely everything. It is not essential to cover every yard, but there are certain things that should not be missed. A checklist for the Convento do Cristo consists of six musts: the sixteen-sided Templar church; the vast Manueline nave and *côro-alto* that adjoins it; the Cemitério Cloister; the immense convent dormitory; the Cloister of João III; and the astonishing west windows. Seeing all of these means embarking on a lesson in Portuguese history as well as architecture. Royal alterations have never interfered with the continuity of purpose. Here one finds reflected national concern, attitudes of pomp and humility, independence, and accommodation with the rest of Europe. These appear in a variety of idioms—Romanesque-Byzantine, Gothic, Manueline, Renaissance, Baroque—always managing to be compatible.

The portal through which one enters the Convento do Cristo is the finest in Portugal. Designed by João de Castilho, it surpasses even the south door of the Jerónimos. Its profusion of sculpture remains strictly restrained. The great door with its carved figures in canopied niches, its borders of stylized foliage, resembles a High Altar glimpsed though a chancel arch, which throws a play of shadows on the stone ornament in a masterful show of chiaroscuro. Records show that Castilho had plenty of skilled stonecutters but that he was often short of stones, or more specifically the oxcarts to haul his granite blocks over nearly impassable lanes. Countless letters from the frantic architect to his royal patron complain how "the works of Thomar remain without stone these three months," pressing the King for a minimum of six oxcarts in order to get on with the job.

The severity of the Templar church belies its interior riches. An octagonal prism with an altar in the center and a sixteen-sided ambulatory, it is built in the purest Syriac plan of the Temple of Solomon in Jerusalem (which Raphael is said to have painted in *Sposalizio*, now in the Brera in Milan). One has no way of knowing how this primitive church was originally decorated; its strong Byzantine flavor dates from the 16th century and Manuel I, a king famous as a dedicated embellisher. It was according to his command that the multi-angled walls were lavishly painted in dull gold, that the carved polychrome statues were placed on Gothic corbels under fretted canopies, and that any open space was filled with ornate frescoes. When it was new it must have been dazzling: even muted by 400 years, it has the voluptuous look of a jewel along with the spiritual force of the Crusades.

Famous as "a museum of Portuguese architecture from the

12th to the 17th century," the Convento do Cristo, unlike most museums, has never been made to fit a chronological order. Instead it constantly backs and fills through the past. There is no formula: kings came, buildings began, kings went their way. It never occurred to them to alter what their predecessors had built. It remained in use or crumbled away. Time was the true master of works.

The Order of Christ expanded, it even changed its stripes—from a military order to a monkish one. All this can be seen reflected in the Convento's lichen-covered masonry. Henry the Navigator found the old Templar church somewhat cramped and added a tiny chapel to the east which he consecrated to Thomas of Canterbury. Fifty years later Manuel I chose a more expansive solution. Without tampering with the integrity of the Templar octagon, he converted it from church to High Altar, adding on the west a vast nave and *côro alto*. For the first time in centuries the whole company of knights was able to attend Mass together. The King hired Olivier de Gand to carve the choir stalls "with large figures on their backs and a continuous canopy with high and elaborate cresting." Unfortunately, the French cooks of Napoleon's armies used them to stoke their fires. To aggravate matters, the spacious nave suffered from what Sacheverell Sitwell calls the "hammer, broom, and chisel" squads of inept Portuguese restorers. Today, as a result, it has an over-scrubbed look, spiritless, and stripped of character, significance, and ornament.

The Cloister of the Cemitério, on the other hand, testifies that skilled restoration can be restorative. This is one of Portugal's loveliest Gothic cloisters, built by order of Henry the Navigator. With its graceful, simple arches supported on slim double pillars with finely carved capitals, bordered with *azulejos*, with orange trees and flowers growing in the quadrangle and Siena-red tiles along its sloping roofs, it has an air of lively meditation

Tomar . . . interior of Templars' sanctuary

which suited a man of Henry's temperament. He was no creature for half-measures: he loved the sea, and when his thoughts were seaborne, he was at Sagres listening to the crashing roll of its breakers; he loved the land around Tomar and knew how to make it rich—no Grand Master of the Order of Christ was more informed in the science of agriculture.

In 1521, when João III came to the throne, he altered the emphasis and the spirit of the Order of Christ from a quasi-military body of knights, bound by some specific vows, into a community of monkish regulars. The knights used the Convento do Cristo as a headquarters, not a permanent place of residence. The King's friars, however, had to be provided with housing. Being both royal and Portuguese, João scorned any modest solution. He probably chose as his yardstick the Hospital Real at Santiago da Compostela, and built a vast edifice 3,000 feet long, with a T-shaped corridor off which open hundreds of small cells. Grim, repetitive, and impressive, João's dormitory has a single splendid ornament—a chapel at the intersection with a coffered ceiling and sculptured panels which Watson calls "the finest Renaissance carving in the country."

João had been bitten late by the building bug. His next venture here at Tomar, which he did not live to see finished, combined monastic purpose and royal pretension. This was the great two-storied Cloister of João III (sometimes referred to as the Cloister of the Felipes because it was here that the usurper Philip II of Spain is said to have been crowned King of Portugal).* It was begun by João de Castilho; in 1557 a new design was ordered from Diogo de Torralva, and the work, obviously inspired by Palladio, was finally finished by Filipe Terzi. Perfection is perhaps the major flaw in this extraordinary cloister, which, as Sitwell says, has a "degree of grammatical correctness . . . incessant shunting and coupling of the pillars [which]

* See page 59.

becomes noisy and monotonous." It does indeed, while at the same time it is immensely grand, splendid and romantic, with its ghostlike circular stairs—skeletal in their sparseness—fitted into the corners leading up to a terrace from which one has a first startled look at the west elevation of Manuel I's addition to the Templar church.

This sight is possibly the most troubling architectural statement to be found anywhere in Europe. Brutal, outlandish, it is also mystifying and beautiful; the exterior of the great nave by Diogo de Arruda has been compared by Reynaldo dos Santos to a "ship returned from the Orient with the flora and fauna of the seven seas on its hull." The masonry seems to drip with nets and floats, barnacles and sea anemones, coral roots and knots. Nowhere else is Manueline as extreme, as exuberant, as flamboyant, or as near the edge of madness. All the while it is powerfully composed. Here is a complete iconography of the ocean, of discovery, of danger, reward, and faith. There is a hint of Hindu, of Moorish (there were Moors on the payroll, men called Omar, Mafamede, Bebedim), but in the last analysis, the statement is Portuguese—bespeaking bravado, wealth, power, stubbornness, guts.

Two immense round buttresses, fluted at the base, soar upward to become entangled in octapus-like tentacles. These in turn are caught up in frayed halyards, the one on the south end, bound in the strap and buckle of the Garter which Henry VII bestowed on Prince Henry the Navigator. In place of the usual rose window, a giant stone porthole is set in a deep splay carved to suggest bound sails just starting to fill. Farther down the great wall, even grander, more bizarre, and fantastic, another window stuns the eye. Around a formidable bronze grille appears a galaxy of stone ornaments: symbols of faith and majesty—crosses and armillary spheres and crowns repeated endlessly—and symbols of the sea—cork floats, coral roots, seaweed, anchors, and knots that seem to tie and untie themselves before one's eyes. At the very bottom there appear an elephant's trunk (Manuel's image of exotica) and a tiny mariner dwarfed by the terrors of the unknown which surround him. The spirit of tenacity, of inquiry, of raw courage—that puny man reaching across the world. These stones of the Convento do Cristo are a monument to the imagination of mankind.

Tomar . . . the Manueline west window of Convento do Cristo

Tomar . . . detail of west façade of Convento do Cristo

CHAPTER VII

Five Royal Palaces . . . Sintra, Mafra, Queluz, Pena, Ajuda

THESE ROYAL residences are clustered within a radius of thirty miles of each other and of Lisbon. Each speaks clearly of its times. They share little in common, except for having served as royal domiciles, along with that depressing lack of privacy that plagues most palaces. But there the likenesses end.

SINTRA PALACE

The oldest of the five, Sintra, dates back to the 13th century, a great eccentric structure in what Beckford refers to as a "fantastic oriental style," with windows that he describes as "crinkled and crankled" but that have an immense allure. This is more of a country house than a palace, more Moorish than Manueline. Its appeal depends largely on one's knowledge of the arts of Portugal. Nowhere is there a greater wealth of eclectic *azulejos* or ornately painted ceilings. The exterior is exotic, in spite of its stalwart air; seen by moonlight, it is suggestive of some great caliph's tent. Eça de Queiroz, in his perceptive 19th-century novel *The Maias*, describes its façade almost exactly as it appears today: ". . . this massive, silent palace without fleurons or towers, seated patriarchally among the houses of the town, with those lovely windows that give it a noble and royal look, with the valley at its feet, leafy, dense and fresh, and on high its colossal chimneys, disparate, summing up everything as though that residence was all kitchen built on a scale to suit the gluttony of a king who daily devours an entire kingdom."

Once the palace appeared more like a stronghold than it does now. A great stone wall surrounded the entire square, isolating it from the townsfolk. Then the town was a mere village stitched onto the royal apron strings; forests were all around, thick with boar, wolves, stag, and partridge. Portions of the building are known to have existed in the reign of Diniz (1279–1335), but nothing survives today that accurately pre-dates King João I, who came to the throne some sixty years later. Architecturally one encounters a bewildering medley of styles and textures running right through the 18th century, although those that predominate date from the 200 years between João and Manuel. Consistently Moorified (as opposed to Moorish), it bespeaks skilled artisans from "the Afrique shores" known to have been employed here. Even in defeat, they cannily imposed their culture on the Christian victors.

Two early documents identify most of the rooms that were in existence at the close of João's reign: an inventory signed by his heir, Duarte, has been preserved in the Carthusian monastery at

Évora; and a collection of 14th-century drawings, *The Book of Fortresses*, by Duarte de Armas, in the Tombo (the Lisbon Archives). Another invaluable document, by the 16th-century Superintendent of the Royal Domains, lists work completed between 1507 and 1510, along with the names of many of the builders and craftsmen employed at the palace.

It is hardly surprising to find that the Paço da Sintra, with its long history, has been many things to many kings. To João I and his court, it was filled with pomp and circumstance along with high spirits. To Afonso VI it was a cruel prison in which he spent the last nine years of his life, confined to a small room by a brother who had robbed him of throne and wife. No wonder that this poor captive fretted and wore down the tiles of his meager quarters with ceaseless frustrated pacing. Other rooms testify to lighter matters, to a father's affection for a daughter, or a royal rebuke. The Chamber of Magpies is a notable reprimand. According to legend, the King was caught by his strait-laced Queen Philippa kissing one of the ladies-in-waiting. At sight of Her Majesty's raised eyebrows, the royal spouse muttered defensively that he had done no harm; in fact, he had merely been doing the lady a kindness. Fortunately, he quickly regained his wits and the offensive by recalling the royal maxim, *Por Bem* (all for the best). The Queen was both amused and mollified, but whispers persisted in the court. Tired of the chatter, João ordered the room in which the incident had taken place closed "for repairs." To show his dispraisal of gossips, the King ordered its entire ceiling repainted with magpies holding his motto, *Por Bem,* in their beaks.

Another enchanting room has a ceiling decorated with twenty-seven life-size portraits of swans. Each bird wears a golden coronet and collar, each is in a slightly different pose against variations of the same background. The effect is ravishing. Although there are several versions of how and when this ceiling was painted, the most likely attributes it to Manuel's reign—an affectionate gesture toward his daughter Beatrice, who had a special fondness for those proud creatures. The walls of the spacious room have a limpid look to suit the elegant birds, contrived by a use of early green-and-white *azulejos* set in a checkerboard pattern which plays tricks of perspective around doors and windows. A patio adjoining this great chamber—small, intimate, full of greenery and the sound of splashing water—is as seductive as verses of the *Rubaiyat*. The Portuguese love of practical jokes is evident in its pretty Grotto of Baths, located at one end, where lavish *azulejos* conceal water spouts which courtiers enjoyed turning on unsuspecting guests.

No more imposing or restless room exists in all Portugal than the Armorial Chamber of the palace. Thirty-six feet square and crowned by the most singularly shaped dome, it consists of a mixture—of ornament, style, texture, and strong color—totally alien to any other country. The dome, which rises to a height twice that of the walls, is richly painted in scrolls and arabesques, foliage and geometric forms which suggest a Moorish origin. This is merely a background for painted stags, each one bearing a shield on which is displayed the heraldic arms of the King, the Infantes, and seventy-two of the noblest Portuguese names. This explosion of decorative zeal might be thought to suffice, but, below it all, walls paneled in blue-and-white *azulejos* portraying hunting scenes fix the already over-agitated eye.

Azulejos are the major glories of Sintra palace, collected examples dating back to the 15th century—rare Moorish designs, tiles executed in bas-relief, in *champlevé*, patterns like prayer rugs of faïence, armillary spheres, the 18th century's elaborate polychrome tiles. Because of their richness, the rooms require little other furnishing—which is just as well, as little remains: some Portuguese Chippendale chairs, fine Chinese porcelain dishes shaped like geese or carp or boars' heads, an interesting portrait of the widowed Catherine of Bragança, quantities of inferior Venetian glass. Perhaps there was never much more, for Beckford, writing some 200 years ago, remarked that he "saw no furniture worth notice, not a picture or a cabinet." It is indeed difficult to imagine that anyone ever lived here. That is, until one comes to the kitchen. This vast hall with its ogival windows and great pyramidal chimneys—covered with pale gray tile—seems merely slumbering until the chef comes back from vacation. The silhouette of the great conical towers that crown the chimneys like desert tents is often attributed to Moorish influence. Such towers, however, were specifically designed for the preparation of foodstuffs in quantities to satisfy the mammoth appetite of medieval nobles; similar towers appear in the great illuminated calendar of the Duc de Berry for the month of September.

MAFRA PALACE

This enormous Baroque structure, the largest and most imposing monument in Portugal, was built to satisfy a double life—part palace and part monastery. Its construction resulted from the concern felt in 1711 because King João V, after three years of marriage, had sired no legitimate children. Worry over the succession was a principal topic of conjecture at court. It was not surprising, therefore, for the Grand Inquisitor to mention the matter to a distinguished Franciscan friar from the Arrábida *conventos*.* This venerable monk remarked succinctly, "The King shall have offspring if he so desires," and strolled away, leaving a somewhat startled Inquisitor. When he regained his

* See page 294.

aplomb, this powerful figure sought out another courtier as witness and together they challenged the friar to be more precise. "Let the King promise God to erect a convent in the village of Mafra dedicated to St. Anthony and God will straightaway give him children," they were told. A daughter was born before the year was out and it was generally considered that a miracle had been wrought. After all, the King had proclaimed, "I am pleased to grant permission that a convent dedicated to St. Anthony be founded in the village of Mafra; the number of friars to be limited to only thirteen." And a princess had been born.

By the time the first stone was laid in 1717 the contemplated size of the monastery had grown to eighty monks; and thirteen years later, when the building was consecrated, there were facilities for 300 monks and 150 lay brothers and novices, and a palace had been tacked on to boot. This giant enterprise employed a minimum of 15,000 men, with as many as 45,000 working during peak periods of activity. A wooden shanty town was erected to house this horde, and a hospital in which some 17,000 sick and injured were treated. The entire country joined in trying to please the King by speeding up the progress of the building. According to an article by Dr. Robert Smith, "All over the country bricks were being made and were being distributed from the towns of Santarém and Alenquer over especially built roads to Mafra. . . . They were piled in such mountains that 'there seemed to be enough to make a city of them.' " Eighty-six teams of oxen and 650 men were needed to place the great stone that closed the dome, a feat that was said to have been accomplished in under two hours. All the records show the element of haste involved in the building of Mafra—obviously João was impatient for results.

The guidebook cliché of the past hundred years has been that Mafra was built in imitation of or competition with the Escorial. The notion was first contradicted in 1908 by Walter Crum

Watson, and recently blasted by Dr. Robert Smith. Both structures were commissioned by ostentatious rulers, both hoped to meld palace life with monastic peace, both were designed according to a gridiron plan. Aside from that, as Dr. Smith states, "The style of the two monuments is so entirely different that there can have been no borrowing."

The architect for this colossal enterprise, surprisingly enough, was a young German-born goldsmith turned architect, João Frederico Ludovice, son of Peter Ludwig, a government clerk in a small Swabian town. Young Ludwig, as he was still called, went to Italy, where he changed his name, recanted his Lutheran faith, married an Italian girl, and lived in Rome. Here he worked as a goldsmith at the church of the Gesù, where he was to "show dazzling virtuosity in the handling of metal." He must have spent considerable time on the side in the atelier of some master architect in order to absorb the fundamentals which were later to serve him and Portugal so brilliantly.

There is no evidence that he had built anything before receiving the Mafra commission. Ludovice and his family arrived in Lisbon in 1701; there he was under contract to the Portuguese Company of Jesus for a seven-year stint "to make silver and metal work for our use in monasteries, colleges, and other establishments." The conjecture as to how the building plum of Portugal fell to him left many false trails: some said that Bernini's rejected plan for the Louvre had passed through his hands; others, that he bought the contract from a venal minister; still others thought the Jesuits had contrived to get the job for their protégé—this was highly unlikely, as it cost them an invaluable goldsmith. The truth was, as it usually is, much simpler. Mafra had been conceived as a modest venture for which the King desired someone who had caught the flavor of the contemporary school of Rome; Ludovice had come to Lisbon highly recommended by the Jesuit fathers there. Had João envisaged anything as grand as what he finally commissioned, he would probably have imported the most distinguished talent in Europe—money was no consideration with the steady flow of diamonds and gold coming from Brazil.

Mafra appears from a distance as a city of palaces, set in rolling, often wooded country, with the Atlantic behind. Only when one stands at its feet does it appear of a piece. And what a magnificent piece. Statistically speaking, someone has counted 5,200 doors and 2,500 windows. The main façade is some 750 feet long with a *pavillon* at either end—one for the King, the other for the Queen, with miles of corridors between; except where his dynastic obligations were involved, João mostly loved nuns. One writer notes, "Fifty nuns, a hundred nuns . . . he was a very pious man." The King went to Mass three times daily and it was said that two tons of wax candles were burned every month he was in residence at the palace-monastery. Lord Byron allows his hero Childe Harold to describe these goings-on at Mafra as follows:

> . . . and church and court did mingle their array,
> And mass and revel were alternate seen;
> Lordlings and freres—ill-sorted fry, I wean.

Today one looks at Mafra's exterior grandeur with respectful awe; nor can one avoid feeling pleasure in its basilica and library. Ludovice was a genius in his use of stone—regardless of whether it was the local *pedra lioz* building stone or ornamental marble. Robert Smith compares him to Mansart at Versailles in teaching his colleagues the techniques of fine stone-cutting, and links this insistence to Ludovice's early training as a goldsmith. He says, "Capitals, flutings, brackets, and all the paraphernalia of architecture were cut with the care and exactitude of a setting for a gem." Mafra is daunting and surely was meant to be. But it has its light touches as well. The platform and stairs leading up to

Mafra Palace . . . the library

the church are strikingly grand, yet this basilica's prideful dome is possessed both of lightness and elegance. On either side are two towers rising some 200 feet into the heavens which reminded Beckford of St. Paul's in London and which, he said, "contain many bells of the largest dimensions, and a famous chime . . . which was set playing the moment our arrival was notified." When João V ordered the carillon for his new palace, the Antwerp firm held up the order long enough to inform the Portuguese monarch of its great cost. João, furious at what he took to be a doubt as to his solvency, immediately doubled his order with an advance payment in gold. (On certain Sundays in August, these carillons are still played.)

In order to enter the exquisite Baroque basilica, one passes through an atrium lined with statues of saints and martyrs wearing marble gowns that appear to billow in a non-existent breeze while their martyrdom looks more fashionable than painful. The church interior is so perfectly proportioned that one is almost unaware of its size. Even Beckford was impressed. "Never did I behold such an assemblage of beautiful marble as gleamed above and below, and around us," he wrote, adding, "The pavement, the vaulted ceiling, the dome, and even the top-most lantern, is encrusted with the same costly and durable materials. Roses of white marble and wreaths of palm branches, most exquisitely sculptured, enrich every part of the edifice. I never saw Corinthian capitals better modeled, or executed with more precision and sharpness, than those of the columns that support the nave."

This is no mean praise. Beckford was a purist. On the other hand, he took a critical attitude about the great library, which is in fact quite dazzling. A very narrow and long room—just eleven feet shorter than a football field—it contains some 36,000 books bound in golden calf and lettered in gold leaf. As morning light streams in through windows running its full length, the lofty white stuccoed ceiling acts as a reflector to every sunbeam.

Along the walls, carved bookshelves are painted grisaille, white, and gold; the floor is a subtle mixture of red and white marble; the general effect is that of a Baroque ballroom rather than an academic retreat.

João V was totally disinterested in gardens or *fêtes champêtres*, but Ludovice laid out a small, formal, green monastic garden within the rear courtyard, a little gem of convoluted topiary that became the model for Portuguese gardens of that time and this.

QUELUZ PALACE

This is the prettiest pink palace in the world as well as the most important and charming example of Rococo architecture in Portugal. Although at first sight it suggests something straight off the confectioner's shelves, there is nothing sugary about it. The pink plaster façade with its faded green accents may suggest sugar-coated almonds, but the stone ornamental trim—window hoods, door lintels, roof decorations—provides a solid look of reality along with dramatic vigor. Kubler and Soria, the authors of *Art and Architecture in Spain and Portugal*, call attention to a commonly held misconception. "The guidebooks praise Queluz by comparing it to Versailles"; in reality, they go on to say, "Mafra is the Portuguese Versailles, and Queluz is the anti-Versailles."

There is indeed a look of privacy, of intimacy, of human scale to the exterior of the palace—architectural legerdemain, for this is in fact a capacious establishment. But wherever a hint of pomp and circumstance arises, it is immediately dispelled. There is an amusing use of different levels of construction, an adroit departure from ordinary rules of symmetry, all contributing to a sense of beautiful insouciance. Two architects are known to have been involved in this project for Pedro, João V's younger son. The first, Mateus Vicente Oliveira, a disciple of Ludovice's, is credited with the handsome, two-storied north wing that faces the entrancing parade ground. Jean-Baptiste Robillon, a French engraver and decorator who had worked with the master silversmith Thomas Germain in Paris, designed the two-storied west wing with its monumental staircase; he also laid out the formal gardens. An unknown talent might be responsible for the one-storied wings along this garden, with their hipped roofs and ogee pediments. Here the tone of voice is most characteristically Portuguese, the statement pure ravishment.

Inside, the rooms are small (palatially speaking), strung out in *enfilade*, usually decorated with beautifully painted and/or gilded walls and ceilings. The chandeliers are sumptuous. The floors, often made of waxed rust-red tiles used in many noble houses, add a down-to-earth flavor that contributes to the durability of Portuguese Rococo. Queluz is a kind of architectural wink. Phoenixes set in the *boiseries* look down with an amused expression, the caryatids supporting the ceiling of the ballroom appear ready to shift their burden for a quick waltz, the gun room is painted to simulate a rain forest. Pervaded by a sense of light and sophistication, the palace resembles a Parisian *hôtel particulier* in the time of Louis XV. The Queen's dressing room is lined with painted panels of children dressing up in grown-up clothes; the Chamber of Picnics (Merendas) was named for painted panels depicting fashionable 18th-century *déjeuners sur l'herbe*, the work of a talented tease with a sardonic tongue in his cheek.

These interior delights are rivaled by outdoor enchantments. Few gardens have ever achieved such ingenuous sophistication—a combined use of complex topiary gardens, exquisite statues,

Queluz . . . stairway at southwest corner

elegant balustrades, intricate stairways, and masses of naïve, everyday flowers, petunias, heliotrope, geraniums in artful, subtle colors—usually based on a palette of pale blue, faded pink, and mauve which looks like painting on fine Saxe porcelain. Water lilies abound in ornate fountains in which the Princess of Brazil and her ladies dangled their toes after running races along the paths. There are a summerhouse built of closely clipped green vines, stands of lemons and oranges, great *allées* stretching in all directions, a canal and bridge lined and faced with *azulejos*—yellow, blue-and-white, and the color of diluted plum juice. This park façade, the work of Robillon, is immensely grand with its coupled Doric columns and a profusion of statuary. But again wit triumphs over grandeur—cascading stairs descend diagonally in a surprise change of phrasing.

Designed as a fabric of gaiety, joy, and enchantment, Queluz was fated to know little of either. The Infante Pedro, for whom it was built, married his niece, daughter of the heir apparent, later José I. At the latter's death, she became Queen and as King-Consort he assumed the title of Pedro III. Maria was never particularly stable and soon showed signs of religious mania. No wonder that when her husband, her son, and her confessor all died within a short time, all remnant of emotional stability vanished. Beckford, in an account of a visit to Queluz, recalls how just before his departure he was frozen: "The most agonizing shrieks—shrieks such as I hardly conceived possible . . . inflicted upon me a sensation of horror such as I never felt before. The Queen herself, whose apartment was only two doors off from the chamber in which we were sitting, uttered those dreadful sounds: 'Ai Jesous! Ai Jesous!' did she exclaim again and again in the bitterness of agony."

Queluz . . . garden side

PENA PALACE

The most agreeable way to visit Pena is to hire a horse-drawn carriage in the main square of Sintra. The road up is as pretty a drive as anyone might wish for, and the palace park is a horticultural curiosity which Richard Strauss called "The veritable gardens of Klingsor and above it is the castle of the Holy Grail." Be that as it may, with its pools and ponds, its rare trees, its camellias of great size and age, its formal gardens, the Pena park is indeed superb and on a par with the gardens of Monserrate between Sintra and Colares. (The latter can be visited only on foot, and by the sure-footed.)

Architecturally speaking, Pena Palace is a joke, but a resplendent one. Constructed in 1840 on the remains of an early monastery, it is pure Saxe-Coburg Moorish, a style inspired by Ferdinand II, who was a cousin of England's Prince Albert. No Wagnerian *papier-mâché* stage set has ever attempted such a crenelated, be-escutcheoned, be-moated fantasy as this. Queen Victoria might have had just cause to think that her beloved Albert and Balmoral were being upstaged: indeed, she would have been right, for Ferdinand held the title of King Consort, and Pena made the Queen's Highland castle appear deadpan and over-straightforward. Pena is grotesque, comical, and rather wonderful. Set on the crest of the Serra da Sintra, its silhouette is visible on a clear day from the outskirts of Lisbon. As for the views from Pena's parapets, they are nothing short of stupendous —the universe, land and ocean, stretching out as far as the eye can reach.

The interior is a medley of extreme 19th-century conceits: the walls of one apartment are of plaster, painted to look like pickled wood paneling, while the furnishings are made of Meissen porcelain. (There apparently was a rage for fake wood, and Ferdinand's second wife, the Countess Edla, had a cement chalet built and painted to simulate knotty pine and cork oak.) There are only two things of intrinsic beauty in the palace, both relics of the ancient Hieronymite monastery. One of these, a tiny double cloister with a patio in the center, has the soft look of a seraglio. The other is the great carved altarpiece in the chapel, which is by Chanterene. That great 16th-century sculptor used alabaster and black marble for this complex composition, which unfolds like a medieval passion play. Its central figure, an exquisite Christ, seems to be slipping off his tomb, only just restrained by the gentle hands of angels.

AJUDA PALACE

Compiègne, the favorite retreat of Napoleon III and Eugénie, is the only palace in Europe that compares with the Ajuda as an example of Second Empire interior decoration and luxury. Most experts go further, claiming that Compiègne is relegated to second place. The decor of the Ajuda reflects the taste and determination of Maria Pia, Princess of Savoy, who came to Portugal as the beloved wife of Luis I. The King was unable to deny her anything, as were his English bankers, and his ministers at their posts throughout the capitals of Europe. Britain, Italy, France, Belgium all vied with each other to supply *objets d'art* for the Queen. She collected rare pieces of 18th-century Portuguese furniture, at the same time encouraging craftsmen and artisans to produce contemporary work for her palace. The immensely knowledgeable Ayres de Carvalho, curator of the Ajuda, works among innumerable letters, documents, sketches, bills, all from these 19th-century sculptors, painters, decorators, upholsterers, and gilders. There is a sense of the Queen's personality on all sides. Chairs or sofas are richly covered in tufted velvet and sometimes leather. Pianos are concealed under damask. Tables and chests are inlaid with Saxe porcelain. There is gaudiness in the air. Chandeliers glitter above Aubusson rugs, Winterhalter portraits, and table decorations by François Thomas Germain and Thomier. There are adequate bathrooms and even a hint of privacy. The King was a bad Sunday painter (and every day was Sunday) who worked in a two-storied studio paneled in dark, carved wood in a style that is thoroughly Neo-Gothic Manueline. The Queen's winter garden is a jewel of its period —with aviaries, simulated bamboo chairs, lattices, and hanging baskets, all gilded and usually filled with green maidenhair ferns. The trend has long been to scoff at this 19th-century past, but it is rapidly coming into its own; granted the contemporary eye must adjust, the smile learn to be affectionate rather than scornful. There is no better museum of the decorative art of the period in which to learn this lesson than the Ajuda Palace.

In a special section of the palace one is sometimes permitted to see the Crown jewels—dazzling objects studded with magnificent gems set by master jewelers. Maria Pia's diadem is easily the prettiest crown any queen ever wore with its twenty-five huge diamond stars set in gold; the King had forty-three diamond buttons in case he needed them. There are huge royal decorations, 18th-century French tea and coffee services made of gold, and magnificent salvers in gilded silver, heavily carved by 16th-century Portuguese silversmiths. The work of at least one such master craftsman of the period has sometimes been hopefully, but not surprisingly, attributed to Cellini.

CHAPTER VIII

Journal

February 1

LISBON

Lisbon's individuality is evident from the air. At 10,000 feet it looks like itself and nowhere else in the world. The surrounding hills are like inverted teacups. The recently completed steel suspension bridge over the Tagus River looks like a rust-red ribbon tying together colonies of red-tiled roofs on either bank. The great Convento do Jerónimos seems like a table ornament, a very valuable one, possibly by Cellini. Our descent was almost accomplished and the plane rushed low over a flower bed laid out to tell time. It said exactly 10:50 on a resplendent morning. The wheels touched the ground and the big Pan American jet engines reversed to brake their speed. It had been a pleasant, smooth, seven-and-a-half-hour flight from New York.

Luggage was produced creditably fast and cleared through

customs even faster. I let Mosey, my small Norwich terrier, sniff airport gardens bursting with primroses and iris. My elation at being back was somewhat subdued by flight fatigue, but it was only a twenty-minute drive to the Ritz Hotel, where I planned to have a drink, a hot bath, light nourishment, and, optimistically, a nap. The last two failed to come up to expectation: the vegetable soup, *caldo verde*, was a lukewarm, pallid facsimile of the brew it purported to be. The dog's food, however, was just the reverse and a tribute to the national affinity for animals and decoration—on a silver salver lay three precisely alternating rows of carrots, rice, and beef, all chopped to exactly the same consistency. Mosey, unimpressed and preferring sleep, spurned food. I swallowed my tepid soup and lay back tensed as if expecting some hypothetical attack. It was just as well that the telephone started ringing. I decided to go out and get my bearings, which for me in Lisbon means going to the Jerónimos.

This great Manueline abbey,* which could exist only in Portugal, never loses its impact for me. Familiarity with it, far from breeding contempt, seems only to deepen my sensual and spiritual satisfaction at seeing it. The late afternoon sun that slanted in seemed turned on for my delight, calling attention to the contrasts of starkness and elaboration. One is made aware almost at once of the immense height of the interior, which seems to soar to heaven. Standing beneath the *côro alto*, the visitor's eye normally projects toward the church chancel. But not here. Those high, slender, intricately carved columns insistently draw attention upward as if to heaven. This is as good a place as any to get a first inkling of something characteristic about Portuguese churches. They seem designed primarily for the delight of God, not of his bishops.

If one accepts this as a basic fact about churches, then unquestionably Portuguese cloisters were built for the delight of

* See page 160.

monks. (Nuns apparently demanded a different kind of architectural indulgence.) To my mind, the cloisters of the Jerónimos are second to no other in Portugal, a land of cloisters. Almost every section of carved stone along the four sides of this two-story retreat is different in design. But because the theme is consistently maritime, these sculptural variations meld into a great stone symphony of Manueline exuberance. Here, especially, one is struck by a highly sophisticated restraint applied to sculptural braggadocio.

Dinner with an English friend, V., a retired partner of Sotheby's, at the Aviz, my favorite restaurant. My biological clock was still shaken, but two excellent martinis helped restore me. Then smoked swordfish (how delicious it is, and how prettily served with quartered lemons tied in tulle tutus); with it we drank a Vinho Verde Vilacelinho. Then lampreys cooked in red wine (they taste like a cross between chicken liver and mushrooms) followed by a queijo da Serra—a good, runny, mountain cheese, with which there was a marvelous Dão Reserva 1954 (at under three dollars and like a young Haut Brion). Home to bed, where I found that V. had left wildflowers at the porter's desk to be put in vases in my room—pussywillows so fat they seemed ready to purr, long-stemmed orangey narcissus, and iris—hardly what one expects as wildflowers.

February 2

LISBON

They were wildflowers all right and dead in the morning. Lunched with Lady E., an Anglo-Portuguese and my oldest friend in Lisbon. Went to Tavares, which was attractively full of men. Generally speaking, Portuguese ladies lead a rather private life. Wonderful *presunto* (smoked ham) and melon, *santola* (a spider crab), and *toucinho do ceu* (a honey-and-almond dessert), which is particularly well made by this chef.

This turned out to be my afternoon for doing things most tourists do but which I never had gotten around to in all the past four summers. Low priorities on my sightseeing list but nevertheless oversights worth correcting. I went up to the Castelo de São Jorge, which is nothing but a maze of ruined walls, all greatly restored. This was the formidable Moorish stronghold that Portugal's first king, Afonso Henriques, had to subdue in the 12th century before he could take Lisbon. History aside, there are two reasons for going there today: from this vantage point one has a spellbinding panorama of Lisbon and its immediate environs; and, second, the imaginative liveliness that has been bestowed on these medieval fortifications by a succession of gardens planted inside their moats, keeps, and roofless guardrooms —exotic furnishings of green trees and shrubs, white flowers, and armies of white peacocks. The guards had asked me to carry my dog, Mosey, so as not to frighten the birds. A fine chance there was of that! A platoon of peahens followed us, hissing like a fury of housewives, and the peacocks strutted with an indignant show of disdain, fanning their tails like starched lace fans.

Because Lisbon is built on seven hills, getting from the lower town to the upper sections is arduous. It has not changed much since an 18th-century visitor bemoaned its "cursed ups and downs, such shelving descents and sudden rises." Around the turn of the century, an outdoor elevator was built to cope with such precipitous matters. Its steel frame is pure Neo-Gothic; the passenger cab is spacious, wood-paneled like the saloons on the now defunct Hoboken ferryboats, and has no windows. (Possibly in those relatively innocent days, agoraphobia was more prevalent than claustrophobia is today.) One disembarks at the top of the town onto a steel runway leading into a square alongside the Gothic ruins of the Carmo church. The Great Earthquake of 1755 struck on All Saints' Day while Lisbon was at Mass, and the marble roof of the Carmo tumbled in, killing most of the congregation gathered there. Today the church aisles are carpeted with neatly trimmed grass; only walls and skeletal arches stand, white and still and portentous—a moving memorial to those thousands who died in a world-shaking (literally) disaster.

Dinner at the American Embassy at eight. (Early for Lisbon, where the fashionable hour to dine is more likely to be nine.) Just the Ambassador and his wife, and a charming young Portuguese couple, the V.Z.'s. (His family are in the Port wine business and he was off tomorrow for Yugoslavia to persuade that government to let him erect a neon-lighted billboard in Belgrade.) The Embassy residence looked particularly lovely filled with flowers arranged *à la Portugaise*—all shapes, colors, and sizes, as in the best of the 17th-century Dutch flower paintings.

The reason for dining early was in order to get to the opera—a treat for visitors, as the opera house is small and mostly sold out to subscribers. Evening dress is required and Lisboans, taking this injunction seriously, dress to the nines. We arrived at our box just before the lights dimmed in the jewel-like São Carlos theater, built at the turn of the 18th century by a Portuguese architect, José da Costa e Silva, who modeled it on La Scala in Milan. The interior is all apricot-colored, with muted green and gold, a sparkle of crystal chandeliers, and white cameos on the front of the grand-tier boxes. The President of Portugal has a double box (seating ten) next to the proscenium, where the visibility is practically nil; the royal box (now used only for state visits) is dead center, a peach-colored drawing room with its own chandelier, slightly dimmed during the performance but never extinguished.

A German company presented Mozart's *La Clemenza di Tito:* the sets were particularly effective, somber black-and-white photographic slides of Roman temples; the conductor doubled as harpsichordist when the score required it. Afterward we drove through the hushed streets of Lisbon; in the night light, ocher-colored houses turn to citron, pink ones to russet. It was one o'clock when I got to my room.

February 3

LISBON

Went to buy flowers for the Ambassadress and found a staggering choice. Armfuls of mimosa, or almond blossoms, or camellia branches loaded with blooms, or two dozen calla lilies —for less than two dollars. I settled for the mimosa, enough to fill a room with sunshine. Lunched with a young English couple, the B.'s, then took a much needed siesta. I was due in Sintra for dinner, Colares for tea, and the Tower of Belém—a sturdy little fortress that looks like a chess-piece, and the Coach Museum and Queluz *en route*. I merely paid my respects to the two latter. The collection of coaches is dazzling and I always feel compelled to look in on it to reassure myself that it exists in fact, and not just in my imagination: there is no more extraordinary manifestation of Rococo anywhere. As for Queluz,* the mood is set, rather surprisingly, on an immense pink parade ground designed to encourage pomp, provided it masquerades as frivolity; and the gardens with their fountains and statues are gems of coquetry.

In Colares for tea with V., where his long gallery—mostly furnished with harpsichords and clavichords—today was filled with bowls of fat garden roses. (He advised me never to send calla lilies, as "the Portuguese consider them mere weeds.") At D.'s in Sintra by 7:30 in order to see *her* garden before dinner, which, as an American, she insists on eating early. There were a twenty-foot hedgerow of mimosa dripping with yellow, a few

* See page 209.

almond trees in flower, and camellias everywhere—indoors and out.

February 4

LISBON TO SAGRES (via Sagres, São Tiago de Cacêm, Setúbal)

An early start in order to drive close to 200 miles. I had invited V. to join me, so my chauffeur, Gomes, picked him up in Sintra to make certain he was on time. According to the map, our route took us to the southernmost edge of Portugal and the western tip of the European continent. It was too early for the Serra da Arrábida to put on its full dress show of wildflowers, but this is a spectacularly scenic drive at any season, wilder and just as dramatic as the famed corniches of the French Riviera. White heather and yellow gorse were blooming in profusion and we met no other car the whole way across.

Stopped in Setúbal to see the convent-church of Jesus (another Portuguese church I never tire of). From the far side of the square, beyond a marble cross, one first glimpses its provocative façade: stone fretwork crowning the parapet; a mosaic-like consistency to its unpolished Arrábida marble portal, carved with what for Manueline passes as simplicity. Here at the church of Jesus one senses the clear line of demarcation between architects like Boytac, Fernandes and the da Arruda brothers, who spoke in the true Manueline idiom (having in fact been its originators), and those who prattled its stylistic jargon for the next twenty-six years.

The interior of the convent-church of Jesus, long before I first saw it, had been subjected to the spoilers who call themselves "restorers" in Portugal. Their passion, wherever they are given a chance, seems to be for stripping away all vestige of exquisite 17th- and 18th-century carved and gilded *boiseries*, or early *azulejos*. This church defied them. It is, in fact, an architectural experience—what might pass for 15th-century psychedelic. Six marble columns, each one formed of three twisted stone banyan roots, appear to be hanging *down* from the roof instead of holding it *up*. This produces an imagined sense of sway, a loss of equilibrium, that could easily be an asset in saving souls.

En route from Setúbal south to São Tiago de Cacêm, where we were to lunch, past fields of white daisies, forests of mimosa and umbrella pines, red soil, and cork trees. (Gomes, the chauffeur, said, "Only foreigners and poor people plant mimosa—it takes over gardens like your honey vine." *) Ruined castles were on all sides—turrets, ramparts, hollow shells. The landscape became more barren, empty, except when a twist in the road brought the ocean in view. We crossed strange, dumpy hills where there appeared to be moving rocks—they turned out to be sheep. Lunch at a *pousada* was late and delicious: a spicy Alentejo specialty, pork and clams cooked together; a light Muscatel to drink; and for dessert, succulent tangerines and Azeitão cheese, which looks like Canadian oka on the outside but at this time of year, when it's dead ripe, is runny enough to eat with a spoon. (V. calls it the "congenial cheese—too much for one, perfect for two.") All afternoon we drove from one *serra* to another in wild, stark country. The emptiness accumulated until we reached Sagres, slightly tawdry now except for the memory of Henry the Navigator. There is nothing tangible left of the man, the fortress is mostly restoration; the short film version of his life shown there doesn't encapsulate his magic—how could it?

My room at the *pousada* here in Sagres looks out on what he saw, the cliffs and, just beyond, the open Atlantic—awesome and beckoning. A pair of ravens were sunning themselves along the cliffs. These birds are a part of the Portuguese mythology.

* Honeysuckle.

Setúbal . . . church of Jesus, interior

According to legend, ravens flew the equivalent of an air-force escort over a rowboat empty except for the remains of the martyred São Vicente: once they saw the Saint's body safely beached on Lisbon shores, they flew back to pluck out the eyes of his Infidel tormentors. The surf makes a resonant booming sound here at Sagres, and as the golden sun dropped into the sea it was easy to imagine—as the ancients did—the hiss of its fire as it sank into the cold Atlantic.

After dinner I was drawn again to this window. There was a Moorish moon—just a sliver of a crescent—and the ghost of Henry. Sagres is haunted by the memory of him; like the lonely man, it is barren, relentless, its soul turned toward the ocean.

February 5

SAGRES TO SERPA (via Lagos, Faro, Vila Real de Santo António, and Mértola)

This morning I threw open the blinds to endless blue, an Atlantic which seems uniquely Portuguese. The whole morning was spent motoring across the Algarve, toward Spain. The countryside appeared more Moroccan than European, with flat-topped white houses, and waterwheels operated by blindfolded donkeys walking the pump handle round to draw water. (Once in a while a small boy seemed to be assigned the chore, obviously for the same reason that my generation was made to stand in a corner.) There were geranium hedges and acres of almond blossoms—all pinky-white, tentative, poetic, and profuse. Imagine seventy miles of apple blossoms and it would be almost as dazzling, if not as tender. Seen through these drifts of pink flowers, the gray, bare-limbed fig trees appeared to be cut of granite. In the Algarve, where winds are fierce, fig trees are weighted when young to make them grow close to the ground, spreading out as much as twenty feet in diameter. We drove through a 100-acre fig plantation stretching out on both sides of the highway, the gray limbs curving down in graceful obeisance—like a *corps de ballet* taking a bow.

Stopped in Lagos, Henry the Navigator's holding harbor. The bay is vast and, a guidebook says, "capable of holding 147 ships"; it doesn't specify of what tonnage. Here again little remains but the legend of Henry and a small, finely proportioned customs house off the main square, with an arcaded gallery where his ship captains auctioned off their slaves. The tiny chapel of Santo António (completely unrelated to the Navigator) combines humor with beauty. Its rich Baroque *boiseries* are elaborately carved and gilded in three shades of gold—yellow, green, and red—all of which sparkle in the sunlight that floods in when doors on either side are opened. There are romping angels, mythical monsters, two fighting knights, a stag hunt, fishermen, and cupids busily gathering grapes, one presumes to make the consecrated wine.

I am not by nature a beach lover, but Algarve beaches admittedly have drama. The sea has cut the cliffs into weird grottos, promontories, oceanic cathedrals (which might easily have inspired Manueline architects) bordered by ribbons of white sand. Just outside the town of Portimão we passed shepherds driving apricot-colored "sheep" to market—according to Gomes, they're called *cabras Algarvia*, which means they are more goat than sheep. The dogs working with the shepherds, *Cão laboreio* (again according to G.), are big, handsome, heavy-coated, and golden, with fine heads and a thoroughbred look. (They might be great to shoot over.) In the Portimão market we bought roasted chestnuts, tender and especially sweet with a draught from the Muscatel bottle I carry in the car.

Farther south, at Faro, we stopped to look at São Francisco, an early church, set on a square lined with orange trees ostentatiously full of fruit. Inside there were good Rococo carved and gilded wood and *azulejos*—a combination that is pleasingly rich. Faro was an early seat of learning, with a printing press dating back to the 15th century; here, too, was the Bishop of Faro's great library, which the Earl of Essex looted in the 16th century (at a time when Spain governed Portugal). The loot was given to Oxford, where it became the nucleus of the Bodleian Library; although England and Portugal have been allies for more than 500 years, this treasure has never been returned to its rightful owners.

Between Faro and Vila Real de Santo António (one of several Vila Reals in Portugal) we were slowed down by road-building. Men were fitting broken stones together as I had first seen it done by coolies building airstrips in China for U.S. bombers during World War II. We lunched in Vila Real de Santo António on the quay beside the Guadiana River, which separates Portugal from Spain, in a small, plain fisherman's inn. There were a real *caldo verde*, boiled *cherne* (a white fish somewhat like turbot), and with fruit and cheese, a "strawberry tree" liqueur offered us by the house. This may well be the first prefabricated town, dreamed up by Pombal in the 18th century. Spain had the thriving town of Ayamonte across the river, and Pombal set out to match it in five months. From Lisbon he saw to every detail right down to the stone window and door frames, the black-and-white marble paving of the main square, the façades of the "noble" houses (early examples of a style later called Pombaline). The whole town was shipped from Lisbon by sea and set up by local labor in five months' time.

After a few miles we left the Algarve to start north again, back into the Alentejo. Here flowers were less profuse; there was greater contrast and reality, too. (The Algarve made me bad-tempered—too much of everything becomes tiresome.) At the top of a *serra* we were stopped by goats spread over the highway. A baby goat had been born that very moment. Much to the disgust of V. and the impeccably dapper Gomes, I insisted on taking the mother goat, her newborn, and the twelve-year-old son of the shepherd down to the village. It took a bit of doing to get "Ma" in the back with me, but she followed when the boy and her kid were installed on the seat. It was smelly, but not unpleasantly so, and I had never seen such a tiny goat. There was considerable amazement when our passengers disembarked on the village square; the boy will be talking about it for some time—admittedly I felt foolish and sentimental. Soon afterward we had to stop to let Mosey have a run (she too disapproved of goats) and I picked some sweet, spicy white narcissus growing wild in a room-size patch of loveliness.

Dozed until we came to Mértola, a small town known by the Romans as Myrtalis. Sparkling white houses piled up along tortuous streets which only a skillful driver like Gomes could negotiate. At the very top was a white adobe parish church, dating from the 13th century. It had flying buttresses on one side, six pepper-pot domes along the top (squat but phallic), and a lovely Renaissance portal. The interior walls were painted a deep ocher and broken by four rows of columns that divided a relatively small space into five aisles. (The sculptor who carved the animal and human heads around the capitals appeared to have worked under the influence of an acute Visigothic hangover.) This church had originally been a mosque, and V. found the old Mihrab—as important to Mohammedans as the cross is to Christians—on a wall at the back of the apse.

Directly across the square were the ruins of a fortress said to have been built in 1292 by the first Master of the Order of São Tiago. It was impossible for V. to negotiate with a game leg, but I climbed to the top, tugging Mosey along for company. From where we finally stood, one would have had no trouble spotting a medieval army while it was still a three days' march away. A small boy materialized from nowhere, probably the village idiot, and he made the little dog and me feel uneasy. By the time we scrambled down to church level, there was a man talking to V. He told us that the people here always speak of "going to the mosque" on Sundays.

Stopped for the night just south of Serpa in a *pousada* built in an immense olive grove at the top of the *serra*. The ground around the driveway was thick with fat, squat wild iris. Looking out of my bedroom window, with my back toward Spain, I could see miles of Portugal spilling out before me, sloping down over countless *serras*, always dropping in order eventually to meet the Atlantic. In a last lingering glow of daylight there were olive trees, and the red earth of the Alentejo, and a sense of mystery.

On the dinner menu the English translation of the fish course was "soused minnow"—meaning slightly pickled. Quite good.

February 6

SERPA TO CASTELO DE VIDE (via Beja and Évora)

Serpa is a somewhat bigger version of Mértola, another walled town, very white, with a hint of minarets to its church spires. There were the remains of an aqueduct and another ruined fortress, part of King Diniz' defense line, and three churches similar to the one in Mértola. The church of Santa Maria, however, is quite different—austerely lovely, and, like the castle, dating back to Diniz.* The exterior is transitional, Romanesque to Gothic; the interior plain, with finely carved capitals and a font that goes around one of the columns—apparently an Alentejo custom.

Driving out toward Beja (north and west of here), we left Serpa through two towers of the town walls—round and massive, and built for defense. There is something immensely com-

* See page 22.

pelling about walled towns, sparking a nostalgia for the days when walls spelled security; they still suggest safety, like drawing the curtains at night.

We crossed a narrow bridge used for either a train or a car, depending on which gets there first. The country grew rocky, and barren except for ancient olive trees growing right out of the boulders, with black pigs and sheep feeding around them. Before long there was another change in the landscape and we drove through immense cork plantations. At first glance these trees might be mistaken for olives, although their leaves are less silvery and their bark is craggier, except, of course, for those that have been harvested—stripped, as it is called. Again, with no transition, rather like bursting through a paper screen, the vistas opened into the rich plains for which this part of the Alentejo is famous. Big landowners around here use tractors to plow their fields of corn and wheat. In winter when most Portuguese countrymen wear a short sheepskin jacket with a red fox collar, the peasants and shepherds of this part of the Alentejo favor ankle-length brown wool coats with three tiers of capes to the waist—warm and immensely elegant. They take their food to work in cork baskets with well-fitted lids, as good as any thermos jug for keeping things hot or cold.

We drove through rows of eucalyptus trees, big and pungent. Everything was bright and sharp in today's overcast. Storks stood on one leg in the fields and sometimes one caught sight of their basket-size nests high up in a eucalyptus. In the distance the castle crowning the town of Beja contributed to its pyramidal appearance as it rises off the plain. For years I've longed to see the convent of Nossa Senhora da Conceição in Beja, and it lived up to expectations. The stone fretwork around its parapet seemed airier than in most Manueline construction, possibly in deference to the nuns who lived here. The convent and its chapel have become a regional museum, closed on Mondays according to Portuguese custom. Of course it was Monday! But with a little persistent rapping on doors and doleful comments as to "how far we had traveled," keys turned in locks. Custodians in Portugal rarely turn people away. In addition to the great beauty of the chapel, the curious design of its cloister, the rarity of the chapter-house *azulejos* (like a Persian carpet), there is a provocative note of scandal attached to these walls. It stems from the 17th-century publication, in Paris, of *Love Letters of a Portuguese Nun*, purportedly written from this convent by Soror Mariana Alcoforado to her lover, the Chevalier de Chamilly, a French officer. The convent is one of many belonging to the Chagas order, most of them famous for richly decorated chapels and the status of the ladies cloistered within the walls—rich, high-born, often royal, and referred to by the English as "Poor Clares."

The chapel of Nossa Senhora da Conceição in Beja may not be the finest property under Chagas rule, but it qualifies as the liveliest. Its giltwork, according to a young curator, was applied in two ways—in a powdered form, and in gold leaf. "That explains its subtle variation of texture and color," he said. And I might add its sophistication, too. Within the abstract convolutions of the Rococo carving there were the figures of countless baby-sized angels and angel heads, the wickedest *putti* in the world, and the most deliciously gay—all flirting, dancing, or scowling. Our guide went on to say, "Portuguese artists of those days competed among themselves in carving such 'live babies'—it made them feel as creative as women." The wood-carvers who worked in this convent were masters of liveliness and delight; even the main altarpiece, consisting of one gold box piled up on another and yet another, combines dignity with exuberance—careful never to become solemn and frighten the *putti*.

We passed out of Beja through a Roman arch set in the double ramparts of still another castle. I wanted to see Santo Amaro, a little Visigothic church, one of a handful of pre-Romanesque

A stone corn crib

buildings in Portugal, but after waiting for twenty minutes for a man to fetch the key I satisfied myself by peeking through the enormous keyhole at some columns with fluted capitals.

Coursing hare is still popular in this part of the Alentejo, and peasants as well as landlords own handsome greyhounds. V. persists in the notion that all these dogs stem from a pair brought over by Wellington during the Peninsular Wars. The English see an English influence on everything from dogs to architecture; the French are just as convinced that they see their own image. But the fact is that the Portuguese have a long record of successful assimilation . . . taking from the French, the English, the Italian, the Arabic, or the Oriental, and making it all their own, and all Portuguese.

We lunched in Évora,* one of my favorite towns, a storehouse of architectural diversity. (On this visit I placed a firm check on my enthusiasm, as we still had some distance to go before night.) On the way to Gião's, the restaurant where we were to eat, we passed the Temple of Diana, the most complete and grandest Roman ruin in Portugal, and the 16th-century Aqueduto da Prata with its graceful gazebos along the top to aerate the water. Évora is very white, a town of handsome squares, of superbly simple marble fountains and splendid ironwork balconies, of palaces and churches. We ate well, a local version of codfish and scrambled eggs, and a tartly sweet dessert which they told me was made with carrots puréed with orange peel, then cooked in light syrup and rolled into balls.

I was curious to have a look at two nearby monasteries. The first, built for Carthusian monks in the 16th century by Terzi, an Italian architect who worked mostly in Lisbon, seemed too stylish for this austere order; at least that was my impression of what could be seen through its closed gates. (Carthusians have

* See page 85.

recently been permitted to take back this property, and visitors are now forbidden entry.) Farther down the road we came to São Bento de Castris, a huge and rambling monastery with a church consecrated in the 14th century. Now run by a pair of stalwart priests, it is an orphanage caring for 160 boys. The padre who escorted me around, was a big, earthy man committed to the splendor of the ancient buildings and the youth of the boys in his charge. There was immense vitality and serenity to the plain two-storied cloister and refectory, both of which were of a size to accommodate the whole community of monks, although the church could hardly have held a quarter of them. I asked if I might give something for the orphans, and the priest suggested an extra dessert for the week of carnival preceding Lent. When we left he removed his beret and made a courtly gesture of farewell. We no sooner hit the road than the car came to a stop. I thought it must be a flat tire, but the sentimental Gomes had a speech to make. "Thank you for those boys," he said.

There is something insidious about motoring in this country. The roads are good, the distances between towns are short, but this very combination produces in Americans like myself a kind of euphoric invitation to loiter, to look at one more thing. I admit to being a sucker for this, and inevitably find myself at close of day far from my destination. We had planned to stay at Castelo de Vide and there was still the Serra de Ossa to cross; rising more than 3,000 feet, its sides terraced and recently planted with tiny eucalyptuses, this mountain range is an impressive piece of Portuguese reforestation.

When we finally got there, Castelo de Vide turned out to be a curious town with a fine castle. (There must be more *castelos* per square mile in Portugal than anywhere else in Europe.) There were Baroque squares, and town houses, and a wealth of medieval stone doorways and windows. The *estalagem* is clean and comfortable enough for a night's stay.

February 6

CASTELO DE VIDE TO LISBON (via Marvão, Estremoz, Vila Viçosa)

There was no hope of sun today, in fact a pea-soup fog plagued the morning. We drove up to Marvão, where I had wanted to spend last night, but, according to the tourism people in Lisbon, the *pousada* there was not open. A mountain fog was so thick that one could do little more than get an impression of what I suspect is one of Portugal's finest walled towns—fortunately, still not tarted up. The *pousada* was "unofficially" open —typical Portuguese hair-splitting—and we had a second breakfast there. I felt like an eagle on my escarpment as I looked out a big glass window. Except for this *pousada*, practically nothing has been built in the town for over a century, and little has really changed since the Middle Ages, when it was a strategic outpost. People on the streets appeared economically better off than one might expect in such isolated barren country. Gomes explained this in a word: "Smuggling." He added that until recently the traffic paid off "from Spain to Portugal; now it's the other way round."

I was astonished by the number of new primary schools that have mushroomed throughout the country, where the law requiring seven years of schooling is stringently enforced. We passed little girls playing during recess in white smocks under which they appeared to wear bright red or blue leotards (right out of Bemelmans illustrations) and drove through the next town of Estremoz without stopping. Estremoz marble was used by the Romans for the columns of the Temple of Diana in Évora, and the Spaniards imported it to build the Escorial. Locally it is cut up for paving blocks, used for house fronts, light stanchions, bathtubs, and ash trays. The town is also famous for earthenware jugs and dishes used for cooking and carrying water. Some of these terra-cotta jars are big enough to hide Ali Baba, and their design and texture almost identical to those of the Phoenicians. Hedges of heather bloomed along the highway outside the town where I gave Mosey her midday run. The buzz of bees struck a frenetic pitch. We stopped in Vila Viçosa for an adequate lunch. (Although Portugal is not a gourmet's country, most of the time one eats well enough, sometimes superbly, and such occasions are more numerous than the traveler might expect to find in America.)

Vila Viçosa's importance stemmed from the Bragança, particularly in the period before 1640 when this rich and powerful ducal family was summoned to the throne. Five generations of pre-royal dukes are buried in the chancel of the pink and green marble church of Agostinho, in identical marble sarcophagi resting on dark-green marble lions. There were several other churches to see in Vila Viçosa, and a ruined castle, part Moorish, part medieval, with Roman foundations—all of which we failed to explore. One runs the risk of seeing too much to remember anything or, equally hazardous, falling prey to what William Beckford noted as the prevalent sin of travel books, which "like peerage-books and pedigrees, are tenderly inclined to make something of what is next to nothing." Having vowed, however, not to miss a Chagas convent, I refused to pass up the one in Vila Viçosa, even though it had been converted into a school. Small desks had been installed in its elegant rooms, rich in *azulejos* and painted ceilings. Stairs leading up to frescoed loggias had the appearance of obstacle courses. One picked one's way between pairs of children's shoes—all pointing up just as the youngsters stepped out of them on their way to class. Like all these retreats for Poor Clares, the chapel was richly gilded and decorated with early paintings on wood—badly in need of expert care.

But to go back to the Braganças and their palace, which was begun in 1501 and only finished a 100 years later. Its butter-colored marble façade, broken by three rows of twenty-three windows, looks out on a truly royal square with crowns on every marble lamp post. This was a private palace until 1640, when João, Duke of Bragança, was invited to become King João IV.* After that the great house was abandoned except during royal shooting parties. There remain splendid things inside, although much of the best was taken to Lisbon by the new royalties and subsequently lost in the earthquake. What remains is an unholy mixture—from Baroque to Victorian, from good to worse. Antique tapestries, however, are magnificent and so are the Rococo furnishings. One object, referred to as the Bragança Cross, deserves close inspection: it is a five-foot ivory spike—a narwhal tooth, turned snuff color with age—set in chased silver. Presented to Catherine of Bragança on her betrothal to Charles II, it contains relics of the murdered Thomas à Becket. My favorite room, however, was the huge kitchen with its marble floor and over 600 copper pots, pans, and other utensils. The palace grounds include a 200-year-old boxwood garden, a lovely water tank, an exquisite Alhambra-like cloister nowadays frequented mostly by peacocks. The Braganças not only were patrons of the arts but actively dabbled as contributors—particularly in painting and music. V., who is knowledgeable regarding 17th-century music lore, insists that João IV composed the tune for "Adeste Fideles."

It was a two-hour drive back to Lisbon, through woods bright with mimosa. The only traffic consisted of donkey carts loaded with fresh vegetables—stacked according to color—headed for the capital's markets.

February 7

LISBON

Loafed until time to get my hair done, afterward a glass of Port with a charming Portuguese author and financier who

* See page 59.

Marvão

describes himself as "a journalist of the Right." It was natural to speak of international affairs. Lunched with one of the d'A. sisters at Tavares; she knew almost all the bankers and government big shots there. The only other women in the reastaurant were a group of mini-skirted Spaniards and Amalia Rodrigues, the famous *fado* singer. She's wonderfully plain, with good, strong features, big eyes, no make-up, and an amused expression.

Afterward I went to look at Madre de Deus, the most beautiful church interior in Lisbon and an example of how rich Poor Clares could be: blue-and-white *azulejos*, extravagant gilding, a wealth of paintings, a magically controlled extravagance with dazzling 18th-century details—the golden grilles which might have been woven for Cartier, and the high Baroque golden pulpit.

Over a drink with a liberal and authoritative American diplomat, I discussed recent figures published by the *Wall Street Journal* which estimate the average Portuguese income as $350 annually. B. placed the sum at $410, which he considered in line with basic costs. "One can live damn well, two servants and all that, on $6,000 a year," he explained. "As for the poor, they are far better off than people in our city ghettos, or the Mississippi poor . . . these children are not suffering from acute malnutrition." Wages are rising and labor shortages exist, but he emphasized that "the crunch is on the white-collar workers who are buying luxuries on credit—mostly electrical appliances." B. went on to say that some emigration was encouraged in order to sharpen skills. When I told him about the hotel maid's family in Brazil who had written: "If we had worked as hard at home as we do here, we would never have needed to leave," B. smiled. "There's less status pressure here . . . a man is what he is," he said.

February 9

LISBON

Stopped in at the Museu Nacional de Arte Antiga to look at the masterpiece of Portuguese printing, the great polyptych by Nuno Gonçalves. There has been a dearth of great painters in Portugal, but this work by Gonçalves (discovered in a remote corner of the convent of São Vicente de Fora in 1882) is a splendid 15th-century masterpiece. Gathered in the company of the patron São Vicente is everybody of any importance in Portugal of that day, some sixty personages including the King and Queen, Henry the Navigator, Jewish moneylenders, the Augustinian monks of São Vicente, fishermen, and carpenters. More wondrous still, each face is a portrait. Little if anything is known about the artist. Mystery surrounds his identity; his date of birth has never been pinpointed. (The date most commonly used would make him court painter at fourteen!) Some circles attribute the picture to Van Eyck, although that great Flemish artist left Lisbon forty years before the polyptych was painted. None of this matters, nothing adds to or distracts from the impact of a great work of art.

Dined alone in the hotel. The Ritz only pretends to a great name and is satisfied by Hilton standards.

February 10

LISBON

Lisbon's thieves' market, the Feira da Ladra, is held on Tuesdays and Saturdays in the square back of the great church of São Vicente de Fora: this being Saturday, I decided to take a look. The accumulation of broken china, plastic containers, and cheap synthetic wearing apparel that crowds the stalls could hardly tempt the most indiscriminate kleptomaniac. Nothing to compare with the marvelous São Pedro-Sintra market on the second and fourth Sunday of every month. As I had forty minutes or more before meeting the Ambassador and his wife at the Aviz, where I had asked them to lunch, I decided to revisit São Vicente. This enormously grand Italianate church was designed by Terzi, the architect for the Carthusian monastery outside Évora, and is definitely better suited to his talent for grandiosity.

Immediately following the earthquake, which demolished São Vicente's marble dome along with many others, a temporary replacement of marbleized wood was installed. Now, some 200 years later, it looks fairly permanent. One of the marvels of the church, however, is its great 17th-century organ set between two monumental angels which form a part of the *baldacchino;* this morning it was brightly and badly lit—like Roxy's theater—and the organist appeared no bigger than an ant. That is, until he began playing, for Francis Chapelet, the young Canadian organist, is an accomplished technician. What glorious sounds these ancient organs can produce! They speak with many voices, all lyrical. Their message rings out clearly, whether jubilant, tender, militant, or sorrowful, quite different from the mushy sound of modern organs.

As I sat listening I was only half aware of lights coming up in the side altars as a few old women praying at the front of the church were asked to move back. When ladies with egret feathers in their hats drifted in on the arms of short men in dress uniform—with swords and gold epaulettes extending beyond their well-padded shoulders—I still remained engrossed in the music. But by the time the church was a quarter full of such 19th-century personages I began to wonder if I had lost my way into another century. Feeling uneasy and out of place, I left, bemused.

At lunch the Ambassador listened to the account of events in the church, took a quick look at his pocket diary, and explained what had been going on. "It was a memorial service for the late Duchess of Bragança, who died recently." The cloister adjoining São Vicente leads to the Bragança pantheon, where all the kings of that dynasty were buried.

February 11

LISBON TO ABRANTES (via Golegã and Tomar)

As far as Lisboans are concerned, Setúbal, the fourth-largest town in Portugal, is "on the other side of the river"; and anyone heading in the general direction of Oporto, the second-largest city, is "going to the north." For the next couple of weeks I plan on traveling to the north, motoring in a gray Opel sedan, alone except for Mosey and Gomes, a courtly man with a brush mustache—the former relying on me, and I relying heavily on the latter, two acts of faith that I'm convinced will be justified.

We started out from Lisbon today, driving across the Ribatejo, that heartland of Portuguese cattlemen, cradle of brave bulls and Peninsular horses. The grass looked green enough for me to eat. The rich black soil was laced by rice paddies, fields of corn and other cereal grain, vineyards, eucalyptus, tamarisks, and sometimes cactus. Friends in Lisbon wanted me to visit the Quinta de Alorna, one of the luxurious ranches of the area; the owner was not in residence, but his herdsman had been alerted. Mauricio, as he was called—like cattlemen everywhere, be it on the plains of Texas, the Landes of France, the pampas of the Argentine—had enormous pride in his work and little interest in anything outside it. Fortunately, we hit it off, as cattle talk had been a part of my early life. In the bull barn (all beef cattle, no fighting bulls at this *quinta*) I admired a 2,600-pound Charolais, a great white mountain of beef who reluctantly got to his feet when Mauricio gave him a slap on the rump. A young Hereford bull calf, recently arrived from America, sulked, and although he refused to move, I remarked on his fine head. It is hoped that by breeding such bulls to Tourino heifers the standard of Portuguese beef cattle will be improved. With my phrase book in hand, I asked about the use of *artificial criar*, the closest I could get to artificial insemination. Gomes looked uncomfortable, but Mauricio after an imperceptible pause got the gist and answered, "Not yet." We turned from bovines to equines and I fell in love with two Peninsular * stallions, unbelievably gentle, with great aristocratic heads and big, expressive eyes. The day was wet and chill, wood fires burned in open fireplaces at either end of the big stone barns. It was tempting to linger near the crackling wood, enjoying the warm animal smells, but I was curious to see a collection of 19th-century coaches for which the *quinta* is famous. Mauricio said there were more than forty of them, all brought back to mint condition, ready to be driven at a word from the Alorna family. There were a spider-cart made in New York State, a tonneau with a Rolls-Royce body, suspension coupés, broughams, phaetons, victorias, dogcarts, governess carts, shooting brakes, wedding carriages—their paint and bodywork refurbished, brasses sparkling, and with the appropriate tack hanging alongside.

As usual, one was offered coffee; then we were on our way. Going through the country town of Golegã, I spotted the Manueline door of the church of Nossa Senhora da Conceição and asked Gomes to stop. Most guidebooks stress the Golegã fair held in November, but ignore the church, a more permanent source of interest. Thought to have been the work of Boytac, its portal is magnificent, rich in stone carving; inside, there are a handsome wooden barrel ceiling, a great Manueline chancel arch, and on the right of the entrance, a stone stairway with a finely carved

* More about this breed on page 77.

railing like a caravel's halyard. Portuguese churches are often locked, and it is sound advice to stop whenever one sees an open church door; this can become wearing, of course, if taken indiscriminately.

At the next crossroad I found myself on the horns of my chronic dilemma. My destination for the night was the town of Abrantes, and here I was about to get there by lunchtime. This seemed foolish with Tomar * only a twenty-mile detour away, too close not to look again at the Convento do Cristo, the most bizarre of the Portuguese monuments. (Gomes delights in my enthusiasm for his country, not just because such detours add excess mileage and ultimately lead to a bigger tip.) Lunched in the *estalagem* at Tomar, set in a park beside the little Nabão River. Here I was again, stuffing myself over a glass of Port and the excellent local bread made of corn and wheat. Restored by this and grilled chicken, I set out for the Convento do Cristo, which at first glance always seems too formidable for immediate acceptance. But I did climb to the top of the old castle keep, along with some romping twelve-year-old boys who were wagering on whether I'd slip and fall. For miles around, one could see only lands which once belonged to this powerful quasi-militant religious order.

Stopped at the little church of Nossa Senhora da Conceição, its elegant Renaissance façade by Diogo de Torralva set just below the Convento in sharp contrast to the grandiose fortress-church. Farther down in the town, on a quiet square, I visited the Romanesque church of Santa Maria dos Olivais, with its colonnaded atrium at one side and its provincial belfry some yards away; then to the church of São João Baptista, on the black-and-white main square, with its fine Manueline limestone portal and carved stone pulpit.

* See page 186.

Spent a comfortable night in the hotel at Abrantes in spite of eating too much under the eye of a *maître d'hôtel* who wanted me to sample each of his vast array of cakes.

February 12

ABRANTES TO THE SERRA DA ESTRÊLA (via Castelo Branco and Monsanto da Beira)

The narrow road up to the Abrantes castle had no guard rail and last night's rain gave it a slippery look, with a valley uncomfortably far below; Gomes and I decided to forgo closer inspection. These fortified castles appear exactly as portrayed in children's books—innocuously grand toys rather than medieval fighting machines.

It was raining by the time we came to Castelo Branco, but even the wet couldn't dampen the exuberance of an 18th-century bishop's garden. Never have there been such overfurnished outdoor rooms. Clipped box in topiary shapes (urns, spheres, obelisks), monumental stairways, stone personages of both sexes (kings, saints, virtues, and continents), orange trees resplendent with fruit, stone arabesques set in water tanks—like floating window boxes filled with heliotrope. It left me with a kind of horticultural vertigo.

It did not, however, prevent my taking another detour to see Monsanto de Beira, touted by a tourist bureau as "the most Portuguese village in Portugal." On the contrary, the town is impressively eccentric and worth the trouble of getting there. We lost our way, ended up on a road under repair in barren country, but finally, at the top of a mountain one glimpsed what appeared to be a village. When we had gone about three quarters of the way, we entered a weird world of green moss: twenty-foot boulders swathed in what looked like green velvet; dry-stone fences carpeted (wall to wall) in that same springy green

stuff. It was dramatic and a little unpleasant, and I was glad when it disappeared as we entered an Iron Age community of bare gray rock clinging to an escarpment. Squat stone houses were lodged between huge boulders that served them as walls on either side. Russet tile roofs looked like patchwork squares. A Misericórdia church,* possibly the smallest and poorest in Portugal, stood on a tiny square not far from an elegant pillory. Obviously the car was meant to go no farther. Mosey and I walked past the 15th-century Lucain Clock Tower up the Rua da Castelo (its only wheeled traffic was a wheelbarrow), which we followed 300 feet straight up the mountain to the ruins of a truncated castle. With some astonishment I passed a "social welfare" office and squashed myself into a doorway to allow a loaded donkey to pass. These "streets" apparently had been hacked out of the living rock. There was no sign of running water or a sewage system, although everything had a scrubbed look, rugged and fiercely proud: there is something awesome to the courage of people who go on living in such remote, barren places. In a shop on the way down a man was working with a lathe under a bare electric light bulb. As I stood watching he invited me in. With his wife he works and lives in this two-room abode with boulder walls on three sides; it was warm in the same way an Eskimo's snow house is snug. Although there was a chilling rain outside, here the brazier burned cheerfully, the smoke going up through the tile roof. There was an agreeable smell of drying herbs, fresh straw bedding, and wood shavings.

As I came out the door, I faced a distraught Gomes. "My lady, you are a big responsibility," he said in the familiar tones of an irritated Nanny. I described the warmth of the carpenter's hut, and Gomes said, "In Portugal the poor people are often warmer than the rich." Palaces rarely have central heating, and

* A church-hospice for the indigent sick.

their big, high-ceilinged rooms tend to be drafty compared to the carpenter's house in Monsanto de Beira.

We drove along the barren tops of several *serras*, with an occasional clump of orange trees or olives, surprising to find at this altitude. It was spring lambing time, and shepherds carried the newborn animals under homespun ponchos. The sheepdogs of this region, the famous *Serra da Estrêla* (they appear to be a cross between a mastiff and a husky), are sleek, golden creatures that look as though they breed true to type. The region abounds with wolves, and the Estrêla sheepdogs display impressive vigilance, possibly inspired by traces of self-interest—often they suckle the ewes, which may account for their luxurious coats and bright, smug eyes. Suddenly we entered another world, thickly wooded on one side, like the Dolomites. Vineyards stretched up the opposite slopes, intricately terraced, rising from the valley like a giant's staircase.

It was almost dark when we reached the *pousada* isolated in a magnificent spot. Not a light showed on the outside. Two Estrêla dogs barked in menacing tones. Gomes leaned on the car's horn until someone opened the door. Yes, we were expected, although the empty fireplace and unlit rooms appeared unwelcoming. The radiator in my room was stone cold and remained so. At dinner it was apparent that there were no other guests. Gomes and I ate at opposite ends of the dining room, which was barely lit so that the proprietor, his wife, and their maids could watch television. No one inquired as to whether this gloomy arrangement was agreeable to me, the paying guest.

The wind howled outside. The setting was appropriate for a murder, and it disturbed me enough to ask Gomes if he thought we should leave. "My lady, I took the liberty of getting a room across from yours in case you need me . . . and I told them the American Ambassador was telephoning you from Lisbon in the morning."

February 13

SERRA DA ESTRÊLA TO VISEU (via Belmonte and Guarda)

I slept poorly. The wind shook the building like a terrier with a rat most of the night. Even in sunlight the place retained its uncongenial air and splendid views. Leaving was a pleasure.

In Belmonte we drove up a small hill to see a ruined castle and an early church. The castle, one of King Diniz' impressive network of fortresses, looked huge and formidable, except for a stylish Manueline window that had been cut into its curtain wall in the 16th century. On a nearby square stood the tiny Romanesque church of São Tiago (the villagers call it *Igreja Velha*, the old church) where Pedro Álvares Cabral (the 16th-century courtier who accidentally discovered Brazil) was baptized. A charming little campanile stood alongside; inside the church are early frescoes, a Gothic tomb chapel, a stone pulpit and canopy so small they were surely designed for a doll of a priest.

On to Guarda, where we arrived at 12:04 to find the Sé (cathedral) closed until two o'clock. Handsome, austere, uncompromising, it looks like a dour Norman church and has none of Boytac's usual flourishes and grace notes. Although it has splendid gargoyles, I was unable to find the "rude" one facing Spain. (Are there polite gargoyles?) Gomes finally borrowed the key from a sacristan who was placidly eating his lunch. The interior was lofty, with heavy groining and an un-Portuguese look of obsessive nobility. The Misericórdia was also closed, but Gomes obtained that key almost at once. What a profusion of carved and gilded woodwork, of color, ornament, and curved lines, in that joyous place of worship. While I was admiring this, Gomes went off to buy food and drink—a bottle of wine,

Washing lines near Viseu

tunafish, sausage, cheese, and bread, which we later ate alongside a lovely mountain road at granite picnic tables.

When we reached the *estalagem* outside Viseu, one of Portugal's lovelist show towns,* it seemed sensible to "clear my eyes" instead of looking at anything more today.

February 14

VISEU AND ENVIRONS

Thanks again to friends in Lisbon, it had been arranged for me to visit two great Baroque *quintas* in the vicinity. Twenty kilometers away from where I was staying, in the village of Castendo, we were directed to the Casa da Insua, a noble house built by an Albuquerque in the first part of the 18th century. At a respectful toot of the car horn, huge iron gates were thrown open for us to drive into an imposing courtyard. At first the house appeared to consist of two wings joined in the center by a marvelous Baroque chapel, but it became apparent that one of these wings was the farm building. A stunning carved stone doorway bespoke the entrance to the main house; a domestic (not in uniform) let me into a hall, where I was greeted by a small, elderly woman dressed in nondescript black. No introductions were proffered, although she welcomed me in French, but the assured manner with which she slipped her small-boned arm through mine made it clear she had been born Albuquerque. She explained that she lived here alone except when her nephews came to visit, or her bachelor brother, the heir.

This grand house, full of rare objects, is pervaded with the feeling of being enjoyed. There were huge, ornate Baroque stone chimneypieces in almost every room, with wood fires burning—comforting in this spell of rain I am encountering.

* See page 112.

Although the rooms were big and lofty, they retained human scale. The coffered ceilings were painted in white and gold or in rich Italianate designs adapted by a Portuguese artist. Silk-paneled walls, crystal chandeliers, thick needlepoint rugs (worked in the Arraiolos stitch of Portugal), everything (except for plumbing, telephones, electricity, and television) had been commissioned in the 18th century along with the house. Family portraits, of course, often predated it. Huge Lowestoft *jardinières* stood along the floor, sometimes even under tables. Immensely elegant chairs, carved of a dark wood, with a shell pattern picked out in gold, appeared to have been ordered by the gross. *Reposteiros* or *portières*, with the family arms embroidered in gold thread on blue or scarlet cloth, hung over most of the doors. Along with opulence, a trace of shabbiness made everything seem real, alive, functional.

My companion drew me to the windows to admire the gardens. Camellias trimmed into towering arches and obelisks ten feet high were covered with blossoms—they seemed as artificial as the flowers wired on trees for Long Island debut dances. In the dining room the table was set for one: a white damask cloth, blue-and-white Lowestoft plates, matching *bonbonnières* on ormolu bases filled with pink camellias. There was a napkin in a heavy Rococo silver ring. When I admired the porcelain, she explained how she tried to use only flawed pieces when she was alone. "But most of it is perfect, still," she said with an abashed smile. She explained that the property remained a working farm, and the peasants were still making oil from the '67 olive crop. Many of the original intricate parquet floors had been laid with hard woods growing on the place; she showed me a sample board of a dozen varieties still growing there from which she could choose whenever repairs were required. I had the feeling that a resident cabinetmaker was part of the establishment.

We looked in the library at an elephant folio of early Brazilian maps which just recently had been gathered together and catalogued. (Goodness knows what bibliophilic treasure may lie among these shelves.) We went into the chapel, a miniature basilica with an elaborately painted dome; patting Mosey, who watched from the car window, she remarked on the "suitability of traveling with a female dog" (I was hard put to follow this subtle point of manners) and seemed loath to see me go. Great houses are no place to live alone.

In Mangualde, where I was to visit Anadia, the house turned up unexpectedly on a simple village square where its huge pink Baroque façade seemed incongruously elaborate. Again we drove through a courtyard, less grand than the one at Insua. The Conde de Anadia was not in residence, but a liveried manservant took me around. The rooms on the ground-floor level were mingy in size, sparsely furnished: Portuguese Hepplewhite in the drawing rooms, stiffly arranged against the walls. The bedrooms were almost Spartan. Whatever warmth there was came from some portable electric heaters. I was almost feeling sorry for the absent owner when we emerged into another, very different world of extreme grandeur. Obviously, all the lavishness lay on the street side, with a reception hall of enormous splendor. Stone stairways with elaborate stone balustrades and magnificent blue-and-white *azulejos*—depicting mythological fantasies—curved up to a landing and a grandiose granite door.

After crossing this noble threshold, a stone statement of immense bravura, I walked through a succession of reception rooms, each more magnificent than the one before. The walls were hung with 17th- and 18th-century family portraits. There were fine porcelains, dazzling Portuguese 18th-century furnishings, carved and painted ceilings. There were no fireplaces, no electricity in the great crystal chandeliers. The palace appeared in a trance.

Although I love Viseu,* this time I must concentrate on those portions of Portugal that are less familiar. In spite of a quickly fading afternoon light, there was still time to drive around the cathedral square—a kind of theatrical mock-up for a grand third-act opera finale.

Dined at the *estalagem.* I ate a purée-of-carrot soup, an *escalope* of veal with anchovies, and a thick-skinned orange that the waiter peeled with one deft, circular gesture of his knife. The proprietress and her Belgian housekeeper sat with the guests after dinner, sewing on napkins they were making for the summer rush. *Estalagems* and *pousadas* often retain a kind of simplicity and flavor that suggests 19th-century travel. One converses with the management or one's fellow guests (there's no escape) on arm's-length topics—the weather, highway conditions, local curiosities—without ever a hint of one's own interests.

February 15

VISEU TO ALIJÓ (via São João de Tarouca, Lamego, and Vila Real)

Having been misled all too often by the phrase "you mustn't miss that," I take the considered risk of saying: *Don't miss São João de Tarouca.* It is all too easily by-passed, lying as it does a few miles off the main road along a lane that runs through a village where strangers are still curiosities. The first indication of something extraordinary ahead is revealed by the intricate terracing of the land. The Cistercian monks for whom São João was built in the early 12th century were the first of that order to come to Portugal. Expert agronomists, they left evidence of agricultural prowess on every strip of land under their control.

* See page 112.

Little remains of the old monastery building except for one ruined wall with its row of twenty-nine windows—elegantly spaced and proportioned—facing the church. We arrived shortly before noon just as the *padre* was locking up; he was the same one who had been here two years ago, only this time he was freshly shaved. Extending his hand in welcome, he said, "It is not often visitors pass this way a second time. . . . The church smiles on you, Senhora." The sun came out as if on cue! Afonso Henriques is said to have attended the consecration of São João de Tarouca; the name of the architect and the date—Froilac, 1171—are chiseled on the façade.

Inside there are staggering riches. Two great borders of *azulejos*—placed one above the other, with no transition to tie their abstract design together—produce a daring visual counterpoint around the church walls. There is a fine painted ceiling. Gilded salomonic columns and carved *boiseries* adorn six side chapels as well as the High Altar. The organ case is covered with rioting golden angels, scarlet-and-gold traceries, simulated marble and lapis lazuli. And sixteen double rows of handsome choir stalls on either side of the chancel are backed with portraits of early abbots—libelous, one suspects, as the monks whose names are inscribed in golden letters are portrayed as effete, supercilious, conniving.

Two curiosities also exist here: a giant stone coffin, and a controversial painting. The Gothic sarcophagus containing the remains of one of King Diniz' many natural sons is awesome in size, and covered with a detailed bas-relief carving of a boar hunt. The painting, in a side altar at the right, depicts St. Peter wearing a Papal crown, and is practically identical to one from the Viseu Sé now displayed in the museum. Considerable dissension exists among art historians over which was painted by Grão Vasco, the 16th-century Portuguese master.

Arrived in Lamego in time to lunch at the hotel opposite the pilgrimage church of Nossa Senhora dos Remédios. An excellent meal of *acepipes* (hors d'œuvres), a beef casserole, fresh local cheese, and a half-carafe of red *vinho verde.* (Very dry, with a taste of granite, and a tendency to be highly intoxicating.) For some charming and unknown reason they presented me with a bottle of *porto branco* (white Port) as I was leaving. Before this junket ends, I may find that I need fine copper wires and Port-wine infusions to sustain me. We are headed into the mountains of the north, where it sometimes snows, and the chains which "weren't ready" when we left Lisbon and were to be "picked up at the Viseu post office" have of course never arrived.

Lamego's pilgrimage staircase, rising up the height of the mountain, is a delicious Baroque extravaganza that devout pilgrims climb on foot. Intricate stone balustrades, huge vases, spheres, obelisks, gazebos, grottos, and seven majestic fantasy kings (dressed in Oriental robes and classic draperies) stand on either side of nine landings and 470 steps. This whole granite entourage appears to move in and out down the length of the mountainside, like dancers executing the movements of a quadrille.

The Sé in Lamego is full of style and styles. It has a Romanesque lower tower, a Renaissance cloister, what remains of a Gothic façade after a wealth of 18th-century additions and alterations by Nasoni, the master of northern Portuguese Baroque. There is considerable panache to the interior, with its painted ceiling and immense gilded pelmets over doors, windows, and arches. In the museum next door the sculpture is particularly fine, much of it from the local Chagas convent that was allowed to crumble, so that eventually it had to be torn down.

The church of Chagas, which somehow just survived, has a startlingly somber exterior, with four rugged granite crosses set flat against the white façade—three on one side, one on the other. A disdain for symmetry is one of the Portuguese talents! The interior fully endorses my conviction not to pass up anything associated with those Chagas girls. There are a great painted ceiling—an architectural composition of columns, balustrades, a red cupola, with lots of flowers and people looking down; gilded retables to flank the chancel; and flower-painted stone, all adding to a joyousness that has little to do with piety. Lamego is a Baroque town; even the police station is tucked away in its Baroque palace, very daunting for provincial cops.

Now that we are motoring in the mountains, Gomes has taken to crossing himself at every roadside shrine and there appears to be one on every blind curve. There are vineyards on every side, climbing to the very tops of mountains and stretching down to the edge of streams. The work that went into building these stone terraces is staggering to contemplate. I planned on going through Vila Real without stopping, but we needed gas, which gave me an alibi (to myself) for seeing the Capela Nova or Clérigos chapel. This elegant, bizarre, and wedge-shaped structure—set on a kind of promontory between two streets—has a pair of huge columns on either side of its Baroque façade. A flyaway pediment is secured by a figure of St. Peter and saintly comrades standing on top.

One advantage in the Portuguese sweet tooth is the ease with which one finds freshly baked pastries in towns or villages. I bought some little sponge cakes, while the gas tank was being filled, to eat with a swig from my new bottle of white Port. Mosey and Gomes stuck to cakes, but everyone felt restored. It was just as well. This early in the year Alijó, which is at the end of nowhere, is startled by strangers. The *pousada* there was clean, if chill, and the bedding turned out to be damp. I spent most of the night fretting over spilled milk—in this case a lack of chains.

Lamego . . . Stairway of the Kings at Nossa Senhora dos Remedios

February 16

ALIJÓ TO MIRANDA DO DOURO (via Mirandela and Bragança)

No hot water this morning, and Gomes for the first time was in a filthy mood. In the five days since we left Lisbon, I have worn the same suit and pink tweed topcoat; he has alternated among three different suits and two overcoats. He said he was "too annoyed at the management to eat their breakfast." We stopped in Mirandela to restore his equanimity.

Spent most of the morning mountain-hopping—just by-passing the snow—from range to range in the province of Trás-os-Montes (literally "in back of the mountains"). One would be deep in Spain before one penetrated beyond these mountains. It's wild, rough country, bare except for a few trees—chestnuts, willows, flowering mimosa, a hardy almond—growing in sheltered hollows. Otherwise it remains wind-swept, a golden-reddish cast on the turf as far as the eye can see. Shepherds tending their flocks wear folded homespun blankets looped over one shoulder. The oxen wear fur headpieces on the order of the fur hats favored by fashionable ladies. The oxcarts with their big, solid wooden wheels might have driven out of early Roman friezes except for the noise they produce, a kind of piercing scream that Gomes says the peasants encourage, to keep the oxen awake and moving. The mountains suddenly smoothed off into a high, arable plateau as we approached Bragança.

In the center of the town, the Sé (formerly just plain São João da Baptista) fails to achieve Sé caliber. The pillory, on the square opposite, a salomonic column with a special richness of stone grapes threaded through its spirals, is the handsomest I've seen, but I find it difficult to view such punitive objects purely aesthetically. Although the Misericórdia church has a bleak exterior, inside there is an impressive retable—very tall, with carved and gilded figures in high relief which have the intensity of portraits. It was lunchtime as we drove past the granite façade of São Vicente, made dour by its proximity to an elaborate fountain—effulgent in royal arms—which seemed to be trying to push God's house off its foundations. I asked Gomes to find a local bistro rather than seek out the *pousada* on the edge of town: one gets a better feel of a place eating among the town folk. My lunch consisted of a cold dish of chick-peas with chopped raw onions, scrambled eggs and ham (especially well smoked around here) and *pudim flan* (caramel custard), which is almost a national dessert. A woman eating alone in a restaurant is an oddity, and the Portuguese make such a point of appearing not to notice, that I am getting to feel like a ghost.

Of nine churches in Bragança, the two finest are kept under lock and key. It was fortunate that the priest who happened to be passing as I came out of the restaurant turned out to be the man I needed. Small, swarthy, and full of enthusiasm, he directed us to his house in order for him to pick up the necessary keys—ancient and too big to carry around in one's pockets. He lived on a daunting "street"—something between a ramp and stairs leading straight up to the walled citadel and never intended for wheeled traffic. He suggested a better way for us to go, and that I visit the ruined castle while he made a sick call which would be brief. The keys to the castle and its Homage Tower (an edifice celebrating some event—the birth of a first son or a battle victory) were in secular hands, but Gomes was quick to get them opened. From the top of the old ramparts I looked down on range after range of mountains rolling out below, and the secrets of their valleys were exposed to me as they had been for centuries to the sentinels guarding Bragança.

Father X rejoined me and together we walked a scant hundred yards to Santa Maria, a delicious small church with a white façade and gray granite ornaments—salomonic columns, bat-winged volutes, and four niches topped with granite rollers. The interior has a good painted ceiling, deep and rich in color and so original in design that one overlooked the familiarity of theme —an Assumption of the Virgin. Less than six yards away from this church stands the extraordinary Town Hall, which was built in the 12th century and since restored. It is one of the few Romanesque civic buildings still in existence. Stone steps lead up to a tile-roofed chamber with stone benches running around on all sides; a water cistern under the floor can be seen through iron gratings; there are no walls, only a succession of rounded arches resting on pillars. Any discussion among the city fathers could be overheard by citizens outside, and perhaps was intended to be as a safeguard for government integrity.

From here we walked within the walled area through a community of poor dwellings which are to be cleared away "because they aren't of the right period," Father X. said. They burst with life, and their demise will leave the medieval citadel embalmed in antiquity. At least a dozen snot-nosed little beggars dogged my heels until I gave them a handful of coppers; the priest then ordered them home to "wash your faces" with such severity that they fled. On the way down to the lower town we passed a strange pillory consisting of a plain granite spike thrust through the body of a prehistoric carved boar. These stone boars, prevalent in this part of Trás-os-Montes, are generally thought to have been pagan fertility symbols; this one is most unusual with its Christian spike, perhaps intended to drive out heresy.

Farther on we came to São Bento, a 16th-century church with a lovely Renaissance door, a stocky stone figure of the patron saint in a niche, and elaborate royal arms. The key turned in the lock with that solid sound associated with iron hardware, and the interior proved to be marvelously gay, with a painted ceiling, a decorated chancel arch, and a gilded High Altar—a kind of ecclesiastical jungle-gym filled with gilded angels, many of them wearing black cloaks.

Instead of going straight to my destination, which was Miranda do Douro, I asked Gomes to take a road in the opposite direction, toward Vinhais. An authority listed this as "not to be missed," and a friend in Lisbon shrugged his shoulders; the truth lay somewhere between. Clinging to the side of a mountain in Vinhais was a massive façade to which a pair of churches were attached; a man sitting at the wheel of a black sedan proposed himself as my escort, and he turned out to be the driver for the Archbishop of Bragança. The lower church, now a seminary, had simulated marble *boiseries*, fine polychrome saints, and a ponderous gilded altar stacked with relics in glass boxes. (They always put me off and so did the smell of drains in the sacristy, where I otherwise might have spent more time looking at the handsomely carved vestment chests.) In the upper church there were an airy vaulted ceiling painted with balustrades, flowers and urns, all on a creamy ground, and more good polychrome saints. I voiced the hope that the Archbishop would keep them right where they were instead of turning them over to a museum.

The road back to Miranda do Douro was mostly under repair; the rugged-looking workmen were full of smiles and cavalier bows for the rare passing motorist. We arrived in Miranda just before dusk, and found the *pousada*—a contemporary marble palace set on a high cliff looking down a gorge onto a new hydroelectric dam. The furnace was out and no one at the dam was able to get it started: "An expert is expected from Porto in a day or two." In the meantime, fires burned in the round fireplaces of the public rooms, boiling water was carried up for my bath, and at bedtime a *saco de água quente* (hot-water bottle) was tucked under the covers.

February 17

MIRANDA DO DOURO TO SERRA DE MARÃO (via Bragança, Mirandela, Murça, and Mateus)

I went up into Miranda immediately after breakfast to

find crumbling 16th-century houses and what's left of a beaten-up castle, all dominated by the Sé. An elegant, stark, and assertive building, it could be by the Renaissance architect, Diogo de Torralva, who designed the famous João III cloister of Tomar. (The *Guide Bleu,** the most complete French-English-language guidebook on Portugal, credits the Sé to one of the Arruda brothers.) Some Portuguese acquaintances speak of it as being "sad," but I found it quite the contrary. Big and lofty, with fine carved and gilded woodwork (mostly high relief such as I saw two days ago in Lamego), it seemed a lively, happy transition of late Renaissance into Baroque. Two things were unusual: the elaborately carved choir stalls backed with landscape paintings in a kind of chinoiserie of blue-and-gray-and-white grisaille; and the big organ with a fierce head of the wind dominating the rest of the decoration.

As we had to go back through Bragança, I stopped there to try to buy one of those handsome homespun blankets the shepherds wear, but with little luck; we happened to meet the same priest who took me around yesterday; he said peasant women only make them during the winter months for their men. On through Murça, only taking time to look at another of those curious stone boars. Then outside Mirandela I saw a sign—the only one I've seen in Portugal—promoting regional dishes served at Maria Rita da Romeu. Gomes took a dubious view, but seemed reassured by a peasant woman—who probably had never eaten there—whom he asked about the quality of the food. "*Esplêndido,*" she said with a big smile, a response which encouraged him. The inn, part of a model village, was designed and run by the owner of the surrounding vineyards, a charming middle-aged man, Manuel de Araujo Menerès. He told me restaurant profits supported a kindergarten for forty pre-school children, then ordered my lunch and my wine (from his vine-

Windmills

yards) and later offered me a glass of twenty-five-year-old Port along with the biggest peach I ever ate, and the sweetest.

Just before Vila Real we turned off the highway in order to go to the Quinta de Mateus,* where I had been invited to tea. Clearly visible from the country road on which it stands, the great house is set behind iron gates, a short sweep of drive, and a pond with swans. A double staircase curved up its astonishingly beautiful façade in stately fashion. The *quinta* is quite unlike the way it is portrayed on the labels for Mateus *rosé* wine bottles, where it looks like a Baroque barracks. In real life, Mateus is three-sided, with two wings at right angles to a central façade considered by many to be Nicolau Nasoni's architectural masterpiece.

A maid opened the door and led me into a squarish room with a high-coved ceiling made of dark chestnut wood, caught up by knots of carving at the corners. A fire burned in a small, plain granite hearth. Almost immediately the Conde de Mangualde appeared, walking lightly on the balls of his feet and apparently pleased to receive a guest on this winter afternoon. He led me briskly through several rooms, all large and almost square, with the same kind of ceilings except for the carvings in the corners, which were always different. Finally we entered a room in which a tea table was set and comfortable chairs had been drawn around a fire. With a cup of good black Portuguese coffee in hand, I was able to absorb something of my surroundings as my host talked of wines and vineyards. He said he only produced the grapes from which Mateus is made. (Five million bottles are sold annually, most of it abroad.) As we chatted I tried to estimate the dimensions of the room in which we sat, which was similar to those we had passed through. (My host later told me the average size was eighteen feet square with twenty-one-foot

* A good concierge can sometimes arrange visits to the Mateus gardens.

ceilings.) I counted eight still-life paintings of fruit and flowers on one wall with plenty of empty space around them. In terms of an average New York apartment each picture would have been wall-size.

The Portuguese, who often seem aloof and withdrawn at first encounter, can make the most instantaneous transference to friendliness, and by the time my host and I embarked on a serious tour of the house, we had reached this easy stage. I failed to count the rooms we passed through as he held back the *reposteiros* to let me cross from one threshold to the next. Objects, not mathematics, are my long suit, and the objects were dazzling. Antique porcelains and Arraiolos rugs; 18th-century Portuguese furniture (*estilo* João V); a William and Mary cabinet and long clock, intricately inlaid and painted; an early Mozarab cabinet that a Portuguese king had given one of Mangualde's ancestors in exchange for a sapphire necklace that had caught the eye of an acquisitive lady whose favor the monarch sought.

Surplus bedrooms recently had been converted into bathrooms. "My daughter is married to an American," he explained. A couple of reception rooms have been turned into a kind of museum, and the verve exhibited in its installation suggested that the owner had missed a career as a curator. There were rich vestments, church silver, a gilded altar from a ruined chapel on a far corner of the property, jeweled swords, family memorabilia. One case contained a copy of Camões' epic poem *The Lusiads* in a late 18th-century binding with illustrations said to be by Fragonard, commissioned by an ancestor to be printed in a limited edition. Along with the book were the drawings submitted by the artist, the copper plates used for engraving, and acknowledgments from personages to whom these luxury copies had been sent—including Talleyrand, Metternich, and Czar Alexander II of Russia.

I wanted to walk around the outside of the house while there was plenty of daylight. There were four topiary gardens, 200-year-old camellia trees, flowers blooming in granite troughs along the foundation line of the building, and a tunnel of cedar trees that ran a 100 yards down the garden—smooth as a green velvet sleeve. My host suggested a whiskey and we walked up the great stairway together. He said that Nasoni had been called in as a kind of afterthought to do the 18th-century face-lifting on the central block. What an afterthought! Granite urns, finials, balustrades, statues, all gray on white—a staggering display of exterior decoration.

The *pousada* which by all accounts was only fifteen kilometers away turned out to be twice as much—time and distance are not a Portuguese strong point.

February 18

SERRA DE MARÃO TO BRAGA (via Amarante and Guimarães)

The *pousada*, high up in the *serra*, is one of the best of those I've stayed in. Driving down the mountain, we passed people dressed in Sunday clothes walking to small village churches that dot the slopes. The drive to Amarante is splendid and sinuous, through semi-wooded country down to the Tamega River spanned by a Regency bridge—enormously festive with its urns and obelisks, and unexpectedly sophisticated in a town of 3,000 people. Amarante may well be the least provincial town of its size anywhere.

From the approach to the bridge, churches appear to grow out of each other's rooftops as though painted by an artist who never bothered with perspectives. As one closes in, things begin to sort themselves out, and the monastery of São Gonçalo moved into the foreground assertively. Its tiled roof seemed to be made of

Chaves . . . courtyard in northern village

finely shirred fabric. The smooth golden stone of the façade provides a perfect foil for an extravagant portal and loggia, two otherwise unrelated architectural devices. The loggia, at third-story level, is populated with 17th-century stone personages, flowering plants, and obelisks on the roof. The portal is a late Renaissance fantasy with elegantly carved and fluted columns, pendant bosses, and a company of saints-in-waiting on a Virgin, who appears like the twin of Venus, this time *under* a half-shell and fully clothed.

This is what I call "gold country," and the interior of São Gonçalo is an undiluted golden delight. Two gilded pulpits serve as soapboxes for angels carrying PAX banners. Stone columns on either side of the chancel arch are painted with flowers and gold festoons. The organ is supported by cloven-hoofed giants decked in red, green, and gold raiment. The High Altar is a kind of golden stairs with salomonic columns on either side and a gondola in lieu of a throne. A mass meeting of *putti*, some with powdered hair, look down from the top, while life-size polychrome angels, acting as a celestial Altar Guild, appear to rustle their robes and their wings. Mass was being said, and black-clothed peasants and town folk seemed to enjoy this ballroom atmosphere for piety.

There are always women praying in the tiny chapel of São Gonçalo, the patron saint of marriage, but I've never seen a man about. A painted stone figure of the saint reclines on the sarcophagus, his head cushioned on two red stone pillows with tasseled corners. Apparently the town celebrates feast days in his honor, at which time bakers traditionally sell cakes shaped like phalluses which are exchanged between the sexes. Even the town's name suggests a link between the Trás-os-Montes fertility rites and the Latin verb *to love*.

Similarly high-spirited approaches to God are apparent in two other Amarante churches: São Pedro, with its high, narrow façade, has a lovely coffered ceiling and more angels competing for celestial best-dressed lists; and São Domingo, which is tiny, round, and overwhelmingly rich. (It is usually locked, but the sacristan at São Gonçalo has the key.) In almost no space at all, without appearing overcrowded or unduly ornamented, there is a gamut of ecclesiastical furnishings: a High Altar, two side altars, two pulpits, a pair of giant grotesques staggering under cornucopias bursting with plenty, and an organ fitted into a corner and supported by baby tritons—all adding up to an enchanting Rococo fantasy.

Late lunch at Guimarães in a kind of bar-and-grill where local families having Sunday dinner were working their way through a six-course table d'hôte. When I settled for *acepipes* (a vast selection to choose from), a pork chop with a lemon sauce, and a dessert called *papos d'anjo* (literally "angels with double chins," a kind of vanilla custard cake), the waiter inquired whether I had recently been ill.

Guimarães considers itself the cradle of the nation largely because the first Portuguese king, Afonso Henriques, was born there in 1111. The town's legends are even older, the most important being that of Wamba, a Visigothic chief who was chosen to be king of the Goths. "Never," he said, "not unless leaves grow from this ancient staff." The staff immediately sprouted in a demonstration of the 6th century's political draft and Wamba became king; a little Gothic pavilion with ogival arches was built 800 years later to pay honor to this event.

The ancient church of Our Lady of the Olive Tree (Nossa Senhora da Oliveira) also commemorates Wamba's miracle; originally a 10th-century abbey, it was rebuilt in 1385 by João I in thanksgiving for his strategic victory over Castile. Today the church door was shut and a sign posted, "Closed for Repairs." While Gomes went in search of a key, I sat on the steps recalling my last visit and anticipating the pleasures awaiting me inside:

the grisaille ceiling, the lavish crystal chandeliers, the swags of carved and gilded musical instruments, the twin pulpits with delicate white-and-gold stairs spiraling up. It was just as well memory did not fail me. Gomes returned with a young priest, who said a "restoration" was in progress but I could go inside. Now I wish I hadn't. The chandeliers and the gilded side chapels, along with one of the pulpit stairs, had been consigned to a museum; everything else had been ruthlessly torn down. The second pulpit stair hung disconsolately, broken in two. The exquisite paneling that had lined the church walls had been ripped off as if it were rotted timber and lay in piles ten feet high along the sides. Only the white-and-gold altar and choir stalls remained intact, lost in Romanesque-Gothic gloom. "They haven't decided what to do about them," the young priest said. He was equally uncertain as to the future of the moribund *boiseries:* "Maybe the masons will sell them to *antiquaires*, or burn them." No nation should treat such treasures as firewood; restoration is preservation, not destruction. I sat there stunned, grieving for this lost beauty. The church's new look will be that of a woman who has had her face lifted until she can no longer smile. What will discourage Portuguese authority from this folly which international art historians have bemoaned for half a century? There are better examples of Romanesque and Gothic elsewhere in Europe, but nothing anywhere like Portugal's golden churches.

I left Nossa Senhora da Oliveira vowing never to return and walked across the square to the old Town Hall with its battlemented roof line and medieval arcade. Framed in the arcade's ogival arches is another square lined with Gothic and Manueline houses teeming with people, hung with laundry, loud with children playing and dogs barking, and not much changed in the past five centuries.

Although my heart wasn't in it, I went to the museum in the chapter house to one side of the church, where I saw fine gilded

Amarante . . . Romanesque Pietà on apse of São Gonçalo

altars removed from a Chagas convent (was everything else burned?). No matter how disappointed one may be, it is impossible to ignore some of the objects exhibited here: a great Manueline monstrance, a 12th-century chalice, the gilded triptych given by João I to fulfill the promise of his "weight in precious metal" in return for victory at Aljubarrota, and the cassock he is supposed to have worn beneath his armor at that momentous battle.

When I came out, I found Gomes and the young priest still discussing my despair over the "restoration." Just as one offers a treat to a despondent child, the priest suggested taking me to see Santa Marinha da Costa, a wonderfully overdecorated 18th-century convent little over a mile out of town. After that he left us, and I went to look in São Francisco, a church that is erroneously overlooked by many guidebooks. Its Gothic portal is almost always locked, but Gomes arranged for me to get in through the convent next door. A former palace with a lavish façade of blue-and-white *azulejo* and granite volutes, it is now used as a convent-hospital for what appeared to be mental patients. A formidable nun shooed these unfortunates away as she led me down long corridors into the big, sophisticated church with its yellow grisaille ceiling, its enormous gilded chancel arch, its elaborate pelmets, its gilded pulpits with unusual black accents —a subtle combination of riches and aloof dignity.

Those responsible for the restoration of the 15th-century palace of the Braganças went berserk and added mansard roofs; there was no use for me to waste time there. But the little Romanesque chapel where Afonso Henriques was baptized is a moving fortress of prayer, although stark and obviously stripped of that accumulation of wealth which would normally belong to a royal chapel.

When we arrived in Braga late in the afternoon, we had trouble finding an open gas station, as everyone was at a soccer match. Friends in Lisbon had written the Banco Português do

Atlantico asking if I could be invited to stay at the Paço de Palmeira, which the bank owns and where it sometimes puts up friends and directors. It was on the opposite side of town, which gave me an excuse for driving past the great Sé. (It was too late to stop today and my itinerary calls for my going farther north tomorrow.) One is struck by the wealth of church towers, of noble houses and great fountains in Braga. The Paço da Palmeira is a huge pink country palace hidden behind miles of pink stone walls, originally built for a bastard son of João V. When he became Archbishop of Braga and Primate of the Spains, it served as his summer residence. Then, as now, it was quite an establishment, with a central hall some 200 feet long from which rooms open on both sides. The Archbishop, it seems, liked to pace its floor. Mosey, after the constraint of the car and small *pousada* rooms, indulged in racing up and down as if she were playing tag with the ghost of His Eminence.

Apparently this semi-royal prelate thought of everything: sitting in his summerhouse along the riverbank, he had a clear view of the front door of the palace and could signal whether or not he chose to receive those who presented themselves there; just outside his bedroom, a corridor with an elaborately painted ceiling contained a hidden stairway. "In case of brigands or other unwanted visitations," he could retreat to an upper chamber, pulling the stairs up behind him. I was put up in a huge bedroom with an equally large bath—obviously converted from an extra chamber as at Mateus. Friends of the bank had come from Oporto (an hour's drive) to join me for dinner. It was an immensely pleasant evening.

February 19

BRAGA TO VALENÇA DO MINHO (via Ponte do Lima)

Sr. and Sra. Burmester Martins spent some of the morning with me, during which we made a tour of the gardens, where two men were tidily sweeping up a carpet of camellias that had fallen during last night's rain. The camellia trees were not only huge but several of them were obvious exhibitionists—they bore both white and pink blossoms. The bank wanted me to see the *pousada* it runs for its employees, each of whom annually is entitled to a free week's vacation (with family) here at Palmeira; I found it attractively set up, and its kitchen was the most modern I have seen in Portugal.

The Burmesters proposed taking me to see the interior of the Casa dos Biscainhos, a noble house built in the early 17th-century recently acquired by the city of Braga to be converted into a museum. The crusty old aristocrat who lived here until his recent death had two daughters, one of whom married conventionally, while the second, and favorite, child eloped with a *cavalheiro*, much to her father's wrath. It appears that the groom was a top-ranking bullfighter, a nice fellow, and the couple were exceptionally happy. But the unforgiving father spent his last years parceling out his wealth to the "good" girl, although she had no interest in the family home.

One enters the Casa dos Biscainhos through an enclosed, roofed-over courtyard designed for privacy as well as shelter; a stable along the same inner court made it possible for guests in coaches to come, go, or stay unnoticed. The interior of the house, reached through a double stone staircase, is in parlous state. Painted or gesso-decorated ceilings and painted linen wall-hangings have suffered from leaks, but fine things survive. Many rooms have *azulejos* up to the chair rail and rich mantelpieces, and a geometrically designed 17th-century iron balustrade leading to the second floor looks as contemporary as the best of Saarinen. One room that seemed unscathed had a rich Italianate painted ceiling—flowers, figures, and architectural details flowing in from the corners—gilded wall brackets with naked angels wearing feathers in their hair—styled for a Mo-

Braga . . . stairway of Bom Jesus

hawk war dance. I was puzzled by the abstract design of *azulejos* along the kitchen walls until I realized it was made up of leftover tiles from the rest of the house. In the gardens at the back, 100-year-old camellias were planted to form a summerhouse under which stood benches and tables.

I said good-bye to the Burmesters, whom I look forward to seeing in Oporto, where they promise to take me around the antique shops. From Braga north we traveled through the Minho, one of the loveliest parts of Portugal. The country is green, rich, and tidy, smiling even in the rain. The Minhotans are genial and have a firmer handshake than people in the south. Their oxen are bigger and cleaner. They store their corn in coffin-like stone houses (*canastras*) set high on granite posts. The hills are snow-tipped with white heather. We stopped for a picnic lunch in Ponte do Lima, where Gomes parked the car with a view of the Lima River on one side and the old jail on the other: the jail must be empty, as there was no sign of the crude needlework bags the prisoners usually let down through the bars in hope of receiving cigarettes, coins, or food. I asked Gomes to make sure of getting me some *broa*, a tough-crusted bread made with corn; it has an unusual taste, and after eating a modest piece one feels thoroughly nourished. Across the river, the white silhouette of Santo António da Torre looked like a Ballet Russe stage set with its onion dome and dark ribbing of Minhotan granite.

Three miles farther to the north, in a tiny village, I stopped at the convent-church of Refoios do Lima, its dark granite outline drawn by a confident hand. With sparse and emphatic ornament and a slender onion-topped steeple, it expresses all the understated elegance of northern Portuguese Baroque. The interior is very rich, as if to contradict exterior restraints, and seems to explode with carved and gilded ornament: a late Renaissance retable; shells and festooning around the chancel arch; richly gilded corner altars; twin pulpits tipped with scarlet; pelmets dripping with gilded fringe.

From here to Valença do Minho was an easy, pleasurable drive through a verdant countryside. Valença is a walled town (the walls built considerably later than the rest of the town) with some nice 15th-century houses and a Romanesque church. From my window at the *pousada*, I watched a dozen boys with wooden swords playing at war along the ramparts, and below, the Minho River with the Spanish town of Tuy on the far bank. For dinner I had lampreys cooked in red wine and tiny pancakes filled with lemon custard for dessert.

February 20

VALENÇA DO MINHO TO OPORTO (via Caminha, Viana do Castelo, Barcelos, and Vila do Conde)

Driving from Valença to Caminha in the rain, we came upon peasants dressed in straw raincoats that made them appear legless, like moving haystacks in the fields. I could not resist stopping and asking to try one on. It was cozy and absolutely waterproof as far as it went—just below my knees—and my appearance caused considerable mirth.

Caminha is a pretty town on a peninsula formed by the Minho and its tributary, the Coura. In the main square there are a clock tower, a Town Hall and battlemented castle, and tucked away on a street off to the right, the Igreja Matriz, a noble, rustic 15th-century structure, part Manueline, part Renaissance. Inside there are a smashing Mozarabic ceiling, Manueline carved stone side altars with *azulejos* over the arches, and a Tree of Jesse. (Jesse, lying on his side, seems to say, "Get a load of me . . . I started it.")

On to Viana do Castelo, once a major shipping center for the Port industry. Although for me the town has an unfortunate tendency toward folklore—native dress and hearts-and-flowers embroidery—it boasts of many stylish buildings. The principal square—in fact a triangle—is rich in architectural variety, with a crenelated Town Hall built over a spacious arcade; a Baroque Misericórdia church; an ornate hospice with incongruous caryatids supporting its two upper stories. My favorite churches in Viana are both Rococo: the tiny chapel off the Malheirão Reimão Palace, which is even fancier than the Clérigos in Vila Real and similarly shaped like an arrow's head; and Nossa Senhora da Agonia, bat-winged with granite eyebrows over the portal. Inside one encounters small-scale grandeur, a neat and pleasing trick encompassing a gold pulpit, gold side altars, and a tiny Rococo organ loft.

Although I had always heard praise of the Campo Feiro (fair ground) in Barcelos, to me it is too big—a quarter of a mile square—to have definition. I stopped at the octagonal domed church of Senhor da Cruz, its exterior decorated with balustrades and stone flambeaux; inside there were *azulejos*, black-and-white marble floors, an elaborate organ, and altars like gilded grottos dripping with tassels and fringe. Gomes bought some little cakes, *suspiros* (sighs), which were welcomed enthusiastically by Mosey and me, and restored, we went on to Vila do Conde for lunch. Later I visited the immense convent of Santa Clara with its 18th-century aqueduct (999 arches from the convent to the springs). Founded in 1318 by demi-royals, Afonso Sanches (one of King Diniz' * many bastards) and his wife, Teresa, who wrote the rules of admission, primarily this was to be a refuge for impoverished noble ladies. It also welcomed the rich. The less socially prominent were occasionally accepted, provided they would "do honor to the order." The convent church is unusually shallow, wide, and lofty and con-

* See page 22.

Viana do Castelo . . . Nossa Senhora da Agonia

tains the founders' tombs and that of Brites Pereira.* At one end of the church, great iron grilles separated the nuns from the rest of the congregation; here the Poor Clares, disdainful of worldly vulgarity, sat in gilded glory below an especially rich painted ceiling. In another part of town, I stopped at the Igreja Matriz. King Manuel I ordered its Manueline portal; inside there are an appropriate wealth of gilding, and a life-size polychrome angel on the right of the altar who seems to be making a haughty attempt to hail a taxi.

The Infante de Sagres Hotel in Oporto is provincial Edwardian and thoroughly comfortable. A note from Van Zeller asking me to lunch tomorrow, from the Burmesters to go antiquing, from the Port-wine firm of Cockburn (pronounced without the *ck*) to visit its lodges, from our Consul General for cocktails, and from a distinguished art historian to dine. Am almost too tired to sort all this out, but I must. Dined extremely well in the hotel on fresh Minho salmon, *scallopine* of veal, and white asparagus.

February 21

OPORTO

Burmester met me at ten A.M. and we went looking for antiques, a routine he follows twice a week; he also wanted to stop in at one of the silversmiths. I had no idea of what beautiful silverwork they do, in a 19th-century idiom. Lunch with Van Zeller at his club: lampreys with a full-bodied silken Evel; and with Serra cheese, a quince marmalade, and a Wood Port "of the 1937 vintage." † After that we set off for Vila Nova de Gaia,

* Daughter of the great Constable, Nun'alvares, and wife of João I's bastard son, the Count of Barcelos.

† See page 154.

where the da Silva lodges are located, across the Douro. Van Zeller, his brother, and his uncle were patient and kind in discussing Port with me. After an hour of concentrated listening, it was agreed that the next step in my education involved tasting eight different samples—from 1894 to 1966. Sniff, sip, and spit into an oblong brass kitty-pan. Eight tulip-shaped crystal glasses, about a quarter full, stood on a table; one at a time was picked up by the stem, the wine twirled to leave a silken coating on the glass, and then passed to me. The first and the last wines clearly were too young or too old; in the middle years the subtleties were too refined for a tyro's taste buds to describe. Port experts concede that as a rule the wine improves over a twenty-five-year period, after which the curve tends to be downward.

It was nearly four when I left. Before returning to the hotel, I stopped at the Sé, stern, forbidding, and mostly Romanesque with a curious carved granite snake balustrade striking a neo-pagan note. Inside there are splendid choir stalls, a noble chancel, and in the chapel on the left of the High Altar a massive chased silver altar, block after block of metal carved in bas-relief. (It was whitewashed during the Napoleonic wars to prevent the French from making off with it.) Then on to look at São Martinho de Cedofeita (literally, "quickly done"), an early church known to have existed in 1120; the capitals of its Romanesque doors have carved animal heads, but restoration of the interior gives it an over-scrubbed appearance. In the Soares dos Reis Museum I looked at an eclectic collection of Limoges enamels, fine ceramics, paintings by Grão Vasco, Frei Carlos, along with a Magnasco, some flimsy Pillements, and two panels attributed to Clouet. Just time to rest before dinner at an *estalagem* outside of town with Dr. Robert Smith, an eccentric, immensely knowledgeable American known to his fellow art historians as "Portuguese Smith."

February 22

OPORTO

I set out early, as I wanted to visit my favorite churches, Santa Clara and São Francisco, while my eyes were fresh. São Francisco is next door to the Bolsa (stock exchange) and inside looks as if the brokers kept their bullion slathered on the elaborate wood carving of the church walls. A side chapel's gates are carved to resemble cork. Others have extravagant pelmets and altarpieces with salomonic columns. In anticipation of Lent, next week, the aisles were crowded with life-size processional figures—saints and saintly monarchs (St. Louis of France and Santa Isabella of Portugal appropriately garbed in taffeta, velvet, and ermine). I was astonished by men shouting from the High Altar—services are no longer held here, but still the sound of rough voices struck a discordant note. It appeared they were trying to hoist a great crucifix into place with the aid of a block-and-tackle—evocative and awesome.

If São Francisco is called the "golden delirium of Portuguese Baroque," then Santa Clara is its golden ecstasy. Set in an austere façade, the interior of the convent-church of Santa Clara translates the elements of lyric poetry into design. Harmony envelops one—the gilded grilles, the twin altars, the elegant pulpit, the golden bosses—all variations on a heavenly theme. Sacheverell Sitwell speaks of Santa Clara as a "golden grotto," of its ceiling as "golden rain," but for me it is more jubilant still, like living on a sunbeam.

By noon I was at Vila Nova de Gaia again, lunching with the directors of Cockburn. I was welcomed by a charming Englishman wearing a chemist's white linen jacket over a sweater (apparently the directors' uniform, from which they switch to tweed for lunch). We did a quick tour of the cooperage plant

Oporto . . . stone snake stairs to the Sé

before the workmen quit for lunch. Another delicious meal and lots of articulate wine lore. It made me giggle at the prospect of telling a New York liquor store to "open a bottle of Vintage Port with hot irons, decant it and get it to me before six this evening." *

Driving back from Cockburn, I asked Gomes to take me by the Palácio do Freixo, a great house designed by Nasoni and two of his famous churches—the Torre dos Clérigos and the Misericórdia—all wonderfully stylish except in the rust-colored stain on their stone façades, which produces a very un-Baroque effect. (Gomes, who hates Oporto, kept growling about the "filthy town.") I had been asked to look in the British Factory House, a non-club "club" built in the 18th century to the specifications of the English consul and the English wine factors. The thoroughly Anglicized rooms are filled with Waterford chandeliers, Chelsea and Wedgwood porcelains, English silver, Chippendale furniture, some of it (the least attractive pieces, too) made and signed by the master. Oporto is a Dickensian town translated into Portuguese.

February 23

OPORTO TO COIMBRA (via Arouca and Aveiro)

The Cistercian convent of Arouca was founded in the 12th century, only to be shaken up some fifty years later by the arrival of a royal lady, Princess Mafalda of Portugal, the divorced wife of Henry I of Castile. The embittered former Queen, taking umbrage at the carryings-on in the convent, proceeded to enforce stricter rules. (She was later sainted.) Mafalda died in 1256—how, and where, one is not told, but according to legend there was some uncertainty as to whether her body belonged to the Arouca convent or to a sister house in Oporto. The dilemma was resolved by placing the sainted corpse on her

* See page 154.

favorite mule, which headed straight for Arouca.

As befits this royal enclosure, the convent church is richly ornamented, in particular the nuns' stalls, each one backed with paintings of saintly events depicted in court dress of the 17th and 18th centuries. Looking down upon all this finery from second-story niches are figures of nuns in pleated white plaster habits (that seem to be made of chiffon), like radiantly beautiful mannequins, their faces lightly touched with make-up. (The Ancient Monuments Commission takes a Puritanical attitude toward this and is constantly threatening to scrub these lovelies.)

After we left Arouca, the hills we have been driving through vanished as if a curtain had fallen over them. We were headed toward Aveiro, situated in strange moonish country, below sea level. Canals that run through Aveiro streets suggest Holland more than Venice. The lagoons are edged with salt pyramids, more gray than white, some of them covered with straw, like huge hayricks. There was a smell of seaweed, mimosa flowers, oleanders, and pungent eucalyptus. Lunched in town on *mexilhões* (mussels) cooked in broth, green peppers stuffed with scrambled eggs, and *ovos moles*. A woman at the next table held a four-month-old baby—pink cheeks, blue eyes, blond curls—to whom she kept spooning heavily sugared black coffee.

Aveiro's convent of Jesus is generally considered the apotheosis of all the Poor Clares' wealth. It seemed sensible to save this treat, as children do, for the last. On the Praça de República a pink-washed Town Hall built in the late 18th century has a generally unbusiness-like charm. Nearby is the Misericórdia church, with blue-and-white *azulejos* covering the entire façade except for a two-tiered Renaissance portal which looks as if it had been stuck on at the last minute; inside there are graceful gilded pelmets, blue-yellow-and-white *azulejos* on the walls, and an organ painted black and white and gold. The 18th-century Baroque chapel Senhor Jesus das Barrocas has Rococo decoration applied to its otherwise austere sides; there's enormous elegance to these octagonal churches which inevitably appear to be built with ample space around them and corresponding space and light inside. The Carmelite church (sometimes referred to locally as Vera Cruz) is so plain as to be almost ugly outside; but the carving within is of unusual quality and patina, a rubbed-down, naked look to its gilding. São Domingos (or Nossa Senhora da Glória, or the Sé, depending on whom you ask) is stylish inside and out, with a flourish of Renaissance ornament on the façade and high oval lunettes which pour light over carved, painted woodwork simulating marble, malachite, and lapis; to one side, a delicious little console seems to invite one to leave a visiting card for the Almighty.

The convent of Jesus (or of Santa Joanna) is a Rococo happening. The ambivalence of its name stems from 1472, when the Infante Joanna, daughter of Afonso V, took her vows here. (She was canonized in the 17th century.) The chapel is a temple of carved and gilded wood which one is tempted to compare to Santa Clara in Oporto. There is a likeness and a difference; in both one feels, literally, boxed in gold, but the inventiveness of 17th-century design gives each a separate personality. The *côro alto* here is particularly elegant with its red-lacquered organ and the red chinoiserie backs of the choir stalls. The Infante of Portugal, turned nun, spent fourteen years of her life within the convent and died in an upper chamber—small for an Infante, large for a nun. Around its walls is a series of 17th-century paintings related to incidents of her life, swathed in regal sanctity, including her deathbed, which is portrayed as if it were a court levée.

The rest of the convent has been converted into a museum, crammed with gilded altars, crêches and other church furnishings, beautiful, but lifeless seen out of context. Two things are of special interest: a huge stone statue, the Menino do Jardim

Oporto . . . golden church interior of Santa Clara convent

(Youth of the Garden), like an early Adam with a snake around his arm; and a portrait of the sainted princess supposedly by Gonçalves (more likely his school) portraying an obviously elegant manic-depressive in a kind of Modigliani idiom.

I bypassed Ilhavo, where the famous Vista Alegre porcelain is made—I was afraid of being tempted. It's lovely, fragile stuff—so delicate, in fact, that it is said to have been shipped to Lisbon on camels as late as mid-19th century.

Coimbra * just in time to change in order to dine with some academics—an Englishman, and an American who teaches linguistics and Arabic. It had been my idea to stay a couple of days in order to see something of university life, but, as it's Carnival, the students are on vacation until next week. I have been asked to return for the awarding of three science doctorates in the great ceremonial hall called Sala dos Capelos.

February 24

COIMBRA TO SINTRA (via Lisbon)

I could not leave this morning without looking into the Machado de Castro museum at the ravishing and girlish St. Michael. Gomes is suffering from a fierce toothache, which he did little to assuage by trying to perform a do-it-yourself extraction. As things stand, I plan to lie low in Sintra for a couple of days and try to sift out all these impressions. Passed the great abbey of Batalha † without stopping, but even driving by at sixty miles an hour, this heroic pile of masonry is impressive.

Sintra at last and the Seteais Palace Hotel—what a delicious spot, with accommodations for only twenty guests. Built as a *quinta* for the Marialva family in the early 18th century, it has a theatrical and ornate arch linking the two wings which com-

* See page 97.
† See page 173.

memorates a visit paid the aristocratic owners by the Prince and Princess of Brazil in 1802. The interior is a·delight, with public rooms often said to have been painted by Pillement.

February 25

SINTRA

What a perfect spot to lie doggo; from my bed here in the Seteais I look out onto the *serra* crowned by the ruins of a Moorish castle and the fairytale spires of Pena Palace.* In spite of his toothache, Gomes' pride prevents his taking the day off, so I settled on an outing to the village, forgetting about the hazards of the Carnival parade, which kept us hemmed in for close to an hour. There were decorated floats and heralds blowing trumpets off key, a royal progress of courtiers, a king and queen, all of them looking both sheepish and amused in their rented finery, pursued by masked children.

February 26

SINTRA AND LISBON

I went in to Lisbon to have my hair done, then stopped in at São Roque to look at the pretentious chapel of São João Baptista, which João V commissioned at a cost of more than a million dollars in 18th-century currency. A masterpiece of the lapidary art if not an aesthetic tour de force, it was made in Rome, taken to pieces, and shipped to Lisbon in three vessels. With some difficulty we finally found the mysterious Capela de Santo Amaro—right where Gomes and I knew it should be, although none of the residents of that part of Lisbon seem to have heard of it. A handsome 16th-century Renaissance church, this octagonal structure has a splendid view over the Tagus, a

* See page 214.

lovely, airy interior, and an atrium lined with 16th-century *azulejos* in bold designs.

February 27

SINTRA AND ENVIRONS

Lunched at the Cozinha Velha (old kitchen) of the palace at Queluz, such a pretty setting for good food: *acepipes*, a cheese soufflé, glacéed carrots, and fresh pineapple. On to see the Gulbenkian treasure, a marvelous collection that includes paintings by Guardi, a Rembrandt, a Quentin de la Tour; a pair of appliques made by Gouthière for Marie Antoinette; silver mustard pots made for Mme. de Pompadour, shaped like barrels and wheeled by angels dressed in gardeners' aprons; art-nouveau jewels created for Gulbenkian by his friend René Lalique; and an extraordinary collection of Oriental rugs. Thomas Hoving, director of New York's Metropolitan Museum, once told me that Calouste Gulbenkian would pay as much as a million dollars for an Oriental rug "provided it had not been walked on."

February 28

SINTRA

Lunched with V. at a little fish place, Tirano's on the Cascais road, where they serve the best seafood I've ever eaten. Started off with a plate of *presunto* with the Port, followed by platters of crustaceans—shrimp, prawns, *lagostinas*, *lagostas* (served cold but not chilled), and a kind of barnacle that I can take but would just as soon leave alone. This place is family-run, and I was introduced to brothers, wife, grandmother, a year-old baby (who looked exactly like the Beja angels) and, of course, the owner, who is said to be a former member of the secret

Lisbon . . . azulejos in Capela de Santo Amaro

police. Everyone but ourselves was Portuguese, including a long table of men quite obviously suffering the pangs of last night's Mardi Gras excesses. Dined at the Marquesa de C.'s and afterward listened to a young and brilliant Brazilian pianist playing Brahms in the drawing room of this grand and comfortable house. There were family portraits on the wall, great Lowestoft *jardinières* flanking the fireplace, *azulejos* up to the chair rail, an Arraiolos rug in a contemporary design, a small painting by Rubens, and a television back of the arras.

February 29

LISBON

I had a rendezvous at the Romanesque Sé at 10:15 this morning to see the treasures of the cathedral which one hopes soon will be exhibited to the public. Monsignor Dom João de Castro (a prestigious name with the prefix of Dom, most often reserved for royalty), who was to show me around, met me at the handsome portal of this impressive, stern edifice. He is one of those charming worldly prelates often found in the Roman Catholic hierarchy. As the Patriarchal seat, the Sé still has dazzling possessions, although most of Lisbon's church treasure was destroyed in the great earthquake. We looked at silver and vermeil chalices, monstrances, croziers, crosses, and patens, many of them dating from the 15th century; the most ornate, however, were 18th-century, stemming from the munificence of João V, the spendthrift monarch who tried to outdo the splendor of Louis V and the Papal See. I saw church vestments that were more like armor than cloth of gold, weighed down with gold-thread embroidery—emphatic as bas-relief sculpture and finished off with massive gold fringe entwined in bangles. I asked whether these precious garments were used by the Patriarch and was assured that they were. "How are they kept in repair?" I asked. There appear to be "rich and aristocratic aged ladies who do this work themselves."

March 1

SINTRA AND LISBON

Nothing but frivolity this morning, mostly shopping in Sintra. Then in to the Benfica district of Lisbon to see the Casa dos Marqueses de Fronteira, a private house with extraordinary gardens that one can usually arrange to visit. As in most great Portuguese houses, there are the ubiquitous topiary gardens, but these are set in immense splendor among walls lined with *azulejos* portraying the legend of the Twelve Gentlemen of Portugal,* and a great water tank with stone busts of kings and nymphs. The ensemble is a tour de force. According to the American art historian Hellmut Wohl, the large niche in the wall behind the tank is a representation of Parnassus; the Twelve Gentlemen were modeled on Velásquez' equestrian portraits; and the concept as a whole was designed as a classical nymphaeum.

Before lunching at the Aviz, I drove up to the Capela de Santo Cristo, a jewel-like chapel by Boytac, set on a hill back of the Jerónimos. This extraordinary structure, small, grand, and more than 400 years old, still speaks in an architectural idiom of today. Unfortunately, it is shut except for an eleven-o'clock Mass "*some* Sundays."

March 2

SINTRA TO THE ARRÁBIDA CONVENTS (via Azeitão and Bacalhoa)

M. and I took off around eleven this morning to see how spring was progressing along the Arrábida. She wanted to

* See page 38.

give her cook a lift to the village of Azeitão, where the woman likes to spend her monthly day off. We were a stone's throw from the Quinta da Bacalhoa, which I longed to see again but felt it would be painful to M., as the owner, her dearest friend, recently died there. My dilemma was resolved when M. tactfully suggested I take a look at the *quinta* gardens while she went off to buy a bottle of Muscatel and an Azeitão cheese to add to our picnic provisions.

Sacheverell Sitwell, writing of this 15th-century house, which once belonged to Afonso da Albuquerque, the son of the first Viceroy of the Indies, called it "a lovely half-caste of the East and West." It has melon domes, second-story loggias, topiary gardens, and off the water tank an exquisite seraglio-like summerhouse filled with precious *azulejos.* (Although there is no evidence that the great Italian Renaissance architect Andrea Sansovino had a hand in Bacalhoa's design, the legend persists that he may have.) Thirty years ago the *quinta* was in a ruinous state, but it fell into the hands of an American who set out rebuilding it stone by stone—lovingly, with concern for authenticity, and no fudging allowed.*

I rejoined M. in the car on the street outside the *quinta* and we set off for the Arrábida convents, which perch on a side of the *serra* with the ocean below and seven tiny chapels—God's sentry boxes—dotting the hillside. There is a meditative atmosphere enveloping the whole place even today, long after the monks' departure. It isn't oppressive, but it tends to make one speak in a whisper. The convent cells are small, but not punitively so; the cloisters are shaded by huge box trees (a horticultural rarity, I have been told). Most of the Serra da Arrábida belongs to the rich and powerful Palmela family, and one of their long-time retainers is employed as the convent's caretaker. Recently, the

* A good Lisbon hotel concierge can often arrange a visit through the gardens of Bacalhoa.

The caption for the photograph facing page 296 should read:
Lisbon . . . Capela de Santo Cristo.

Duke of Palmela decided to promote the old man to an easier job and summoned him to the Palmela Palace in Lisbon. "I went all the way to Lisbon," the old caretaker said, stressing the length of the trip (forty minutes by bus), "where His Grace told me what he had in mind. I said I was most grateful, but asked if this change meant leaving the convent." At this point the old man allowed for a pregnant pause in his narrative. "His Grace said indeed it did, and I told him that that was quite impossible. 'Leave my trees? I know every one of them. I thank Your Grace, but no, I cannot leave them alone, they would miss me.' "

It is still too early for the *serra* to put on its full-dress show of wild flowers but it provided a wealth of early spring delights: golden gorse, wild daffodils, creamy lupin, pink cistus, and white broom looking as if each frond were dipped in icing.

March 3

SINTRA TO COIMBRA

Left for Coimbra soon after nine along with V. A brilliant sunny day turned into pea-soup fog which slowed us up. We had to stop once for Mosey in the pine woods of Leiria, planted by King Diniz centuries ago, but even so we arrived early enough to stop at the Mosteiro de Santa Cruz. The gray day only added to the definition of the Manueline façade half concealed behind its Baroque portal; as it was the first Sunday in Lent, the church was packed and several small girls wore brass crowns over their white mantillas.

I had invited the J.'s (English) and the H.'s (American) to lunch with us at the Pinto d'Oro; we had *acepipes*, fish, chicken, a sweet, two bottles of an excellent Grão Vasco Dão tinto (red), and the bill came to the equivalent of ten dollars.

From there we went on to the University of Coimbra's main

square, and the ceremonial Sala dos Capelos to see three graduate students receive their doctorates in science. For a while we stood at the foot of the double staircase below the gallery called the Via Latina, awaiting the procession to form across the way. Men in medieval accouterments were dashing about carrying maces and salvers, some of them wearing swords. Many guests were formally dressed, the men in "white tie and decorations," their ladies in brocade and beaded cocktail suits with egret-trimmed hats. My Pucci looked dowdy. Dr. H. thought we had best move into the hall to find seats among this elegant throng. One already caught the strains of a band playing a solemn processional—it sounded like a medley of "Onward, Christian Soldiers" and "God Save the King," with overtones of Tchaikovsky. The Faculties of Coimbra University—one of the oldest in Europe *—walked in reverse seniority, the newest disciplines first; hence, Engineering (light blue and white), Pharmacy (purple), Letters (dark blue), Science (light blue), Law (red), Medicine (yellow). They were dressed in black cassocks, over which they wore small, rufflike, embroidered satin capes (which came just below the shoulders) and fringe-covered spiked hats shaped like inverted flower pots; the capes and hats were in the colors of the academic disciplines. Once they settled themselves in the carved stalls around the room, they became part of a medieval *mise-en-scène;* so did the Rector's wife and some of the more distinguished visitors, looking down from upper-gallery windows. I was grateful that academic Portuguese was outside my scope; there was no need to listen, I could concentrate on looking. The scholars' faces were astonishingly Portuguese—robust, thoughtful, amused; they appeared more rugged than their counterparts on the American or English academic horizon. These faces were straight out of the great Gonçalves retable in Lisbon.

* See page 25.

Dr. H. explained that the men receiving their doctorates had spent seven years on their theses, and he estimated their ages as between mid-thirty and forty. After considerable perorations by each candidate's two sponsors, pages arrived carrying blue capes and flower-pot hats on salvers for the official robing. This done, the new members of the Faculty made their way past their colleagues, by whom they were embraced and welcomed into the academic community. It was done with such warmth that I remarked on the seeming absence of overt academic jealousies. "Why do you think I'm here?" Dr. H. asked. "I have more freedom in Coimbra than I had in three universities I was associated with in America."

Later, in the square, I said good-bye, expressing my appreciation for being allowed to witness this resplendent occasion. I was so preoccupied with what I had seen that the three hours' drive back to Sintra seemed like nothing.

March 4

SINTRA

The Dominican nuns who run a girls' school in Ramalhão, Beckford's *quinta*, let me take a tour of its interior. Rows of girlish cots have partially drabbed down past glamour, time has taken its toll. But the curving double staircase rising from the inner hall, the great painted rooms (said to be by Pillement) retain the essence of imaginative elegance. As at the Seteais, one room is completely enfolded in its painted design—walls and ceiling suggesting a Brazilian forest. Dined with V. at his house along with our Ambassador and his wife. Afterward V. played for us, Scarlatti, Bach, and Mozart, alternately using the harpsichord and the clavichord. At last I found out why the aristocratic Portuguese are listed in the telephone directory under their titles rather than their family names: Portugal is a republic, therefore the title is incorporated into the name.

March 5–8

SINTRA

People have said Sintra is "sad," but not ever to me. For those who seek crowds, gambling tables, cocktail parties, probably yes. But there is nowhere one can "*mieux être à deux*" or find such a sense of peace and serenity alone. I have been told one becomes dotty if one stays too long. But, like Robert Southey, "had I been born in Sintra methinks no inducement could have tempted me to leave its delightful springs and shades."

I've spent the last three days seeing friends. I hate leaving, but my capacity to absorb is exhausted. I fly back to New York this afternoon. It is time to go home, if only to make plans for coming back.

Bibliography

Anderson, H. C.: *A Visit to Portugal*
Atkinson, W. C.: *A History of Spain and Portugal*
Baedeker: Spain and Portugal
Barnes, W. J.: *Portugal: Gateway to Greatness*
Beamish, H.: *Cavaliers of Portugal*
Beazley, C. R.: *Prince Henry the Navigator*
Beckford, W.: *Travel Diaries*
Bell, A. F. G.: *Portugal of the Portuguese*
Bottineau, Y.: *Portugal*
Bridge, A., and S. Lowndes: *The Selective Traveler in Portugal*
Byron, Lord: *Childe Harold's Pilgrimage*
Chandos, D.: *Journey in Spain and Portugal*
Cheke, M.: *Dictator of Portugal: The Marquis of Pombal*
Crawford, O. J. F.: *Travels in Portugal*
Croft-Cooke, R.: *Port*
Deon, M.: *The Portugal I Love*
Fodor: Spain and Portugal
Gordon, J. and C.: *Portuguese Somersault*
Guia de Braga
Guia de Portugal, 4 vols.
Guide Bleu: Portugal, Madeira and the Azores
Hughs, T. M.: *Overland Journey*
Hume, M. A. S.: *Through Portugal*
Kelly, M. N.: *This Delicious Land—Portugal*
Kendrick, T. D.: *The Lisbon Earthquake*
Kingston, W. H.: *Lusitanian Sketches of the Pen and Pencil*
Kubler, G., and M. Soria: *Art and Architecture in Spain, Portugal and Their American Dominions 1500–1800*
Livermore, H. V.: *A History of Portugal*
Macaulay, R.: *They Went to Portugal*
Marden, P. S.: *A Wayfarer in Portugal*

Morison, S. E.: *Admiral of the Ocean Sea*
Murphy, J.: *Plans, Elevations, Sections and Views of the Church of Batalha*
Nichols, R. S.: *Spanish and Portuguese Gardens*
Ogrizek, D.: *Le Portugal*
Prestage, E.: *Portuguese Pioneers*
Queiroz, Eça de: *The Maias*
——: *The Mandarin and Other Stories*
——: *The Sin of Father Amaro*
Sanceau, E.: *Henry the Navigator*
Santos, R. dos: *O Romantico em Portugal*
——: *O Manuelino*
——: *L'Art Portugais*
Sitwell, S.: *Southern Baroque Art*
——: *Portugal and Madeira*
——: *Monks, Nuns, and Monasteries*
Smith, R.: *The Art of Portugal: 1500–1800*
Southey, R.: *Spain and Portugal*
Watson, W. C.: *Portuguese Architecture*

Index

MARY JEAN KEMPNER

As a war correspondent accredited to the U.S. Navy in 1945, Mary Jean Kempner covered the Pacific war theater from the Marianas to Iwo Jima, Okinawa, the Philippines, China, and Japan. Later she visited India as a member of a famine commission, reporting for the Newspaper Enterprise Association. A compulsive traveler, Miss Kempner has ventured to Baffin Island to describe Arctic life for *Harper's Magazine*, and her articles in *Sports Illustrated*, *Harper's Bazaar*, *House Beautiful* and *The New York Times Magazine* have covered subjects varying from the Verrazano-Narrows Bridge to a Russian mystic. Born in Galveston, Texas, she has lived most of her life in New York, and now leases a house in Sintra, Portugal.

RUSSELL LYNES

Russell Lynes was born in Great Barrington, Massachusetts, in 1910, and was graduated from Yale University in 1932. He began his long association with *Harper's Magazine* in 1944 as an assistant editor; after nineteen years as the magazine's managing editor, he is now a contributing editor and writes a regular column, "After Hours." Articles by Mr. Lynes have appeared in many other national magazines, and he is the author of seven books: *The Domesticated Americans*, *The Tastemakers*, *A Surfeit of Honey*, *Snobs*, *Guests*, *Cadwallader*, and *Confessions of a Dilettante*.